To very dear friends.
Barney + Shirley Weinstein
With best wishes
Lou Barish
and, of course, Rebecca

VARIETIES OF JEWISH BELIEF

by

Louis and Rebecca Barish

JD | **JONATHAN DAVID PUBLISHERS, INC.**
MIDDLE VILLAGE, NEW YORK 11379

VARIETIES OF JEWISH BELIEF

JONATHAN DAVID PUBLISHERS, INC.
68-22 Eliot Avenue
Middle Village, New York 11379

Originally published, in 1961, as
BASIC JEWISH BELIEFS
New Material: Chapter 15 and Index
ISBN 0-8246-0242-0

Library of Congress Cataloging in Publication Data

Barish, Louis.
    Varieties of Jewish belief.

    Previous ed. (1961) published under title:
Basic Jewish beliefs.
    Includes index.

    1.Judaism-Miscellanea. I.Barish,Rebecca,
joint author. II. Title.
BN51.B3 1979   296.3   79-9339
ISBN 0-8246-0242-0

PRINTED IN THE UNITED STATES OF AMERICA

CONTENTS

CONTENTS (*continued*)

Where did society get its basic moral and spiritual values? What is the Jewish conception of the origin of man's moral and spiritual values? How are the moral and spiritual values, which emanate from God, communicated to man? What is the biblical account of the revelation at Mt. Sinai? How was the biblical account of the revelation interpreted in the Jewish tradition? How can the word revealed to one generation be meaningful to another? What is the oral law? What are the different views of revelation to be found in Judaism today? Does the scientific study of the bible challenge belief in divine revelation? Does modern science challenge belief in divine revelation? How have Jews responded to the challenge of science and Bible criticism? Why do many Jews believe that God literally revealed the Torah? Must a Jew, who wishes to remain within the mainstream of traditional Judaism, believe that the Bible is literally true?

As scientific knowledge increases, will men outgrow their need for God? How does tradition look upon science? How does tradition explain discrepancies between the teachings of science and religion? Guided by tradition's view of science, what should our own approach be? Does the theory of evolution contradict the biblical story of creation? Can scientific theories ever negate the story of creation? What does the story of creation teach us, which we cannot learn from science? Can science prove that God does not exist? How do Jews today react to the challenge of the theory of evolution? Does Judaism retreat in the face of advancing scientific knowledge? How does Judaism define a miracle? How did the tradition discourage the yearning for "revealing miracles?" Can God break his own laws of nature to perform a revealing miracle? Do Jews today believe in the miracles of the Bible? Can a Jew today believe in God without believing in miracles? How do the three major branches of Judaism treat the belief in miracles?

How shall we understand pain and suffering? How shall we face suffering? Why do the wicked prosper and the righteous suffer?

Since God is good and all-powerful, how can we account for evil? In the light of Jewish tradition, how shall evil be understood? What is the nature of evil? Why do men do evil? How should we react to evil? Do Jews believe in Satan?

Why did Jews believe themselves to be the chosen people? What did the belief mean? Why have the unsympathetic attacked the concept of a chosen people? Do Jews today consider themselves the chosen people? What are the viewpoints of the three branches of Judaism? What do the Reconstructionists say about this concept? Do Jews believe that Israel is the Holy Land?

CONTENTS *(continued)*

CONTENTS *(continued)*

How has Judaism reacted to emerging moral problems? What is abortion? Is abortion right or wrong? Is the embryo or fetus a human being? Where does Judaism stand on this issue? On what authority is the Jewish view based? What is the rabbinic position on abortion in our own time? Why do rabbis reject the idea of abortion-on-demand? What is birth control? What is the traditional Jewish position on birth control? When is contraception permitted? May a man practice birth control? Is sterliization by surgical means approved? What is the Jewish position on population control? What is the position of rabbis today on population control? What is the Jewish view on organ transplants? What is euthanasia? What is the Jewish view on euthanasia? How did the Torah delimit and discourage capital punishment? How did rabbis of the Talmud restrict capital punishment? Why did rabbis of the Talmud tend to restrict capital punishment? What is the position of rabbis today? What is autopsy? Why the reluctance to permit autopsy? Which beliefs reinforce Jewish aversion to autopsy? Is there authority or precedent for autopsy in the tradition? What is the position of orthodox, conservative, and reform Judaism on autopsy today? May a Jew donate part or all of his body to science? What was the early Jewish attitude toward war? Was war ever considered desirable in Jewish history? How was the destructiveness of war circumscribed? In the tradition, who was exempt from the draft? Does anything in Jewish tradition reconcile us to the use of atomic bombs, nuclear weapons, biological, and chemical poisons? What is the traditional Jewish stand on law and order? What was indicated for Jewish living under tyrannical government? Was civil disobedience ever approved? What did Judaism say about homosexuality in the past? Why did Judaism condemn homosexuality?

Index

Foreword

All three schools of Judaism influenced my thinking. I do not feel that the three contemporary movements in Jewish religion are either incompatible or contradictory. Each of them is a valid expression of Jewish experience and a life-enhancing interpretation of man's destiny.

As a student at Yeshiva University, I drew inspiration from such great orthodox teachers as Dr. Bernard Revel and Dr. Pinchos Churgin. Dr. Stephen Wise and Dr. Harry Slonimsky, two great scholars of the Reform movement, stirred my mind and heart when I attended classes at the Jewish Institute of Religion. Preparing for ordination at the Jewish Theological Seminary of America, I was privileged to count among my teachers such great spiritual giants as Dr. Louis Finkelstein, Dr. Louis Ginzberg and Dr. Mordecai M. Kaplan.

My congregations at Fort Hamilton, Fort Jay and Brooklyn Army Terminal raised many of the challenging questions that led to my writing "Basic Jewish Beliefs." To them I express my appreciation.

To my colleagues, the Catholic and Protestant Chaplains with whom I work, I am indebted for their honesty, willingness and interest in discussing with me the Christian viewpoints. I have learned much from them.

Where shall I find words to express, adequately, my profound gratitude to my friend Colonel John K. Daly, Commanding Officer of Fort Hamilton? Unknowingly he encouraged my efforts in many intangible ways. Because he is a man of intellectual and spiritual stature, he has stimulated and encouraged the military personnel of Fort Hamilton to pursue academic study, and created in the community an atmosphere conducive to creative effort.

I owe a great debt to the Chief of Chaplains of the United States Army, Major General Frank Tobey, to the senior First Army Chaplain, Charles McGee, and to Rabbi Aryeh Lev, Director of the Commission on Jewish Chaplaincy, for helping me with personal problems thus enabling me to complete this work. I was encouraged by the warm interest of Dr. Simon Greenberg, Vice-Chancellor of the Jewish Theological Seminary; of Dr. Robert Gordis, Professor of Bible at the Seminary and of Religion at Columbia University; of Dr. Eliezer Berkovitz, Professor of Philosophy at Hebrew Theological College; of Rabbi Jacob Agus, as well as of a host of colleagues, especially Rabbis Solomon Freehof, Max Eichhorn, Alfred Kolatch, Arthur Hertzberg, Julius Mark, Maurice Lamm and others.

This book, of course, could not have been what it is without the invaluable discussions, contributions, creative criticism, and skillful editing of my beloved wife Rebecca.

LOUIS BARISH

Fort Hamilton
Brooklyn, N. Y.

Introduction

The threat of nuclear doom and a new apocalypse make a faith to live by both necessary and urgent in our times. Therefore, we would do well to open our hearts and minds to an examination of beliefs that have given vitality and durability to the Jewish people throughout the generations.

What is the secret of Israel's survival and continuing creativity? What are its resources for dealing confidently with manifold crises? Why does it emerge from disaster with renewed conviction that life has purpose and meaning? What saves it from despair by directing its attention and energies to the challenges which make life a bold and exciting adventure? Wherein lies the inspiration for its spiritual strength? What enables the Jew to say, even in adversity, "This is my God and I will glorify Him?" The answer to all of these is to be found in its faith.

For those who lack either knowledge or spiritual anchorage, for those who seek purpose and direction in our complex civilization, for those who are filled with wonder over the hold which basic values of religion had on their ancestors, for those who yearn for a faith they never had, for those who rejected a faith they neither understood nor cherished fully, for those who are inquiring, for those who want the enduring faith and sustaining values of a rich heritage, this book is written.

This book is an attempt to answer questions regarding Judaism which are most frequently asked by Jews or addressed to Jews by non-Jews. Some of the questions simply seek information: "What do Jews believe? What are they supposed to believe?" Others reflect a desire for justification or challenge: "Why do we believe? What *can* we believe?" Still others reveal an anguished search: "How can we believe?"

Even the questions which merely ask for information cannot be answered simply. Judaism has no authoritative

ix

set of beliefs. Judaism has a tradition which has allowed, and even encouraged, diverse expressions of belief. Even where a generally accepted belief exists, the tradition records variations in it. On sincere and reasonable differences of opinion in matters of belief, the Tradition says: "Both views are the words of the living God."

Views of the Tradition are to be found here and there in the Bible, in the Midrash, in the Talmud and in a multitude of other great classics of the Jewish past. And Jewish belief today follows the traditional pattern of unity in diversity. There is a mainstream of Jewish opinion but it is a well-spring containing a number of vigorous currents of thought. This explains why so many of the questions have no *one* answer.

The answers to questions asking "what?" are split into two main parts: What did Jews believe in the past? What do Jews of the three major groups of today believe? Answers from the past go back to the mainstream of tradition. Answers about Jewish belief today are drawn from writings and teachings of spokesmen for Orthodox, Reform and Conservative groups and academicians associated with their respective theological seminaries. Within each of these movements there is fluidity and diversity. To some degree, there is also overlapping of all contemporary movements.

Those who seek facts will find information. For those who are in search of a faith that can be justified, we have tried to reckon with the need for a rationale. For those who want desperately to believe with their emotions as well as with their minds, we can but stress that if they work at it with sincerity and patience, their hope may be realized.

Part of our glorious heritage is a great faith. That faith becomes ours only if we are able to grasp it. Acquisition of an old faith requires search in the pages of Holy Writ, and in the teachings of the Rabbis and Sages of the Talmud. This faith is the product of centuries of Jewish experience which was fruitful in the past and can be an inspiration today.

CHAPTER I

God—The Starting Point

What is the Most Important Idea in the Jewish Religion?

Judaism begins with God. "In the beginning, God created the heavens and the earth." This is the starting point of the Jewish religion. All Judaic concepts stem from it.

One of the sages asked: "Should not the Torah have begun with Abraham, who discovered God and founded our faith?" Another asked: "Should not the Torah have begun with the Revelation at Sinai where the Torah was given? Why does it begin with Creation?" These wise men were trying to understand life as fully as possible and came to the conclusion that understanding begins with the biblical statement: "In the beginning, God created . . ." This great axiom, the foundation of the Jewish system of faith, is the basic premise from which follow all the principles necessary to render life meaningful and good.

Actually, every system of human thought, including science, begins with a declaration of faith. Each postulates certain basic assumptions as self-evident and necessary truths. Judaism starts with the basic axiom that *God is the Creator*. From this follow two corollaries:

1. The God who creates also reveals.
2. The God who creates and reveals also redeems.

The God who created the universe *reveals* His purpose. All of creation incorporates and reflects His will. The heavens declare His glory and nature represents His genius. The earth spins out its destiny according to His plan and history moves toward the fulfillment of His objective. If we listen, we can hear; if we look, we can see; if we contemplate, we can comprehend God's Revelation. *The God of Creation is the God of Revelation.*

The God who created the universe is *concerned* about His creation and exercises providence over it. He sustains and renews it. He loves His creatures; guides, helps, nourishes, reproves and corrects them. God has granted His children freedom to choose between right and wrong. When they err and wander close to the brink of disaster, God saves them. The God of Creation and the God of Revelation is also the God of Redemption, the God who saves man.

The basic affirmations of Judaism lead to the following conclusions:

1. Life is a gift of God and therefore, we should strive to make the most of it by using its opportunities and blessings wisely.

2. Man was created in brotherhood with all his fellow men. Since we are all equally precious in His sight, we must learn to view each other through the eyes of God. We are our brother's keeper, bound to one another by an act of divine creation, by brotherhood.

3. Men are morally responsible to God Who reveals His Will. He is our Father and we are His children who have been taught that there is a right and a wrong. We are morally accountable for our conduct to Him Who judges us constantly, and we should strive to do what is right.

4. Life has a divine purpose which we must try to understand, and help fulfill. We must rise to the challenge and perform the necessary tasks. Our duty is to serve God's purpose in the world: to help create the good life for ourselves and for our fellowman.

5. Life has infinite possibilities. Therefore, we must never lose faith or interest in it. No matter how disappointing the past or frustrating the present, we dare not feel defeated as we look ahead to the future.

6. Man is not a god. We are not self-sufficient, therefore

God helps; our vision is limited, therefore God guides; we err because we are human, therefore God forgives; sometimes we are overwhelmed by the problems of life, therefore God redeems. The fulfillment of each individual's life and of humanity's destiny is in a redeeming act of God.

The logic of our faith rests upon the one great affirmation: "In the beginning, God." This the major premise and starting point of our religion.

How Did Man Come to Know God?

For the Orthodox, the answer is obvious. The opening chapters of the Torah tell us that in the beginning, God spoke to Adam and Adam understood. God commanded man and man knew when he disobeyed God; God and man "knew" each other and there was dialogue between them; God revealed Himself to man and man responded.

The non-Orthodox find the literal meaning of the Bible unconvincing. They cannot accept the idea of God speaking like a human to a human, and see no evidence of it in their own experience. They search for more plausible answers but none have been completely satisfactory. Their restlessness and doubts find expression in various popular conceptions:

God was born in human fear. Man's terror in the face of darkness and the unknown, and his critical need for help, comfort and reassurance, wrung from man's heart his first wordless prayers. The relief he experienced made him feel he was "saved" by a power not his own and filled him with profound gratitude. In his *fear,* man discovered a faith that conquers fear. He found God.

God was born in human need. Man's first awareness of his own inadequacy was tempered by the discovery of hope and expectation. In his unbearable loneliness, man first felt the companionship of a God Who is everpresent. In his recognition that his life was in the hands of a power greater and stronger than his own, man found the providence on which he could depend for help. In his *need,* man discovered God.

God was born in startling self-awareness. When man realized that he had not made himself, that he must be the object of a Creator, he found himself. He was filled with wonder and gratitude for all that had been provided for his sustenance and care by a God Who is continually concerned about what happens to His creation. In his first flash of *self-awareness,* man discovered God.

God originated in human strength. Belief in God is rooted in the miraculous nature of man—his power to reason. Endowed with remarkable perception, man saw spiritual dimensions of his universe—order, sequence, cause and effect, beauty, design—and responded to the God Who had fashioned it. Belief began when man perceived that life has a purpose, and that God needs man to help fulfill that purpose. Belief grew when man developed a sensitivity to moral demands, and saw "the finger of God" directing him to choose between good and evil. His first stirrings of conscience gave rise to powerful feelings of moral obligation. His first experience at self-mastery gave him a glimpse of the Master. His first victory over fate gave him the beginnings of faith. His first act as creative man brought him awareness of his Creator.

God was known intuitively, through an extra-logical insight. The mystery and grandeur of the universe aroused an immediate, inexplicable response in the human personality. In a sudden revelation, like a flash of lightning, something spiritual inside man found something spiritual outside man: man, with his whole being, "saw" the Source of All Being.

How Do the Orthodox, Conservative and Reform Views Differ?

According to the Bible, man's experience of God is initiated by an act of God. In the beginning, God spoke and man heard. According to the Modernist, awareness of God begins with man. Man experiences God through his own reason, emotion and intuition—through an act of faith.

According to Jewish tradition, both views have validity. God "speaks" in a spiritual sense and man "hears" in terms of emotional, rational and intuitive experience. The idea of God began with an act of God directed toward man, and an act of man responding to God.

The Orthodox emphasize the act of *God*; the Reform, the act of *man*. Some Conservatives stress the former and some, the latter. To most Conservatives, however, the importance of both must be stressed to the fullest in order to achieve a fair degree of understanding of the mystery of God's self-revelation and of man's discovery of Him.

Although vitally interested in all possible avenues to God, Orthodox Judaism stresses the revealed nature of the God-idea: God, in search of man, breaks through to him with suddenness and completeness. Reform, interpreting Revelation as a process rather than as an historic event, stresses the evolution of the God-idea in the mind, experience and culture of man: man, in search of God, discovers Him only through gradual stages. Although one wing of Conservative Judaism leans toward the Orthodox, and another toward the Reform view, Conservatism, by and large, recognizes the validity of both positions as complementary and necessary.

How Can I Find God?

When modern man is estranged from God, he asks: "How can I find God?" He knows *about* God but he does not *know* God. He knows God in the abstract but not as a living, personal God. He wants to believe that God is everywhere but cannot *feel* Him anywhere. Man asks how he can find God; but what he really seeks is to *experience the reality* of God's presence in an immediate, personal way.

Judaism's age-old answer is still valid. Three seemingly distinct roads lead to the Divine Presence; all three must

be travelled, for the three are one. A Jew can find the way
to the One God by

1. Studying God's word in the *Torah*.
2. Seeking God's companionship in *prayer*.
3. Serving God's purpose by performing good deeds.

STUDYING GOD'S WORD IN THE TORAH

Torah is God speaking to man, saying "Thou shalt" and
"Thou shalt not." It is God giving the Commandments and
setting forth the requirements for a good and holy life in
answer to the Jew's question, "What doth the Lord God
require of me?" Study of the Torah is the Jew's way of
saying: "Speak, God, and like our ancestors at Sinai, 'we
will do and we will listen.'"

Study of Torah begins with the study of The Book. The
Book was given to our ancestors for their guidance. Whenever we, in turn, seek to attain a deeper, clearer, and more
complete understanding of our duty and destiny, we too
study The Book—Torah. This search for understanding is
an ever-expanding process, eloquent witness to the eternal
relevance of God's Revelation and of man's wondrously inexhaustible capacity for inquiry. A serious attempt to hear
God's word leads to God.

To profess certainty and finality in "knowing" all there
is to know of Torah is to proclaim one's ignorance. Some
individuals mistake what is actually only a small beginning
in the study of *Torah* as knowing all; still others who do not
have even modest beginnings vehemently reject the Torah's
teachings. Ignorance is a block to true piety. There is no
such thing as a complete knowledge of Torah because the
Torah contains infinite meanings which bear witness to an
eternal God.

A group of sages once met on top of a hill overlooking
the ruins of the Temple in Jerusalem after its destruction
by the Romans. One of them asked: "Now that our holy

Temple is destroyed, where will we find God?" To this, another sage replied: "Wherever men study Torah, *there* will God be found." Men approach God as they devote the powers of their mind and heart to Torah, knowledge of God's word. *Talmud Torah,* in its deepest sense, provides a meeting place for God and man.

SEEKING GOD'S COMPANIONSHIP IN PRAYER

As already noted, Torah begins with the supreme question "What doth the Lord God require of man?" Whether the answer is contained in Revelation or emerges from the divinely ordained human power of reason, it is experienced as God's answer. Because God works in and through man, we feel that God is speaking to us. Conversation with God—prayer—is sometimes man's answer to a question directed to God for an answer. Through prayerful conversation, man comes to feel God's presence in a personal way. Prayer is communication and communication leads to a companionable relationship with God. Man may conceive of God as an idea or ideal, as a process or a power, as something Wholly Other than himself, unknowable and remote; but when he begins to pray, man feels he is in the presence of a God who is very close and alive, personal and related to him.

When words of spontaneous prayer rise from the heart, they lift us up and bring us closer to God. Formal prayer, when recited with humility and an intense desire of the heart to absorb, is even more effective in making us a little more like the image of God. We are carried away from intense preoccupation with self and *our* will, and become keenly aware of God and *His* Will.

Non-verbal prayer, the sum total of ritual, rite and ceremony, binds us to God in love and familiar patterns of beauty. All prayer, verbal and non-verbal, is our confidence in a loving God to whom we can turn at all times. Traditional observance offers abundant reminders of God: the *mezzuzah* on the door, the Sabbath lights, festivals marked by distinctive ritual requirements; these sensitize us, both consciously and unconsciously, to His presence.

The Hebrew word *yodea* has the double meaning of know and love: to know God is to love God and to love is to know God. Through prayer, we express our love for God and in return, come to the knowledge of an attribute of God—His love for us. Prayer makes for a warm, personal relationship between man and God.

SERVING GOD BY PERFORMING GOOD DEEDS

Torah study, service of the mind, and prayer, service of the heart, are very important to our search for God. However, by performing *mitzvos*, or good deeds, we are God's co-workers. By helping to fulfill His purpose in the world, we come, perhaps, as close to God as we *can* come. To fulfill a *mitzvah* is to be with God in deed.

Good deeds are the practical application of functioning laws. The great ethical laws, made for men, must operate in the lives of men. It is as important for us to live by truth as to pursue and discover truth. When we live by God's truth, we are, in truth, with God.

When a man fulfills a *mitzvah* (literally, Divine commandment) he actually approaches the Divine. A good deed, performed solely because it is the right thing to do and untainted by ulterior motives, is both noble and ennobling, inspired and inspiring. God's Will becomes man's will and the resulting deed sanctifies life. Our impulses are purified; our disinterested motives transform our deeds into *Gemilus Chassodim*, acts of loving kindness. A good deed becomes a godly act and we are lifted into a partnership with God.

Man asks: "Does life have purpose?" The answer lies more in his own deeds than in contemplation. In the process of fulfilling *mitzvos*, he discovers that he has a task to carry out, a responsibility to meet, a purpose to forward. Man finds purpose in living purposefully. By living usefully, he becomes aware of his usefulness; by doing good, he comes to realize that life is good. In the process of serving God by fulfilling *mitzvos*, man discovers that his own soul quickens and his life becomes enhanced. When man establishes a satisfying partnership with God, he finds that life does indeed have purpose.

"And now Israel, what doth the Lord thy God require of thee . . . but to walk in all His ways?" (Deut. 10:12). Commenting on this verse and on Deut. 13:15, "Ye shall walk after the Lord your God," Rabbi Huna asks: "How is it possible for man to walk in the ways of the Lord?" Rabbi Huna answers the question himself: "Just as God clothes the naked, so do thou also clothe the naked; as He visits the sick, so do thou also visit the sick; as He comforts the mourners, so do thou also comfort the mourners" (Sotah 14). Man finds God when he strives to imitate God.

When man studies, he is trying to understand God; when he prays, he is establishing contact with God; when he is carrying out a *mitzvah*, he is toiling for and with God. The three ways to God are one.

Where Can Man Find God?

The Reconstructionist prayer book answers this question most eloquently:

"God, where shall I find Thee
Whose glory fills the Universe?
Behold, I find Thee
Wherever the mind is free to follow its own bent,
Wherever words come out from the depths of truth,
Wherever tireless striving stretches its arms toward
    perfection,
Wherever men struggle for freedom and right,
Wherever the scientist toils to unbare the secrets of
    nature,
Wherever the poet strings pearls of beauty in lyric
    lines,
Wherever glorious deeds are done."

The Jewish *tradition* says it in a single sentence:

"God is everywhere but man finds Him where he seeks Him."

Does God Speak to Man?

In the Bible, God frequently speaks to man. Significantly, God speaks to man before man speaks to God. God addresses man more often than man addresses God. For example, "And the Lord spoke unto Moses saying," almost invariably initiates the dialogue between God and Moses. Adam and Eve, Noah, Abraham, the Psalmists, Judges and Prophets alike do not speak to God until, and unless, God first addresses Himself to them. In the Bible, God speaks and His speech is unmistakable.

If God spoke, *literally*, in biblical days, why doesn't He speak to us today in the same compelling way? Those who believe that men actually heard the voice of God offer the following explanations:

1. In the early childhood of the human race, man was spiritually immature and unable to discover God unaided. God, therefore, revealed Himself by a display of supernatural power. God spoke to man until man could learn to speak to God. Such supernatural manifestation is no longer necessary.

2. The generations that were privileged to hear the Divine Voice were *receptive* to that voice. The Age of Revelation was an age of profound spiritual sensitivity: men listened intently in their striving to attune themselves to God. The age that produced Moses, the Prophets and others who could hear God, was an age of exceptional spiritual excellence. Our scientific-minded age can only produce scientific geniuses. We tend to be unreceptive spiritually.

Those who believe that God surely speaks to man, but not in a physical sense, interpret God's speech as follows:

God's speech is real but our description of God's speech is only a *figure* of speech, a symbolic representation. God's speech is a spiritual fact too profound for reduction to mere verbal expression. Any attempt to describe God's speech in physical and psychical terms is as inadequate as the young child's visualization of a concrete God in the physical likeness of his idealized father, or with the moral attributes of his glorified mother. God's speech—how God makes His Will known to man—has been, and always will remain, a mystery.

God's speech is unlike human speech. It does not follow, therefore, that God is speechless. "And the Lord spoke," is no miracle. Surely, God speaks! It is only a miracle that man can sometimes hear and comprehend even a little of what God is saying. The problem is not *whether* God speaks but rather *how* to hear and comprehend His message.

Can Man Train Himself to Hear God?

Tradition never asked, "Can God hear man?" "He who formed the eye, surely sees, and He Who planted the ear, surely hears." An all-powerful God hears even that which a man considers in his heart. On the other hand, it did ponder how man, with his human limitations, could hear God.

Before we turn to tradition's reflections on this question, let us try to adopt the proper frame of mind. We should challenge ourselves rather than Him. The Lord surely speaks, why can we not hear? Are we listening with a sincere desire to hear? Have we done everything possible to render ourselves worthy, therefore capable, of hearing Him? God is not a foolhardy man who must accept a dare or rise to a challenge. When we ask: "*If* there is a God, why doesn't He speak?" our arrogance and doubt have already stopped up our ears with the impropriety of the challenge. Man hears God speak when man asks *himself*: "What doth the Lord God require of me?"

Tradition says that man's ability to hear God depends on man:

Man must have strong will. He must will to use all his

heart and soul and mind to discern the voice of God. Without aspiration to hear, there is no inspiration to listen.

Man must make strong effort. When man inquires with his lips, seeks with his mind, reaches out with his spirit, he may hear God.

Man must have confidence that God reveals. When man struggles to find his way to the Divine Presence and is firm in his faith that God can guide him, he may hear God.

There must be right motive, and moral and spiritual fitness. When man is worthy, he may hear God.

Tradition says that God can make Himself heard when He wills it. Sometimes a man would rather not hear God but he is compelled to listen. He may shut his ears and his heart but there is no escape. The voice of God pursues and batters on the closed doors of his mind and conscience until man lets Him in.

Is It Important to Hear God's Voice?

A rabbi once told the following story:

A musician played dance music which was so compelling and beautiful that all listeners began to dance with abandon and ardor. A deaf man entered the room and, not seeing the musician, could not understand why the people were leaping about with such enthusiasm. Were these not madmen dancing for no reason! So it is with those who are deaf to the voice of God: the music and joy of religion elude them. Those who dance to its music often look like madmen to those who cannot hear or appreciate the age-old chant of religion.

Meaning is the joyful music of life. If there is no musician, there is no music; if there is no God, there is no meaning to life. To the end that our lives may indeed follow a joyful, harmonious, balanced pattern, regardless of the range of experience, we must plan with purpose, operate with ideas and ideals, and strive for a meaningful composition. This is possible only if we are sensitively attuned to the Great Composer. To declare God an illusion is to declare all human striving senseless. Through faith, we cultivate sensitive response to God to enable us to hear Him. Without faith, there is no hearing; without hearing, there is no rejoicing; without rejoicing and understanding, how can life have meaning?

What is the Instrument of God's Voice?

The great prophets, sages and poets of Israel saw and heard God everywhere:

"The voice of the Lord is upon the waters.
The voice of the Lord breaketh cedars.
The voice of the Lord slaketh the wilderness.
The voice of the Lord heweth out flames of fire.
The voice of the Lord strippeth the forest bare."

They heard God in the winds, in the rushing waters and in the pelting rain. They heard Him in the laughter and weeping of the human heart, in the spoken and written word of man, in art, music, poetry; in the quiet song of a burning bush and in the whispered pledge of lovers.

Our people heard His voice at Sinai. We too hear Him speak whenever we gather to study Torah. We come to the synagogues to listen to Him as much as to speak to Him. We hear Him every time we reflect on or fulfil *mitzvos* of our religion. In every man is a miniature Sinai, the conscience, to remind man that there is a right and a wrong, and that he must choose the right in order to live right.

The voice of God is heard in nature and in human nature, in the great events of history, and in the small but significant details of each person's life.

How Can We Be Sure God Is Speaking?

We encounter the voice of God as a spiritual experience: He "speaks" in a divine, universal "language" that each man "translates" into his own cultural and personal vernacular. God speaks in one language which transcends all languages but is expressible in any language. This is no physical voice expressing itself in exact terms. To some, the voice of God is so clear, so close, so precise that they seem to hear very literally; the voice is almost a physical reality to them. To others, the voice of God is too subtle, too universal and spiritual, too distant and hidden, to be interpreted literally; it is a spiritual reality more real than physical reality. To still others, the voice of God is figurative speech or poetry symbolic of reality; the symbol is not reality and the poetry is not the voice of God, but they express Ultimate Reality.

Regardless of the manner in which we experience the voice of God, how do we know that the experience is valid? In a sense, faith is the way and faith is also the test: without faith there is no voice of God; with faith comes a feeling of confidence and certainty. But Judaism insists on the additional test of Truth and Reason. The voice of God can express only moral and spiritual truths. It may go beyond reason but it may not do violence to reason: it must have the ring of truth. If ever we are haunted by the possibility that the voice we hear is not of God but merely a psychic experience, let us remember that there is always ground for reasonable doubt for those who are not dogmatic. That is why we must continually strengthen the structure of our faith. If there were no uncertainty, we would not cultivate and seek certainty; if we begin with the assumption that all is known, there is no incentive to increase knowledge; if faith, reason and truth were finite qualities, we could not comprehend the dynamic universe. A test of the validity of what we interpret as the voice of God is whether it is a clear call for us to realize a little more of the remarkable potential for feeling and understanding that is in each one of us. The final test is whether it leads to the fulfillment of *mitzvos*: deeds that ennoble life, add to its sanctity, relieve suffering, and increase the welfare of our fellowmen.

CHAPTER II

Proving and Defining God

Can We Prove the Existence of God?

No! The existence of God cannot be proven beyond a shadow of doubt. The shadow has its purpose and cannot ever be removed by brilliant exposition or argument. For those who have faith, belief in God is no problem. They are moved, miraculously, by the same spirit that made it possible for a Jew hiding from the Nazis in the darkened shadows of a devastated building in Cologne to write on the wall: "I believe in the sun even when not feeling or seeing it; I believe in God even when He is silent."

Faith transports some beyond the shadow that envelops the brilliant light that is God. By faith, the unseen God is "seen." We interpret the visible in terms of the invisible and the known effects in creation by the invisible Creator. By faith, some men first see the Unseen, then find evidence for Him in the visible world everywhere. Faith needs no proofs.

How Can We Learn to Have Faith?

If a man does not have faith in God, he must construct his own ladder to Heaven. Step by step, in common-sense fashion, he must try to find his way to God. The man of faith proceeds from the unknown to the known; others can arrive at the Creator through the visible effects of His creation. By humbly seeking the evidence for belief, he may be privileged to catch a glimpse of God.

Tradition instructs him to practice the forms: pray, observe and keep the Law. Through repeated action he may, in time, arrive at belief. If a man keeps the discipline of a faith, he may find his way to that faith. Practice is itself an expression of hope and belief that may lead to true faith. According to the prophet, God said: "Would that they had forsaken Me and not My Law."

Believing in God is reasonable and desirable. For evidence that such belief is reasonable, we shall observe nature; that it is desirable, we shall observe *human* nature.

What Are the Classical Proofs for the Existence of God?

1. *Creation implies a Creator.*

Experience teaches us that everything in existence has a maker. It is reasonable to assume that the universe did not make itself either. Ergo, the existence of the universe implies a Creator.

2. *Cause and effect imply a First Cause.*

Just as every effect has a cause, every cause is itself the effect of some prior cause. Experience makes that observation sound enough. If everything *in* nature is the effect of some cause, we must look for some initiatory cause *outside of* nature. This first uncaused cause is the Ultimate Cause of the chain of events which proceed from it. This First Supernatural Cause is God.

3. *Motion implies a Prime Mover.*

A physical body will remain inert unless and until set in motion by some outside force. The universe consists of physical bodies in constant motion. What force is responsible for having started, and maintaining, them in motion? The Prime Mover was the Supernatural God who alone possesses the power to move and make move without a preceding natural cause.

4. *Change implies an ultimate Unchanged and Unchanging Agent.*

Everything in nature is characterized by constant change. Change itself is the result of action *on* something *by* something else and that something else, in its turn, was acted on by still another force making for change, and so on. This chain of changes must have had its beginning somewhere. Logic seeks an initial force for change outside of nature since everything in nature is itself a subject of change. This Unchanged and Unchanging Primary Agent or Force for Change must be the Supernatural God.

5. *Law implies a Law Giver.*

All nature follows natural laws; no part of nature makes its own rules. The laws governing the bio-physical nature of man, for instance, are certainly not of his own devising. The laws governing the complex relationships in nature either emerged by trial and error, or by accident, out of an unthinking nature or were conceived in the all-powerful intellect of God. The latter possibility is far more reasonable: the operation of natural laws implies the existence of a Law Maker Who transcends nature.

6. *Order suggests an Ordainer.*

The laws of nature, as we know them, are human formulations describing the order of nature, its various relationships, and the composition of bodies and forces in it. The physical order of nature either came out of chaos accidentally or was the Will of a Divine Ordainer. But what of the moral order? The aesthetic and intellectual orders, such as beauty and truth? Can all this order be the result of accident and coincidence? Can order automatically come from disorder? It is more reasonable to assume that the order of the universe was produced by an Almighty God than that it was the accidental result of meaningless, undirected, self-determined forces of *unknown* origin. It is, of course, possible to ignore the unknown factor altogether by shutting one's mind. But the whole thing makes no sense unless we trace the unknown origin back to God. The order we find, then, is no longer accident but design; what was meaningless becomes meaningful indeed.

7. *The order of the universe implies a Supreme and Creative Mind.*

The effects of an amazing order and system are discernable everywhere in nature. Our human minds can only *appreciate* the existence of systems and order which they neither created nor introduced. This prevalence of order in the realm of non-thinking things can only be conceived as the work and expression of a Creative Mind.

8. *The ingenious complexity of the universe implies a Supreme Intelligence.*

Darwin, the father of the Theory of Evolution, expressed it in these words, "Another source of conviction for the existence of God follows from the extreme difficulty or rather *impossibility* of conceiving this immense and wonderful universe, including man, with his capacity of looking forward with futurity, as the result of blind chance or necessity. I feel impelled to look for a First Cause, having an intelligent mind analogous to that of man in *some degree.*" The complicated structure of even a single atom, let alone the myriads of galaxies, precludes the assumption of blind, mechanical, non-rational, purposeless forces responsible for its contrivance. It is more reasonable to assume a Supreme Intelligence behind the complicated mechanisms of nature and man.

9. *The demand of logic for an independent entity.*

Everything in nature depends for its existence and its very form on something else. This is as true for the stars as it is for man. Logically, we must seek something outside the natural order on which the entire universe depends but which is itself completely independent. This something is the Supernatural God.

10. *Varying degrees of goodness imply a standard of perfection.*

There is good and there is better but there is no such thing as perfect (best) in earthly experience. Without the existence of a best, the concept of good and better is imperfect. Therefore, the Perfect must lie beyond earthly experience. This Perfect is the Supernatural God.

What Does Belief in God Do For Us?

Belief in God strengthens the moral foundations of life:

A. *Encourages humility*

When God is denied, man assumes that moral law is based on human opinion. Human power becomes *the* decisive moral force, and the world a battlefield of clashing and presumptuous human wills where society and our most cherished values are endangered. When man assumes that he is the sole author and judge of right and wrong, he invites the triumph of the dangerous doctrine "might makes right."

Men who humbly seek to understand God's Will and recognize their dependence on God as the Author of right and wrong are more likely to avoid the dangers of self-righteousness and brutal arrogance than those who "play the god." Humility is as essential to our humanity as to our morality; humility keeps us humane.

B. *Crowns man with dignity*

It is only the moral and spiritual nature of man which raises his status above that of a mere bio-physical phenomenon, the accidental by-product of natural processes. All men, regardless of race or religion, are stamped in the "image of God," making each life sacred and worthy of respect and honor. Robbed of this dignity, man's life would be cheapened to the value of a bug, to be exterminated without regret.

C. *Makes duty a lofty obligation*

Duty becomes an unreliable volunteerism dictated by baser motives such as self-pity, apathetic resignation, prudence, or utilitarian expediency, unless the great and convincing "oughts" of the moral life have their origin in God's Will rather than in human opinion. Man's acceptance of moral obligation must be a free choice dictated by loving commitment, but the source of moral obligation must be God's Will. Unless our moral obligations are conceived as commands of God to be fulfilled in loving obedience to His Will, even the noblest commitments may lead to demoralizing self-righteousness.

There is nothing to prevent man as an individual, or any part of society, or society as a whole, from denying duty and rejecting all moral obligation if the concept of moral duty is man-made and rests on authority no higher than man or human agencies constructed by man. If our sense of duty is simply the internalization of external authorities such as parents, teachers, the state and society as a whole, men have a moral right to reject the moral conscience which they have, or have had, imposed upon them. However, moral law, like natural law, is part of reality discoverable by man but not his creation; it is a law of life above human authority which points to the Ultimate Reality, to God. It is the best way to explain the persistence of the concept of duty and its indispensability to the moral life.

D. *Gives validity to ethics*

If the distinction between right and wrong were of man's making and man were the highest moral authority, men would have a moral right to deny the *absolute* validity of this distinction. If *justification* for the moral distinction between right and wrong, and for the authority behind man's obligation to choose the right, is to be sought in the common good, human welfare, or the collective judgment of society, we would still be in the unjustifiable position of trying to validate an *absolute principle* by authority of a *relative, transient and changeable human judgment.*

The kind of thinking that reduces moral law to a temporary and temporal agreement, or social contract, excuses man from the ultimate and eternal obligation to abstain from violating it whenever he thinks he can get away with it, or rejecting it whenever he sets himself above it. Burning out "the eyes of God" has been instrumental in weakening and breaking down moral certainty and behavior. We are still paying a terrible price for our sacrilege. The existence of a Higher Being, Whose concern is for the well-being of man, gives validity to ethics.

How Does Belief in God Strengthen Man's Will to Live?

Man needs belief in God to strengthen his will to live and to live well. It justifies his efforts to reach intangible goals, to realize the unrealized.

A. *Man needs belief in God in order to live*

There seems to be a vital connection between will to live and belief in God, the Source of All Life. For example, the life of a critically ill patient hangs, at times, on his will to live; where belief in God is strong, so is the will to live. The fields of psychology and medicine offer ample evidence that the individual with strong faith in God is less likely to suffer nervous breakdown than individuals who do not believe in God. For the latter there is no "will to live" a meaningless and purposeless life. Anthropologists say that entire ancient civilizations lost their will to live when they lost faith in their deity.

B. *Man needs belief in God in order to live well*

Belief in God strengthens man's will to make the most of life. To live well man needs:

1) hope and joy, courage and confidence;
2) a sense of personal worth and of the significance of the lives of his fellowmen;
3) to find purpose and meaning in life; and
4) to be morally accountable.

Belief in God inspires man with joyful expectation of realizing progress for himself as an individual and for society. He knows himself to be a purposeful force within a moral structure that encourages his sense of responsibility.

C. *Man needs belief in God to justify his efforts to reach intangible goals*

We have a solid basis for believing that our moral effort has value and meaning only if moral aspirations are part of God's vast purpose. What else explains and justifies the self-denial, self-discipline and strenuous endeavor without which no moral and spiritual growth is possible? It is natural for man to engage in a hopeful search for the purpose and meaning of life when he is confident that God has indeed invested all life with such purpose and meaning. The universe is a dynamic, creative, rational, purposive, conscious, and hope-inspiring reality because it bears the stamp of a loving Intelligence which is God.

How Can God Be Defined?

There's a definition for everything in the dictionary. There's a definition of life. Does any man seriously feel he can say everything there is to say about life? Is any definition final and complete? Man tries to define everything but nothing can be completely and permanently defined. The ancient Greeks had what they believed to be a categorical definition for atom: the smallest particle of matter. Since the early Greek definition there have been innumerable definitions for the smallest particle of matter and no scientist today would maintain that all the possibilities have been exhausted. The simplest words undergo continual change in nuance and sometimes complete change in meaning; abstract words change even more. No conceptual system which must be expressed in words can contain the whole of reality either in its internal composition or external boundaries. The simplest phenomenon defies complete and changeless definition. Always, ultimate source and ultimate purpose elude and confound all definitions. Theoretically, we could completely define anything we ourselves created by our own efforts and substance. But the substance always includes someone else's creation. Even man the creator is God's creation.

The logical positivists say that nothing exists except that which we already know, or that which we do not yet know but which, in principle, may some day become the object of our knowledge. Anything else, that is, anything which is by definition unknowable, is meaningless nonsense and does not exist. This position makes of man the omnipotent God of the universe who determines what exists by what he knows or can know. It leads to absurdity: if man were to disappear from the earth, everything else would cease to exist. Furthermore, what does the positivist mean by "knowing,"—a term subject in itself to many definitions. Some things we know by our powers of reason, but only partially or imperfectly; some things we know as we experience them by powers of our being other than mind. But as we mature our perspective undergoes change. There are many theories and definitions of knowledge, subjective and objective, but these are themselves variables which cannot define "knowing."

Although we know that God, too, is indefinable, our efforts to define our relationship with Him and how we experience Him are a necessary and desirable component of the great search for truth. Many have experienced God, from the innocent child to the mature and sensitive priest, prophet, sage, saint, poet, philosopher, mystic and artist, and their efforts to express God have resulted in the development of countless formulations, ingenious conceptions, endless visions and inspiring pictures. What God *is* we cannot know, but what He *can* or *does mean* for us is very important.

Why Is It Difficult to Define God?

1. The limited human mind cannot define a limitless God. Any attempt to define God leads to some human error. When the pious Jew defines God or ascribes an adjective to Him he humbly adds the word *Kivyochol* (as though it were possible for me to say anything about God). Eager to emphasize God's incomprehensibility and the need for humility in at-

tempting to define Him, Jewish mystics speak of God as *Ayn* (He Who Is Not). In much the same spirit, Jewish medieval philosophers, in particular Maimonides, insisted that we could only understand some of the things that God is not, never what He is. To say something positive about Him is to limit Him. Even to assert that He is absolute is to confine Him within our limited conception of the absolute.

2. Any attempt to define God must be via man-created vehicles of expression. Thus, a definition of God must be either in mechanomorphic (in the image of a machine or process) or in anthropomorphic (in the image of man) terms. Since the most exalted terms available to us are anthropomorphic, we tend to describe God in terms of human qualities but always with the understanding that He is more and other than what we are describing. Human qualities such as mercy, righteousness, goodness, etc., may be attributed to God, or He may be conceived as Power, Force, Process, etc. Words and ideas are simply inadequate to describe the indescribable or to comprehend fully the incomprehensible. All metaphysical speculation must inevitably remain inconclusive, for human vocabulary will never be adequate.

3. We must insist that descriptions of God be consistent with our loftiest conceptions of reality. However, we cannot insist that our best conceptions of reality or of God are, at any time, consistent, accurate or complete. Indeed, when our formulation appears perfect and whole, we should be troubled. We should not be overly concerned that our description of God is inconsistent, imperfect and inadequate because we are thus lead to continue our search for greater revelation. To say that God cannot have any meaning apart from human ideas or ideals is to announce that God can only be interpreted in natural terms. To state that God is supernatural does not define Him but admits that we cannot completely encompass or define Him. We must define

God in human terms even though we cannot arrive at a categorical definition of Him in such terms.

4. The chief difficulty arises out of the nature of God: He is both transcendent and immanent. The transcendent God is the Infinite God beyond the universe: remote, unsearchable, unknowable by man. The Immanent God is reflected in the world, and involved in the very life of the grass underfoot, in every clod of earth. As we start to describe God in terms of His transcendence, we lose sight of Him and our feelings of closeness to Him. In our haste and desire to recapture our loss, we start to describe Him in terms of His immanence only to find that we are out of touch with the lofty aspects of His transcendence. That is, we can think of God as an abstraction or in concrete terms; in terms of spiritual quality or of physical attributes expressed in anthropomorphic or in mechanomorphic terms; as a Force or a Person. Thus, we either depersonalize or overhumanize Him: a disembodied principle or an all-powerful man. Either way, we fail to see God as He is because of our inability to grasp simultaneously transcendent and immanent qualities.

5. We cannot encompass God in any definition because He is *beyond* definition. As the God Who is near to us, He is the Personal God but, He is also the God beyond. He is the God Who "led us out of Egypt," the Lord of *our* history, But He is also the Lord beyond all history. He was the personal God of Abraham, Isaac and Jacob, and is the God of Israel and the personal God of all the world. But He is also the God beyond the world.

How Can a Transcendent God Be Real?

Man defines and redefines but he can never feel or say: "I have *the* definition of God." He must avoid the pitfall of presumptuousness which would make him proclaim in arrogance that he has found God, that he has the final definition. He must also avoid the opposite pitfall of saying, "all of this is too much for me. My God is the God Whom I can never understand anyway." Everyone must strive to make the God "beyond," his personal God. In his search for God, man will always find a personal "god" regardless how refined or exalted. But, the personal "god" points always to the God who transcends our "gods." Beyond our concrete "gods" is the indefinable God drawing us ever toward Him as we exert ourselves to comprehend Him.

CHAPTER III

God Faith and Morality

Do We Need Religion In Order To Be Ethical?

The popular statement, *"My* religion is *doing* good," expresses the widespread notion that ethical conduct is possible without religion, that *doing* good is sufficient. Some adherents of this view may even admit that religion sustains morality. But, they maintain, only those who tend to be weak in mind or character, or both, *need* religion. They say: "A person can be moral without being religious, without believing in God. Look at me!"

Of course an individual can have moral ideals and live by them without believing in God. However, the fact that he has set up moral ideals to live by is already an indication that he is acting under the influence of the moral implications of religious belief. No man can be so arrogant as to believe that his ethical standards were created out of his own head, independent of the background and culture into which he was born. Religious values are an inseparable component of that culture and background.

The real question becomes: "Having extracted the religious ethic, why should I bother with religion and belief in God?" Consideration focuses on a cluster of questions into which this one question breaks down: "Would belief in God affect my ethical stand in any way?" "Does my failure to believe in God have an adverse affect on my own moral life or on society?" "Cannot morality continue, vigorous and sound, without religion?" "Does belief in God add to or detract from ethics?"

What is More Important: Faith or Action?

In the Talmud, the Rabbis discuss a question analogous to the one we have raised: "Which is more important, study or action?" Rabbi Tarfon's position was: "Action is more important. Of what earthly use are fine words and preachments unless they are put into practice?" Rabbi Akiba upheld the contrary view: "Learning is more important because it leads to action." The final conclusion of the Sages synthesized the two contrary opinions into a greater truth: "Study is more important because it leads to action, but study is of no value when it does not lead to good deeds."

In the rabbinic view, the relationship between faith and action is precisely the same as between study and action. Faith in God leads to moral conduct and moral conduct, performing the Will of God, is the whole purpose of faith. At times the Rabbis stressed the importance of good deeds or works; at times they stressed the importance of faith. The needs of the times determined where the emphasis was placed, but it was always understood that both elements are essential.

When the importance of good deeds was being highlighted, the Rabbis pictured God as saying: "Would that they had forsaken Me and kept my law." In other words, the true test of a man's worth is his deeds, not his creed. Thus, they taught that the first question asked of man when he appears before the Throne of Judgment is whether he has dealt faithfully with his fellowman, not whether he had faith in God. "Who shall ascend unto the mountain of the Lord?" asks the Psalmist. "He that hath clean hands and a pure heart," is the answer that he gives.

When the importance of faith had to be emphasized, the Rabbis expressed it in this fashion: "The Holy One, blessed be He, is concerned, above all, with what is in a man's heart." The teaching of the Prophet: "The righteous shall live by his faith," and the counsel of the author of Proverbs: "As a man thinketh, so is he," were heavily underscored.

Commenting on Leviticus 5:21 ("If any one sin and commit a trespass against the Lord, and deal falsely with his neighbor"), the Sages remarked: "No man deals falsely with his neighbor until he denies first the Root (God)."

In brief, faith and action are equally important. They are actually inseparable. Creed that does not lead to good deed is meaningless; and morality without creed is detached from its root (God) and cannot long endure.

How Do Our Beliefs Influence Our Conduct?

Our behaviour is strongly influenced by our goals and values, and by what we are willing to do in order to attain them. Our beliefs condition both our goals and values, and how we exert ourselves for their attainment.

When the world seems without purpose or meaning, man operates as though the ultimate reality is amoral. He is for himself and only for himself (his immediate family is a mere extension of himself). He can be ruthless in exploiting others for his advantage, unconcerned about the needs and desires of others or callously unaware of them altogether as he strives to achieve his ambitions for self-gratification or self-aggrandizement. He is capable of sacrificing anything or anyone that threatens to interfere with his ambitions. In his mind, and in accordance with his code, the end justifies the immoral means. The end may or may not be immoral but it is always unworthy.

When man is unsure of the reality of God, his belief lacks conviction. He pays lip-service to God but is unwilling to make the sacrifices necessary to maintain moral integrity. Hypocrisy is wide-spread in our society because man's belief lacks the strength and certainty to uphold morality when it conflicts with self-interest. It is self-induced moral blindness.

When man feels that his conduct is under the watchful eye of God, the quality of his life is greatly enhanced. His sense of moral responsibility is strong, his conscience is clear, and his will firm. He is inspired to live worthily today because he feels secure in the knowledge that the future is in God's hands. Man is a moral man when he lives in loving awareness of God and is concerned about upholding the worth and dignity of all God's creatures.

Are Ethical Values Man-given or God-given?

Those who disclaim God as the author and creator of morality, those who see in ethics something apart from religion, must attribute morality to man's creation. This leads, logically, to such conclusions as:

1. Men are the supreme judges of right and wrong.

2. All morality is relative since there is no absolute standard for right and wrong.

3. All morality is subject to change depending on what is expedient in a given time and place.

4. Morality in any one society is as good as morality in any other society.

5. In effect, men are not morally responsible. They simply hold themselves responsible to themselves alone, or to social agencies composed of other men, for upholding whatever they wish to regard as right.

6. One man's morality is as good as another man's. Man as an individual and men as groups have a right to set aside a moral law which is man-made.

One of the indigenous elements in the moral consciousness of the religious man or the religious society is the sense of accountability and responsibility to God. Religious people behave with the conviction that they are answerable for their conduct to a Being higher than themselves; they must obey "higher laws," immutable laws, which are independent of man's whim and varying judgment. The basic premise of religion makes us responsible for our conduct to a Judge and to a Law, higher than man and not of his making. This has been a powerful incentive to virtue; and an effective restraint on immoral action.

Agnostics and atheists can live moral lives only because the world has been humanized by religious ideas and ideals for thousands of years. Religious influence pervades the society of which we are a part. Since religion is the driving force behind morality, a decline in religion may very well bring about a decline in morality. If the belief in God, the foundation of moral responsibility, is undermined, then man's sense of moral responsibility may very well be impaired.

How Do Non-Religious Ethical Systems Measure Morality?

Non-religious ethical systems appeal to man's self-interest. Man is encouraged to measure the value of morality by the yardstick of self-benefit. Thus, non-religious ethics tends to promote selfishness, the very quality which makes the training of character for moral responsibility so difficult.

Even appeals to enlightened self-interest are bound to result in weakened morality since morality remains subservient to expediency. For instance, the ethical principal that honesty is the best policy is rational enough: human relations would break down if mutual distrust and suspicion prevailed. However, the degree of adherence to the principle depends on how strongly we are motivated by a rationale that will support and induce honesty even when it does not pay. When morals are treated like commercial values, moral failure threatens our society.

Religion, on the other hand, appeals to the moral conscience of man. It calls upon man to do what is right whether or not it is in his own interest. The only valid principle is a divine principle from a divine source. For instance, man *must* concern himself for the unfortunate because every man is his brother under the Fatherhood of God. Ethical conduct is the religious man's way of expressing love for God and the desire to serve Him. When love of God and the duty to serve Him are no longer the primary motive for right action, man's self-interest dictates behavior based on "What's in it for me?"

The tendency in moral philosophy to enthrone anything or anyone less than God as the highest authority, source and ultimate judge of morality has forced men into the position of adopting lesser gods fashioned by men. Even when man conquers the impulse to set *himself* up as god and final authority, he creates *other* gods: service to the state, a class, a party, an international organization, a political philosophy or some other ideal, and declares them to be ultimate standards by which to judge right and wrong. The effect of such idolatry is to create a confusion in our moral language, contention and disorder in the moral life of man. Non-religious ethics results in precisely such moral breakdown.

Has Religion Helped Man Become More Ethical?

In addition to serving as the source of authority for morality, religion has supplied fresh insights to enrich the content and spirit of ethics. For example, Judaism's acceptance of the idea of the Fatherhood of One God led to its discovery of man as "fellow man," and "brother," thereby revolutionizing ethics. The principle has not yet been fully understood but it remains potentially applicable.

In Jewish religious ethics, all men are children of the One God and, consequently, brothers. Out of His love, the Father instructs His children: "Thou shalt and thou shalt not"; out of their love, the children hearken to the wisdom of the Father and obey. Through obedience to the moral law of God, men acquire a sense of responsibility to do right. Through love of God and of their brothers, men become moral men.

Scientific ethical thinking honors in each man the universal idea of humanity but has little concern with the individual as a person. Its impersonal approach and its organ of expression, the impersonal law, reduces ethics to an intellectual formulation, a scientific prescription. Precisely because scientific ethics makes no attempt to understand man as a person and address him as such, it has but little influence in the moral life of man. It fails to involve him emotionally. Objective, rational, and scientifically formulated principles of ethics, divorced from religion, cannot operate effectively in the lives of men because the great emotions—love, pity, sacrifice, hate, fear—have been belittled or ignored.

Moral ideals become a matter of chance when moral principles are an expression of personal preference or logic: that there is no certainty of their success makes for insecurity. Moral principles laid down by religion are a program written into the scheme of things, God's design of universal possibilities.

Religion predicates a God, a Power that makes for righteousness, and His moral laws are absolute. This God-faith is necessary to help man translate the laws of God into the laws of human life; it offers assurance, strength, explanation, and consolation in the face of indecision, self-seeking, sorrow, or lassitude.

Is Belief in God Wishful Thinking?

Even if the belief in God were *rooted* in wishful thinking, the validity of the belief would not be affected. What we wish may be either true or untrue. Some religious beliefs are, indeed, mothered by men's wishes; some are fathered by their fears; but the roots of religion penetrate far deeper than hope or need. The sources of our religious convictions are love and duty, honor and self-respect, the majesty and mystery of life. We believe in God and follow our faith because of intangible values in the soul which are far more real and powerful than wishes in the mind.

To say that belief in God is *merely* wishful thinking is to imply that the belief is not supported by reason or by any other evidence. But the rational arguments for beliefs in

God are at least as good, and certainly as numerous, as those for disbelief.

What are the Rational Arguments for Belief in God?

We can see how rational is the belief in God by tracing the roots of our faith to its many diverse sources, other than wishful thinking.

1. *Logic.* Any phenomenon can be explained more logically in terms of relationship than in terms of itself. An attempt to understand the whole in terms of only one of its component parts is less enlightening than the effort to see a part in relation to the whole. Thus, when we begin with human motive as an approach to explaining God, we may arrive at the erroneous conclusion that God is a myth, a product of man's wishful thinking. By following the more logical procedure of trying to account for man, his motives, and behavior in terms of a higher order of being, we move in the direction of belief in God. God may be comprehended as the reason or cause for man's wishful thinking rather than as the result. It is more realistic to think of the creature as the product of the Creator than to assume that the Creator is the product of the creature's imagination.

2. *Experience.* Man feels compelled to interpret himself, his fears, hopes, his very being, in relationship to the world outside himself. This need to find a causal category, or principle, to help explain life and the universe is what distinguishes man from the rest of the animal kingdom. He is moved by logic and experience, rather than by wishful thinking, to postulate a belief in God. Unless God *is* real, human goals and strivings are futile and meaningless; moral and spiritual hopes are contrivances generated by wishful thinking; ideals are artificial, and whether or not they are attainable hardly matters.

3. *Intellectual affirmation.* No intelligent person forms his beliefs and convictions on nonrational grounds; no religious person could continue to believe in God if he found it

contrary to reason. A person who is both intelligent and religious is, in a sense, always thinking about his beliefs, subjecting them to increasingly mature evaluation. Belief in God is dynamic, not static.

4. *Considered judgment.* The religious person believes in God not because he wishes to believe but because he is convinced of the value of his belief. He has considered the intellectual, aesthetic, moral and spiritual values, and concluded that belief in God is intellectually satisfying, aesthetically appealing, morally desirable, and spiritually satisfying.

5. *The will of man.* Something in the will of religious man refuses to concede that life is an accident of physics and chemistry, that the universe is a blind movement from nowhere to nowhere. The religious man wills that life should come under the dominion of the moral and spiritual values which he associates with the Divine, and that the universe should respond to the will of a living and loving God. By his very will to believe, the religious man makes these ideas function as facts in his life. To the religious man, God is a reality and functions as such in his life. When the will of man is in harmony with the will of God, the Maker of all truth, then the will of man becomes a maker of truth.

6. *Free will.* From the standpoint of Judaism, all of reality is the product of will, the result of choice. The world came into being because God willed it; what God wills becomes real. The divine image in man makes it possible for man, to a limited extent, to share this power of will and creativity with God. When man's will is in harmony with God's will, he is creative. When man's will is contrary to the Divine will, he is destructive. "Everything is in the hands of God except man's will to believe in God." Man is no automaton: endowed with free will, his belief in God depends on his own choice. It may be wishful thinking but it is creative thinking.

7. *Human hope* that what *ought to* be true *is* true. Rejection of religion may be due to fear of error or to

cynicism. Rather than yield to our fear of being wrong in matters of important moral and spiritual belief, we should yield to our hope that the belief may be true. It is wiser and better to make a positive decision, for only positive decision can lead to positive action. Negative decision as well as indecision lead to nothing. The great formula of religion is: think the best, act for the best, believe in the best, pray for the best, then, have the maturity to take what comes without regret or self-reproach. We are all fallible when we attempt to break paths leading to truth. Our urge is to discover or uncover truths from the Great Unknown so that they may function in our lives for good, and give us purpose and direction.

8. *Awareness of present limitations and future promise.* In the universe are imbedded many truths and a multitude of facts which do not yet function as realities in our lives because we are not aware of them. The law of gravity, for instance, operated for a long time in the world before it was recognized and put to conscious use in comparatively recent times; coal in the earth gave no warmth and light until it was discovered and we learned how to use it. They did not exist for man until discovered and put to use, but they existed, nonetheless. Similarly, there are vast treasures and wonderful blessings in the universe and in man himself of which we are unaware, but they exist nonetheless. They wait to be willed into our consciousness by faith, persistent exploration, action, experience and discovery. In this respect, the will of man is the maker of truth and can transform the character of the world. When man wills that his reality should be a living and responsible one, *that* reality tends to actualize itself in experience as a result of man's thinking and behavior. The essential difference between the religious and nonreligious view is the quality or character of the world, the quality or character of human effort bent on making the most and best of it. The will of man is capable of discovering God.

9. *Faith*. God, the Great Unknown, is not subject to concrete demonstration and verification. And it requires an act of faith on the part of man to transport him beyond the known. Faith and the drive to go beyond what *is* have made discovery, exploration, and invention possible. In this respect, all advances in civilization, even purely material ones, begin with wishful thinking. Certainly in the search for truth, for an enlarged understanding of man and his universe, and in the cultivation of appreciation and creation in the arts, man must *start* with the faith that such possibilities exist and that they are unlimited in an evolving civilization.

How Do We Achieve Faith?

Of course, wishful thinking is *only* a starting point. Partial realization—never complete because each achievement is the starting point for the next, ad infinitum—comes only through intensive cultivation and purposeful, self-imposed discipline: Faith, like all the elevating and humanizing arts, is a spiritual experience, an exquisite refinement of inner response. It is not a free gift; it is not an inanimate possession to have and to hold. It is a living thing which must be nurtured continually in order to survive and grow.

Some people are born with a rare talent for faith just as some have innate and superior potential in music, art, literature, and science. But to realize any potential one must be willing to work at it with persistence, passion, and patience. A spiritual goal is ever-expanding: it grows richer in possibilities, more beautiful, and more rewarding in proportion to the time and effort expended in seeking after it. The creative artist must continually create or he ceases to be creative. Similarly, the man of faith must continually deepen, heighten, and add dimension to the understanding of his faith.

If an unmusical child is given no opportunity to learn

music and is rarely exposed to it, he may discover, in adulthood, that music leaves him cold and unmoved. Would he be justified in asserting that the power of music to evoke exquisite response was a myth? He could multiply himself by tens of thousands and point to these as "proof" that music lacks unique power. Of course, the lack is not in the music but in himself. Had he proper humility and an open mind, he would recognize that, like all men, he has limitations. Yet, people both intelligent and intellectual have had the arrogance to deny God and faith because they had never experienced them. These same individuals would not disallow a scientific theory because they could not follow through the reasoning in all its complexity. They would not deny the evocative power of poetry or art to which they personally are unable to respond. They are being neither consistent nor reasonable when they deny the existence of sensibilities which, in truth, do not exist for them.

What Is The Difference Between Wishful Thinking and Faith?

By simply defining the two terms, we can readily see that they are related. But a world of difference separates them. Wishful thinking may be a starting point for faith but, being static, it is left far behind by the dynamic force which is faith.

What Is Wishful Thinking?

It is passive contemplation of life and the world as we would wish them to be. The contemplator remains unmoved to act, and life and the world go on unchanged. Wishful thinking may be harmless but it may also be tragic when it makes the world appear to be as we wish it to be rather than as it really is. It ranges from fantasy, which is completely detached from reality, to an idle mental position or attitude.

What Is Faith?

In its Hebrew sense, faith is the trust that makes man realize his strength and endurance; it moves him to fulfil *mitzvos*. As a motive power, faith impels man to act in the service of God and lends him the assurance that what man cannot do alone will be done, if it ought to be done, by God. It is the vehicle which enables man to transcend the known, move into the unknown knowable, and to come into communion with the Unknowable; it is the force that illuminates vision, emboldens action and attempts to transform, with confidence. It is a rigorous exercise of affirmation involving man's whole being in thought, feeling and action. It casts light on the significance of the past, gives meaning to the present, and proclaims the confidence that creates the future.

What Are Some Common Misconceptions About Faith?

Faith is belief that brings peace of mind. On the contrary, faith *is not* euphoria which allows us to empty our minds of unpleasant reality and allows us to be buffeted about blindly. Faith *is* firm decision to face and conquer one's fears; declaration of resistance to weakness and laziness; protest against irresponsibility; commitment of self to accept challenge. Faith is the initial step that leads to fulfillment through exertion.

Faith is a one-time leap to belief in God. Once that belief is accepted, we have faith. On the contrary, faith is a slow, steady, rigorous exercise in growth. To be kept alive as an operating factor in our lives, it must be cultivated intensively by purposeful, self-imposed discipline. The degree of maturation it achieves is determined by our own strivings.

In Judaism, Which is More Important—Ritual or Morality?

Ancient religions were almost exclusively concerned with ritual. They concentrated on the forms by which man acts out his relationship to his deity. Since the purpose of ritual was to propitiate the gods, it had to be performed with precision lest the gods take offense. Consequently, all ancient religions had a body of experts, called priests, who were trained to perform the ministrations with exactitude. Their gods may have been wrong, their motives may have been wrong, and their ways may have been wrong, but all grasped intuitively the truth underlying all of man's religious effort: the supreme importance of pleasing God. What they almost completely failed to recognize is what Judaism emphasizes mostly: the best way to please God is via the road of moral living. Stress on the moral law was and is one of the important distinctions between Judaism and other religions.

Judaism does not reject or minimize the importance of ritual. The Torah contains the ritual as well as the moral laws. Both are indispensable. Without piety there can be no vital and enduring morality. Men *must* cultivate spiritual awareness, the discipline of piety and worshipful relationship with God or they lack the sound moral orientation which makes for a desirable relationship with their fellowmen.

Judaism is both priest-minded and prophet-minded. The priests of ancient Israel stressed the punctilious fulfillment of the prescriptions of ritual but recognized their ethical value. The prophets of ancient Israel emphasized personal morality, national integrity, social righteousness but recognized the value of ritual. Rabbinic Judaism welded both views into a way of life in which the controlling motive of doing all things for God elevates all human effort into a unity of high purpose. Sometimes men neglect one; sometimes, the other. To those who tend to make ritual piety synonymous with religion, Judaism says, "stress morality." To those who equate morality with religion, Judaism says, "stress ritual." In Judaism, religion without morality is as unthinkable as religion without ritual.

Judaism maintains that ritual is indispensable to religion but morality is more important than ritual in man's service to God.

What Evidence is There That Tradition Considers Morality More Important Than Ritual?

In cases where observance of the ritual law obviates a moral law, the ritual law is waived. According to the Talmud, all the ritual laws of the Sabbath—no other ritual laws are more important than these—must be set aside if it means saving even one life. The same Talmudic law insists that a Jew must sacrifice his own life if, in order to save himself, he is required to commit murder or sexual immorality. To sum up, all ritual laws may be waived to save a single life but a Jew must be ready to die rather than transgress certain moral laws. Similarly, a man who meticulously observes all ritual requirements but neglects his moral duties is called "one who despises God's name." As a rule, the tradition classifies moral acts as "serious" *mitzvos*, and ritual acts as "light" *mitzvos*.

In the literature and in the liturgy, God's moral attributes are more frequently referred to than His metaphysical attributes. The qualities which should be prominently marked in human conduct are precisely the ones most frequently and conspicuously described as attributes of God. According to rabbinic literature, the ideal that guides man's conduct should be imitation of God. The God of Judaism is a moral God and the godly man is a moral man. This doctrine, the foundation and motive of Jewish ethics, is expressed in various sources. For example, the Rabbis of the Talmud interpreted the verse, "Ye shall walk after the Lord your God," (Deut. 13:4) to mean: "As He clothes the naked, so do you clothe the naked; as He visits the sick, so do you visit the sick; as He comforts the mourners, so should you comfort those who mourn; as He buries the dead, so should you bury the dead." The verse, "To walk in all His ways," (Deut. 11:22) is interpreted as a reference to God's compassion, mercy and truth. The verse, "Whosoever shall be called by the name of the Lord shall be delivered," (Joel 2:32) called forth the question, "How is it possible for a man to be called by the name of the Holy One?" The answer of the Rabbis was: "As God is called Compassionate and Gracious, be you also compassionate and gracious; as God is called Righteous, be you also righteous; and as He is called Loving, be you also loving."

The Doctrine of the Seven Commandments of the sons of Noah implies that man establishes his kinship with God and fulfills this relationship primarily by living morally. In this doctrine, Judaism stated that: 1) a gentile earns Divine approval if he lives a righteous life based on the seven basic rules of moral conduct, and 2) moral men of all peoples inherit the bliss of the Hereafter. This would establish that, in the eyes of God, a man's worth is judged by the quality of his moral life, not by the content of his ritual performance. "I call to witness heaven and earth that on all human beings, whether gentile or Israelite, man or woman, according to their deeds so does the Holy Spirit rest upon them." (Gen. Rabbah 52:11 and Tanna de-be Eliyahu 9).

A heathen once asked the great sage Hillel to tell him the whole of Judaism while he stood on one foot. His answer was, "Do not unto others what is hateful to you. All the rest is commentary." Here, too, is the implication that a man's morality, how he relates himself to his fellowmen, is the test of how man relates himself to God. The same priority of values is implied in the well-known Mishnah: "For transgressions between man and God (ritual), the Day of Atonement makes atonement; for transgressions between man and man (moral) the Day of Atonement cannot atone until the transgressor appeases his fellowman by making amends." (Yoma 8:9)

"The commandments were given only in order to purify human nature." (Gen. Rabbah 44:1) This authoritative statement by the great sage Rav implies that the purpose of the ritual and moral laws of the Torah is to improve the quality of the ethical life. This view is further supported by other authoritative statements in the Talmud and elsewhere:

When the Rabbis of the Talmud commented on the Prophet Micah's statement, "It hath been told thee, O man, what the Lord God doth require of thee: to do justice, love mercy, and walk humbly with thy God," they interpreted all three phrases in terms of moral obligation. Similarly, the verse Exodus 25:6, "If thou wilt do that which is right in His eyes," was interpreted to mean honesty in commerce and all dealings with one's fellowman.

The teachers of the Talmud considered the laws of the Torah to be aids to moral conduct. This is reflected in their statement about dietary laws: "What matters it to God whether the animal is slaughtered at the throat, as the ritual requires, or at the back of the neck? The Torah has been given only to ennoble mankind."

The same view may be found in Book III, Chapter 31, of Maimonides' *Guide for the Perplexed*:

"Every one of the 613 precepts serves to inculcate a truth, to remove an erroneous opinion, to establish proper relations in society, to diminish evil, to train in good manners, or to warn against bad habits."

Where do the three branches of Judaism stand on the question of relative importance of ritual and moral law?

1. *Orthodox Jewry*

Since Orthodox Jewry, by and large, is more interested in pleasing God than in man, it gives primary emphasis to scrupulous observance of ritual. The ritual requirements of the Sabbath or of Holy Days receive much more religious attention than some of the great moral problems of the day. A *Hefsek* (unauthorized pause or interruption) in the rendition of the service arouses much more religious concern than some of the great social issues of our times.

This may be true of Orthodox Jewry in America today but it is assuredly not true of Orthodox theory. The supremacy of *mitzvos bein odom l'chavero* (the moral laws,

Divine commandments operating in the relationship between man and his fellowman) is a *halachic* principle of Orthodox Judaism. Certainly, Orthodox Jews in the *Torah v'Avodah* (religious labor movement) in Israel exhibit creative zeal in applying the moral laws to their society.

2. *Reform Jewry*

Compared to the Orthodox, who act as though religion were ritual tinged with morality, Reform Jews view religion as morality tinged with ritual. Reform Jews rejected most of the ritual laws of the tradition as anachronisms both meaningless and burdensome. Acting, as they believed, in the prophetic spirit, they gave much-needed emphasis to the moral laws of the tradition.

3. *Conservative Jewry*

Conservative Jews have, with some success, maintained the traditional emphasis on morality and ritual as equally necessary elements in the religious life of the Jew. Both are indispensable.

4. *The Current Trend*

It is a hopeful sign for the future of Judaism that Orthodox Jewry is now showing increasing interest in moral problems just as Reform Jewry is becoming increasingly aware of the need for ritual. The Orthodox now recognize the need for more of the prophetic emphasis on morality in the religious life; the Reform, for more of the priestly emphasis on the importance of ritual in the spiritual life.

Does God Reward the Righteous and Punish the Wicked?

Judaism believes that God is a righteous Judge. Therefore, there must be righteous judgment: reward for the virtuous and punishment for the wicked. Because the facts of life often seem to contradict the belief in God's justice, our tradition has frequently re-examined its belief and has always emerged with a new formulation justifying an affirmative answer.

Each exploration of the problem resulted in the discovery of a truth about life, but none of the answers has been definitive or final. Some of the sages felt that it was impossible to explain what appear to be painful discrepancies in God's justice. How can we possibly understand the ways of God? Some of the sages even intimated that true service to God would be impossible if there were no apparent discrepancies between merit and lot. This view is discernible in the Talmudic story (Menachot 29b) describing Moses' ascent to heaven to glimpse into the future. He is privileged to hear the great sage Akiba expound the Torah in most wonderful fashion, and inquires of God: "Thou hast shown me his worth, now show me his reward." On being shown Akiba flayed alive and burned at the stake by the Romans for expounding God's law, Moses shouts out: "And this the reward for Torah?" God answers, "Be silent! This I have determined."

Nevertheless, the tradition affirms that God is a righteous and perfect Judge. We turn now to a brief review of some of the attempts by the Tradition to reckon with the question.

Is Man Punished and Rewarded in This World?

The early biblical writers felt that God's judgment should and does operate in terms of direct material reward and punshment: the reward for obedience to God's commandments is prosperity and long life; punishment for disobedience, failure and death.

Later biblical writers came to the conclusion that despite the logic inherent in the earlier view, it was often contrary to the facts of life. The prophets asked: "Wherefore doth the wicked prosper?" (Jeremiah 12:1). Job asks substantially the same question: "Wherefore do the wicked live, become old, yea, wax mighty in power?" (Job 21:7). The doubts expressed by Jeremiah, Job, and others did *not* put an end to the practice of deducing a man's character from the circumstances of his life. To this day the tendency to explain suffering in terms of sin, and well-being in terms of virtue, persists in the culture. For example, psychiatrists attribute emotional illness of children to the "sins" of their parents. The prophets themselves explained suffering in terms of backsliding and violation of God's moral laws. At the same time, they came to the compelling conclusion that God's justice could not be conceived in simple terms of cause and effect. In the Book of Job, for example, we have a lively debate between one of Job's comforters, who stubbornly supports the old view that suffering is retribution for a man's sins just as prosperity is the reward of the good man, and Job, who points out that since this is, at times, contrary to the facts of life, a more profound understanding of God's justice, and a new interpretation, must be sought.

Is Man Punished and Rewarded in a World-to-Come?

The need to square the reality of life with Divine judgment led to the projection of reward and punishment into the future. Actually, this affirmed the principle that an individual's conduct is rewarded or punished on earth as merited even though consequences might not be discernible immediately. Sooner or later the guilty are overtaken by their guilt and the righteous reap the rewards of their righteousness. In essence, this newer interpretation was identical with the older, save that it stressed patience and the long view. Still, it was undeniable that many wicked died unpunished and many righteous, unrewarded. This consideration paved the way to the next stage of Jewish thinking—other worldly reward and punishment.

Justice eventually works itself out to its logical conclusion: rewards and punishments not given in this world are meted out in the world beyond, after death. In some of the books of the Bible and in the later prophets, the day of reckoning was to be on the Day of Judgment following the resurrection of the dead. This is how it is expressed in the Book of Daniel: "And many of them that sleep in the dust of the earth shall awake, some to everlasting life and

and some to reproaches and everlasting abhorrence."
(Daniel 12:2) The Rabbis of the Talmud adopted this view
of otherworldly reward and punishment. Said Rabbi Eliezer:
"They that are born are destined to die and the dead are
to be brought to life again to be judged."

To the rabbinic mind, it was inconceivable that there
should be a discrepancy between what man deserved and
what he received from the Righteous Judge. Appropriate
punishment and reward in this world might be postponed
but they are inexorable in the world to come. The existence
of a life with perfect justice beyond this imperfect world
was a natural assumption for those whose faith in God's
perfect justice was unquestionable. The same urge that
drives scientists to seek consistency and dependability in
natural law led the Rabbis to persist in their efforts to find
consistency in God's administration of the moral law. Otherworldly reward and punishment was their explanation but
it did not completely satisfy them. Their dissatisfaction led
them to a radical discovery resulting in a remarkable con-
tribution—spiritual reward.

What Is Spiritual Reward and Punishment?

"Pursue even a small *mitzvah* and run away from *averah*
(sin) : one good deed leads to another good deed just as one
sin leads to another sin; the reward of a good deed is a good
and the punishment for a sin is a sin." Thus, the Rabbis
found the reward for virtue in virtue itself. They felt that
the highest form of motivation for moral behavior was the
knowledge that every good deed brings something good into
man's life and into the world. This spiritual interpretation
was further developed and refined. The result was formulation of the view that the highest reward of virtue is finding
the opportunity to serve God, in love, without thought of or
desire for reward.

This is the meaning of the rabbinic statement: "Be not
like servants who serve their master in the expectation of
receiving a reward; be like servants who serve the master

in no expectation of receiving a reward." (Aboth 1:3) In this manner, the Sages liberated Judaism from preoccupation with seeming lack of correspondence between merit and lot, and from an interested self-seeking motivation that corrupts moral effort. To do the will of God became the primary purpose for good conduct; considerations of reward and punishment, secondary. Rabbi Eliezer explained the verse: "Blessed is the man that delighteth greatly in His commandments" (Psalm 112:1), to mean that man should delight in doing God's commandments but *not* in the rewards promised for their fulfillment.

Notwithstanding, the Rabbis continued to believe implicitly that the divine ordination of justice *demanded* just reward and punishment, if not material then spiritual, and if not now then in the hereafter. At the same time they insisted that the desire for reward or fear of punishment must not be the chief incentives to right conduct. A pure, disinterested love of God and a free enthusiasm for doing His bidding must be the motive for virtuous behavior. Here is a splendid example of the logic of Jewish faith: persistence in belief in reward and punishment because it is a morally indispensable, and logically necessary inference from the major premise that a just God rules the world. Instead of permitting doubt to destroy their faith, the Rabbis used doubt as a stepping-stone to a higher, purer and stronger faith.

Their profound grasp of life led the Rabbis to speak of God as both concealing and revealing: God conceals so that man may reveal. (If all were known, there would be nothing more to know). At times, God conceals His moral attribute of justice, involving the dispensation of reward and punishment, in order that man may discover the more important truth: the motive for virtue should be an unswerving, unqualified confidence in the intrinsic value of virtue *per se*. This, of course, is the lesson of the Book of Job. Job's friends defend God's justice by counselling Job to accept his suffering as punishment for sinfulness. Job maintains his suffering is unjust because he did not sin. Both are rebuked. Finally, Job recognizes that God has concealed His justice in order to teach him a higher faith: confidence without complaint and persistence in the virtuous life, even in adversity.

CHAPTER IV

Prayer

Reference to formal prayer elicits questions beyond number. The very shadings of voice in which they are expressed—pleading, humble, curious, warmly inquiring, coldly impersonal and indifferent, contemptuous, truculent—indicate uncertainty and confusion and gross misunderstanding. Here is just a sampling of such questions:

Can I worship God without going to services? Is formal prayer necessary? Can I be a good Jew without attending services? Why should I attend services when I don't feel like attending? Isn't that being a hypocrite? What do you get out of services anyway? Isn't it a waste of time? What's so important about going to synagogue? I can't read Hebrew so what can the service mean to me anyway? The Reform service is in English but I'm too orthodox for that. What's wrong with the services that they fail to inspire me? What's wrong with the prayers that they make no sense to me? Why does Judaism place so much emphasis on prayer? How can I learn to pray without feeling self-conscious? Does God answer man's prayers? Since my Bar Mitzvah, I have attended services only rarely. If I should suddenly start to attend more regularly, wouldn't it seem suspicious? I know people who go to services regularly but they are sharp dealers in business and unethical in their behavior. Am I not a better Jew than they if I try to deal fairly with people?

From the questions it is clear that many may have forgotten, or perhaps never learned or experienced, what prayer is. Some need to learn, others to relearn what Judaism says about prayer. Understanding of Judaism's approach to prayer should make us want to repeat with Moses and the children of Israel, "This is my God and I will praise Him; the God of my fathers and I will exalt Him." (Exodus 15:2)

What Is Prayer?

1. *Prayer is man's conversation with God about his hopes.*

Other than man, all living things are motivated solely by the desire for physical survival. Man is motivated, also, by moral and spiritual hopes that transcend the physical and may even involve his self-sacrifice. Man is distinguished from all other animals by his instinctive feeling that for the realization of these transcendant hopes he is dependent upon some Power outside himself, the Power he calls God. When man prays, he converses with God about his hopes.

2. *Prayer is man's way of talking with God about his burdens and his blessings.*

In the depths of despair, man asks for help; in moments of extreme happiness, he feels grateful. In prayer, man shares with God his sorrows and his joys, his defeats and his victories.

3. *Prayer is man's way of discovering each day that life has meaning.*

It is the soul of man ascending to the source of all souls; the heart of man turning to the heart of God; the mind of man in contemplation of life's holiest purpose and destiny. It is man's conscious effort to associate himself with God in the furtherance of the good life and in the creation of a better world.

4. *Prayer is the process by which man reaches out for his better self.*

When man prays, he turns the telescope, ordinarily used to explore the skies, and the microscope, ordinarily trained on the minute organisms of the universe, on himself. By contemplating *what* he is and what he should be, *how* he ought to behave so he can live at his best, he arrives at the resolution to become what he should be: more loving, more just, more good, more worthy. Through genuine prayer man seeks out his moral weaknesses, spiritual infirmities, social derelictions—the sins that prevent him from attaining the stature of his higher self. He is reminded that every moment is a God-given challenge, that he has something to live for, that he has a duty to perform, and that by performing that duty he rises to his true self.

5. *Prayer is a key to power.*

It opens for man the door to the presence of the greatest Power—God. From this contact with God comes awareness that he is not alone in his encounter with the problems, dangers, and crises that are always with us. Awareness sharpens his insight. This inner vision heightens his resolve and strengthens his determination to tap the reserves of latent power within him. He dares to try, and finds the strength and will to confront courageously the challenges of life.

6. *Prayer is the mood of faith.*

Man is often torn between faith and fatalism. Underlying both moods and outlooks is human awareness of inadequacy and dependence. Man, facing the universe, recognizes that forces and factors outside himself affect and influence his destiny. The mood of faith is, however, more akin to his nature than the mood of fatalism:

A. *Faith implies* that the forces of the universe have the quality of dependability, that they are capable of and designed to support life because they are instruments of the Creator. Governed by the Will of God, they operate in accordance with life's needs. Therefore, whatever ought to be will be; whatever happens has behind it a reason and purpose that make for the best.

Why pray then? Man prays to understand the Will of God so that he may distinguish between the ought and the ought not; so that he may know what to expect and what God expects of him (not what he expects of God); so that he may perceive the Divine purpose and serve it. In the mood of faith, man prays because he knows that God is ever-ready to help. Through prayer, man hopes to and does find that he can also help himself.

B. *Fatalism implies* that man is a prisoner of fate with no hope of escape. The forces of the universe are unconcerned with human welfare; no one can control these inevitable forces; whatever is bound to happen will happen. Any design or direction, any purpose or reason they might appear to manifest are coincidence and accident. When man feels helpless, prayer is absurd and useless: there is no help. Why pray?

When man prays, he cultivates faith, the spiritual approach to purposeful living.

Why Does Man Pray?

From the standpoint of Judaism, it is in man's *nature* to pray. Only the specific forms of prayer are cultural products. Even those who deny the validity of prayer, pray. We do not pray because we believe in God—we believe in God because we pray. The matrix out of which prayer emerges may be discerned in the following:

I. The Hebrew word for prayer means self-evaluation. Man is culturally indoctrinated with specific duties and aspirations but the sense of duty and the tendency to aspire are inherent in man's nature. He reacts automatically to given situations and to his own behavior (relationship to these situations) with spoken or unspoken self-evaluation. "I can," "I should," "I could have," "I didn't try hard enough," etc., are moods, feelings, or meditations that spring from the universal need of man to give account of himself.

2. Man's natural reaction to fear and problem situations is one of hope and faith that what ought to be *can* and *will* be. His instinctive response to threat situations is "Please help"; to success, "I am grateful!" Implied in these natural

reactions to his environment is man's intuitive recognition of dependence on a Power outside himself, desirous and capable of coming to his assistance.

3. The tendency to give account of himself and his natural optimism, or rudimentary faith, emerge as prayer. All over the world, and in every age, men have prayed. Form and techniques have varied, the deities to whom the prayers have been addressed are different, but prayer itself is universal. Man prays because he is a praying creature; even when he is not conscious of his relationship with God, he reacts in accordance with it. He prays silently, even unconsciously, but he prays always.

What Has Weakened Our Belief in Prayer?

The waning of prayer is a reflection of the weakening of our conviction that life has spiritual meaning and, consequently, a diminution of our will to live. If we lose that conviction, considerably more than prayer will be lost. It is essential to our well-being that we discover, and clearly identify, the forces that block the free flow of prayer.

Can we logically attribute the waning of prayer to the modern Jews' conviction that prayer "doesn't work," that the prayers of even very righteous people seem to go unanswered? No. Our ancestors experienced disappointment much more frequently than we, and had fewer physical comforts, yet they were moved to prayer.

Did our ancestors pray because they were more superstitious than we? No. Like everything else in our civilization of abundance, superstitions have multiplied greatly. Multitudes who do not pray, nurse the most senseless superstitions. No ancient hesitated to walk under a ladder or was afraid of Friday the thirteenth.

Did our ancestors turn to prayer because, lacking our technological knowledge, they saw no other way to solve their problems? No. Our problems are numerous, and even more complex than our predecessors', despite our advanced knowledge in every field.

Standing in the way of man's belief in prayer are a number of gross misconceptions.

1. *Misconception of nature*

Modern science, working on the assumption that nature is purely a cause-and-effect mechanism, has been successful in discovering rules and principles that have made modern technology possible. Unfortunately, the common man has confused the nature of science with the nature of nature and, what is worse, with the nature of life. Obsessed with the idea that "cause and effect" is the total explanation of nature and of life, the modern mind views man as a machine ruled by the principle of "cause and effect" in a mechanical cosmos. In such setup, prayer *is* pointless: life has no spiritual meaning, God appears to be a vague fiction and man is bereft of purpose. This widespread misinterpretation abandons man to a vacuum of meaninglessness in which the natural impulse to pray is blocked by the mind.

Man must and will rediscover the moral and spiritual quality of life. Man will again be able to pray with his heart and with his lips. He cannot long deny the considerable evidence for the belief that nature has qualities distinct and apart from mechanical cause and effect, such as, good, bad, useful, beautiful, variable and harmonious and that nature is directed by a Spiritual Power exhibiting remarkable intelligence, purpose, will and coherence.

Man is part of nature. We may rightly assume that the spiritual and mental qualities inherent in man are inherent, in still greater abundance, in the nature of which he is a part, or in the Spiritual Power that directs nature. These spiritual and mental powers indicate that man can exercise choice and can influence destiny, that man requires and desires guidance to fulfill himself as a worthy, creative individual in a universe which is responsive to him and is ever-expanding to meet his needs. Man's quest for such guidance from the responsive Power Who is the source of all spiritual significance, is the essence and substance of genuine prayer.

2. *Misconception of God*

In the synagogue, we see the words *Know before Whom thou standest* inscribed in bold lettering on the Holy Ark. The conviction that we are standing in the presence of God makes it possible for us to pray. If God is not real to us, our prayers are unreal. Men cannot pray to *ideas about God* or to someone else's God. Prayers have the power to inspire only when they are addressed to a Living God, to our own God. Some of our misconceptions about God have made Him intellectually unacceptable or emotionally unsatisfying or both.

We cannot worship a God who is rationally unacceptable. We cannot worship an inherited God who was acceptable to our ancestors but whom we have not experienced. That is why our tradition does not speak of the God of Abraham, Isaac, and Jacob. Rather, it is very distinct in stating the God of Abraham, the God of Isaac, and the God of Jacob. In other words, it is very important for us to *understand* the traditional God of Abraham as the God Who inspired Abraham. Just as Isaac had to *begin* by trying to understand the God of Abraham and went on from there to discover the God Who was to operate as a dynamic force in his own life, Jacob, in his turn, began with the God of his fathers but had to find for himself the God of Jacob. Some Jews today try to accept the God of Abraham, of Isaac, and of Jacob and are shocked to find Him intellectually unsatisfying. Instead of using their knowledge of the God of their fathers as a starting point for uncovering further truths and values that can operate most effectively for them, they reject God. It is as though, unable to fathom the workings of a wondrously complex mechanism, they discard the entire mechanism in contempt. They shut their eyes to the obvious fact that no spiritual experience becomes ours until we make it so through our own efforts.

In efforts to prove that belief in God is not sheer sentiment devoid of reason, intellectuals have over-rationalized and depersonalized God to the point where He elicits no feelings of warmth and intimacy. God has been turned into a cold, hard fact which leaves us unmoved.

The individual must understand and feel the reality of God as an intense personal experience. His conception of God must be both intellectually acceptable and emotionally satisfying: a God to believe in and to inspire, a God to Whom he can pray wholeheartedly.

When we know with heart and mind before Whom we stand, we will experience the reality of God as our God, and prayer as the experience of man speaking with God.

3. *Misconception fostered by psychological and psychoanalytic theory*

Just as scientific theory and method have laid bare many of the secrets of nature, psychological theories and methods have exposed many of the mysteries of the human psyche, and have increased immeasurably our understanding of the mechanics of the mind and the dynamics of behavior.

Although psychoanalytic methods have produced moral healing, they have done incalculable harm at the same time. All ideals, actions, values, and standards were interpreted as expressions of unconscious desires striving for fulfillment or as mechanisms for diverting or checking such desires. When carried to extremes, this led to absurdities: Abraham, Isaac, Jacob, Moses and even God became "father substitutes"; prayer, wishful thinking; ritual, a form of sublimation; God, a super-ego; religion, an opiate or crutch; obedience to God's Will, submission to authoritarianism; social idealism, a symptom of maladjustment or a type of rebellion against an inadequate or tyrannical father image; virtue, a cover-up for violent feelings prompted by guilt reactions.

At best, psychologists treated prayer as either a form of auto-suggestion with superstitious overtones or a means whereby the patient (worshipper) talked his troubles over with his omniscient, white-bearded psychiatrist in heaven. As a result, prayer became unfashionable and rather embarrassing.

The latest thinking of psychotherapists is more favorably disposed toward religion and the value of prayer: failure to pray deprives the psyche of an activity essential to its well-being and estranges man from God. Psychologists today recognize that prayer is a vital, necessary aspect of normal living: man needs a comforting, reassuring, enriching, strength-giving, and demanding relationship with God. This recognition has yet to percolate down to the laity.

4. *Misconception of material success as the supreme value*

When material success becomes the highest good, and man's status (the regard and respect accorded him by society) is determined by his material possessions and resources, it follows that anything which makes for success is good, anything which interferes with it is bad, anything that does not affect material success one way or another is unimportant. Religious ethics give way to expedience, and practical results are the sole test of value. When the supreme value is material success, belief in God becomes unnecessary and prayer irrelevant.

If man's "practical" goal is valid, why is his appetite for continued success insatiable? Why must he "kill time" that is not devoted to money-making or possession-acquiring activity? Why is his feverish existence so restless, tense and joyless? Because, wrapped in his own desires for material self-indulgence, man is trapped on essentially the same level of existence as the animal. But man is more than animal. Therefore, he is miserable with the status to which he has reduced himself. Even he who puts mental exploration high on the scale of values, and is willing to sacrifice material satisfaction, must endure spiritual dissatisfaction. His soul is a moral and spiritual vacuum.

The Rabbis recognized that "if there is no *Kemach* (satisfaction of basic physical needs) there can be no *Torah* (cultivation of intellectual and spiritual resources)." The stress, however, was on the converse: "If there is no *Torah* there can be no *Kemach*." In other words, man knows no peace, no contentment, no joy of living unless his spiritual needs are given the higest priority in his scale of values. If man does not taste the ennobling influence of worshipping God, even his bread will seem tasteless to him.

5. *Misconception of the value of formal prayer*

Even those who attend synagogue services and "pray" often harbor strange misconceptions as to the purpose and meaning of prayer. They think of prayer as a formal exercise in recitation, completely detached from vital experience, and of the synagogue service itself as a monotonous, overlong and artificial performance. Prayer is also explained as a useful form of self-discipline, or communal obligation and celebration; a means of telling God what we want, what He can do for us, what He can give us; a superstitious hope that God will grant us cash if we give Him some credit; an expectation that God will perform miracles for us if we win His favor by sacrificing time for Him. Attendance at services is believed to appease an inexplicable uneasiness and sense of shame in our Jewishness, and to parade the one shred of pride and decency which is dredged up from an abysmal ignorance; or is a good way for the aged and infirm to "kill time"; or affords an opportunity for companionship with others who have nothing better to do or who are feeling forsaken and forlorn.

Thus in both private and public worship, prayer has been reduced to something less than prayer. No wonder so many have turned away from it! For lack of knowledge and training, we do not understand the words and the meanings to be derived from them. We fail to see that prayer increases our insights into life's purpose, that it helps us meet our personal needs as our experience expands. For lack of long, comfortable association beginning in childhood, we do not experience the warm delights and nostalgic memories evoked by familiarity and loving recognition. When prayer yields neither intellectual, emotional, nor spiritual satisfactions, it is indeed a senseless waste of time. The lack is not in the prayer, of course, but in ourselves. In our ignorance and disregard of essential preparations, we form many misconceptions about prayer and synagogue attendance and erroneously conclude that there is nothing in prayer. We need to rediscover the true meaning of prayer. When we do, it *will* be relevant and vital, as it should be.

Is God Influenced by Our Prayers?

The answer to this question, in the tradition, is decisive. Although the purpose of our prayers is to change ourselves, not to influence God, our prayers do move God. Joseph Albo, author of *Ikkarim* (Principles of Judaism), sums up the position of the tradition in these words: "Pious men . . . can change the laws of nature by prayer." Traditionalists are not troubled by what appears to be a discrepancy between our prayers and their fulfillment. They resolve the discrepancy by stating that our prayers are unworthy or that our desires are not in accord with the Will of God, or that we do not understand the answer. The happy confidence that God is indeed influenced by our prayers is expressed with powerful simplicity in the talmudic statement of Hama b. Hanina: "If man's prayers are not answered, let him pray more." (Berochot 32b).

Does God Answer Our Prayers?

From the standpoint of Judaism, God the Creator is concerned about every one of His creatures. He listens to and answers prayers. He does not always answer us to our satisfaction. He does not always do what we would like Him to do. And, of course, He does not answer us in the same manner in which another human being would answer us. But, holds the tradition, to every worthy prayer there is an answer.

What Kind of Prayers Are Altogether Unworthy Of an Answer?

The Jewish tradition designates certain types of prayers as *tefillah shel tiflah*, prayers that are immoral and irrational, and admonishes us to avoid them. A prayer is unworthy IF—

What we seek is contrary to His moral law.

What we ask is contrary to His natural law.

The worshipper lacks sincerity.

What we ask is not good for us or hurtful to someone else.

Our prayers are intended as a substitute for action or an evasion of personal responsibility.

We say, in essence, "My will be done, not Thine, O God."

Is There Evidence that God Does Answer Prayer?

Does prayer bring results? Yes indeed! If our prayers are worthy, they seem to help us physically, psychologically, morally and spiritually. Something in the nature of life, and in the structure of man and the universe, corresponds with and reacts to our prayers. This correspondence is the foundation for our faith that God answers prayers: prayer helps us.

Often, in a state of fear, man prays for help and emerges with new confidence.

Often, in a state of weakness, man prays for help and emerges with new strength.

Often, depressed and troubled in spirit, man begins with prayer and ends with renewed hope and decision.

Often man begins prayer in a state of confusion and ends with new insight, an essential kind of vision of which the eye and mind alone are not capable.

Often man begins his prayer with a question and emerges with an answer.

Prayer quickens our conscience, heightens our resolve, and strengthens our will power.

Prayer keeps the mind and will of man fixed on desirable goals and worthy values.

Prayer helps neutralize the terrible feeling of loneliness by bringing us closer to God.

Prayer relaxes man and aids his recovery from illness. It can spell the difference between life and death, where the will to live is heavily involved.

Thus, prayer addressed to God exerts an influence on man. This influence on man is the Divine answer.

How Does Prayer Work?

Religious Jews today differ in their opinion on how prayer works but all agree that it does produce changes in, *and* external to, man:

1. *Prayer works by influencing God*

Some believe that God listens to and answers our prayers directly: "If they cry to Me, I will surely hear their cry." (Ex. 22:22) Prayer offered from the heart and for the sake of Heaven ascends and pierces the firmament. Spoken words and meditations of the heart break through the seven Heavens and reach the Throne of Glory. God hears our prayers and responds to them directly: He weighs our words of prayer and our motives; He hears our cry and saves us; He fulfills the desires of those who revere Him; He stays a raging flood and ends a drought by rain for our sake. He intervenes by supernatural act in the workings of nature and contravenes nature when it is His Will: God produces miraculous changes for our sake when He is moved by our prayers.

2. *Prayer works by influencing man*

This process has been described in many different ways but basically it is an assertion that prayer makes us increasingly susceptible to God's influence. When we pray, we feel God's presence and are no longer alone. We allow God to enter our lives as we pray, and with Him come many wonderful things. The subject matter of our prayers is our needs, our hopes, our fears, our wants, but our appeal is, "Do not forsake me, O Lord." Our words are an invitation to God to talk to us. As we begin to hear Him, the world and our place in it appear in God's light; the center, which is our self-will, becomes God's Will; our hopes and true aspirations are clarified and brought into proper perspective. We begin by communicating, addressing ourselves to God, and, if we are really praying, end by receiving communication, feeling ourselves addressed by Him. The miracle of prayer is that our words bring God's words to us; the self in prayer rises above the self and attains vision, guidance, courage and healing from beyond itself. The purpose of prayer may be to influence God but the process by which it works is God's influence on us. Prayer transforms us and man, changed, becomes capable of producing change. As we listen to God in prayer, we learn and find new resources within ourselves.

Whatever the explanation of how prayer works, no religious Jew would say that prayer makes no difference and cannot alter physical facts. The Orthodox accept the explanation of God's direct supernatural intervention; many Conservatives do also. Most of the Reform and many Conservatives picture God answering prayer indirectly through the effects of prayer.

Does the Jewish Religion Encourage Petitionary Prayer?

Praying for personal benefits is not the major concern of Jewish liturgy. Most of the prayers are commitments of our resources to fulfill our duties under God, meditation on the wisdom of our sacred writings, expressions of praise and gratitude for the marvels of life, and declarations of trust and confidence in the power of God.

In the Bible, Talmud, Midrash, and Prayer Books are to be found many petitionary prayers and copious references to instances when they were granted. The sages of the Talmud certainly believed that God answers our petitions but these very same Rabbis discouraged some aspects of petitionary .

prayers. For example, R. Joshua ben Levi forbade the use
of Scriptural verse in prayers for healing, yet recited Psalms
3 and 91 (pleas for protection from all hurtful forces and
influences) before retiring. To reconcile the contradiction,
the explanation was given that "for preventive purposes it
is allowed." Maimonides gave this explanation: "To seek
healing through the words of Scripture is forbidden. The
Holy Scripture is for healing the soul, not the body. However, a healthy man may recite Scriptural passages and
psalms, and the merit of this reading may be with him and
protect him from danger and hurtful influences." Referring
to prayers for protection from terrors of the night, the
Rabbis of the Talmud state emphatically that the best protection is a clear conscience, when the mind and soul are in
harmony with the Will of the Creator.

When motivated by materialistic concern with self, petitionary prayer is not worthy unless expressed with the
intention that these material needs—for health and peace,
sustenance, wisdom, etc.—will help man serve God and
improve his soul. Man should pray when he is in need, but
the basis of his prayer must be the desire to attune himself
to the Will of God rather than the desire to derive direct
personal benefits.

Every Jew knows that we do have prayers for the sick
in our liturgy. We petition God on behalf of those who are
ill and even encourage the dying to pray for restoration to
health and useful service to God. We do believe that God is
the Great Healer—ultimately our health does depend upon
Him. Our teachers simply attempted to discourage the sub-
stitution of petitionary prayer for action or human responsibility. The effect of spiritual health on physical health is
acknowledged but the cultivation of spiritual health is not
meant to take the place of the technical skills of trained
physicians. For that reason, the Rabbis maintained that no
one should dwell in a community where there is no doctor.

Petitionary prayers demand that the worshipper concentrate on God's Will rather than on his own. Our petition

for the blessings of life should be motivated by our desire to use those blessings for the glory of God. The Rabbis included petitionary prayer in the Jewish service but they insisted that it be preceded by prayers of praise and followed by prayers of thanksgiving. They sanctioned only those petitionary prayers which begin with petition and conclude with acceptance of obligation.

Also, Jewish petitionary prayers are expressed in the plural rather than in the singular, (Heal us . . . Save us . . . Look upon our distress) in order to sharpen our awareness of others. The Rabbis taught: "Always include the community in your prayers." (Berahot 29b). In *Sefer Ha-Chasidim* we find: "Many a person prays but is not heard because the misfortunes of others did not move him." The normal selfishness of man is sublimated into a moral experience of identification with the concerns of others. Even those prayers which are intended as personal supplications are expressed and interpreted in such manner as to point up the obligations incumbent on the worshipper should his request for blessing be granted.

Petitionary prayer is defined as appeal for strength to help us meet life's difficult situations in order that we may be better fitted to serve God's purposes in the world. Even petitionary prayer should be prayer of appreciation for needs of others, of kindred, of friends, of compatriots, of humanity. Even petitionary prayer, which is essentially self-enlargement, must be voiced in such way as to enlarge our vision of God, of the world and of our role in life.

Can We Believe in Petitionary Prayer?

Some rabbis and thoughtful Jewish laymen have an aversion to petitionary prayer. Their objection is to the kind of petition which reduces the dialogue of prayer to man begging, and God granting special favors and blessings. Wishes expressed in prayers are expected to be carried out by an indulgent God. They set forth the following arguments to explain their objections to petitionary prayers:

1. Petitionary prayers are generally selfish. The purpose of prayer, on the other hand, is to liberate us from childish, excessive concern with our self-centered wants.

2. It is pointless to tell God what we want and need. Moreover, it carries the implication that God does not know what we want and need, what is good for us, and what He will grant us.

3. Petitionary prayer is absurd. The law of cause and effect which God imposed on the universe makes for coherence, dependability and a degree of predictability so that man can order his life intelligently. Life and its events must follow the divinely ordained law of cause and effect. It is wrong to ask God to change or suspend the order of nature when we cannot possibly know the consequences of such change for others, or even whether we ourselves will truly benefit from the change. What we ask is that God should run the universe to suit our whims, disregarding His own law.

4. Petitionary prayer is an evasion of moral responsibility. The purpose of prayer is to help us understand the Will of God so that we may act in harmony with it. The kind of faith that expects God to take care of things once we have, in prayer, acquainted Him with the problem is immoral. For example, some people are content to pray for noble ideals without doing a thing toward their ultimate realization. Some pray for the sick, the needy and the oppressed but do not lift a finger to improve their lot. Some are even known to trust in prayer while refusing to use medical resources to treat their ailments. Prayer should be a concomitant of action, not a substitute for it.

The same thinkers who reject petitionary prayer do believe very strongly in the value of prayer which expresses the high resolve to pursue noble aspirations and to dedicate one's self to the service of God. Prayer should be self-expression in the spirit of: "Thy Will, O God, be done. May I be privileged to understand Thy Will that I may act in accordance with it."

Those who favor petitionary prayer justify their position as follows:

1. Reluctance to confide his needs to God is symptomatic of a lack of man's faith. Alternatives to the faith that God responds to man's needs are the fatalistic attitude that man should resign himself to accepting what comes since it is "inevitable," or the idolatrous assertion that man's destiny depends entirely on himself since there is no providence outside himself. Either alternative is repugnant since it makes man either completely insufficient or wholly self-sufficient. Man is neither!

2. Man should feel free to pour out his most fervent hopes and wishes, unashamedly, to his Father in Heaven. It is an understandable impulse to express his need for God's help in the light of his own limitations. In order to elicit God's help, he must formulate a clear statement of his need and of his deepest feelings. This, in itself, will result in his being helped.

3. Like a child's hopeful request of its father, petitionary prayer carries the proviso, expressed or implied, of humble acceptance of the Divine Will. The request reflects a hope.

4. When man talks over his needs with God the subsequent action he takes to meet the need is greatly benefited. His confidence is strengthened and his behavior influenced for good. To trust only in prayer is to deny our own responsibility. To deny the importance of prayer is to deny the role of God in the events of our lives.

5. The petitionary prayer, properly used, makes sense. It recognizes that the whole chain of cause and effect functions as an instrument of God's Will. With his limited human powers man is able to direct and use the law of cause and effect for his purposes. He can initiate, produce, manipulate and control cause and effect. What man can influence on a small scale, God can influence on a large scale.

Elsewhere in this book it has been pointed out that

prayers which ask God to violate His own laws of nature are unworthy. For instance, to petition God to restore to life someone who is already dead is to ask God to violate His law of nature. It constitutes unworthy prayer. On the other hand, to petition God to heal someone who is dying is to affirm that the law of cause and effect is under His control.

Is It Hypocrisy to Pray When You Doubt the Efficacy of Prayer?

The non-believer will always be able to point to the natural causes of an event and say, "because of these, it would have happened even if you hadn't prayed." The believer will always have the reply: "The whole chain of causes and effects hangs on God's Will. The prayer may have been the decisive factor that determined the happening and its outcome." The real consideration is whether God's Will can, and does, take prayer into account. There is truly an element of doubt in this consideration. If there were no doubt, there would be no free human decision to take a hand in one's destiny. Prayer must be a voluntary act of faith or life loses its quality of spiritual adventure and achievement.

Some people have a happy confidence that God listens to their prayers. They trust the wisdom and justice of God. Whatever He decides is for the best. With such an attitude, they can extract a blessing even from adversity. Confidence in God's never-failing love gives them hope and courage to do what must be done. However, even the most pious must wrestle with moments of uncertainty.

Doubt in itself is neither sinful nor a sign of weakness. By raising questions, we are moved to seek answers. This search, pursued in the mood that we cannot know the whole final truth but we can always gain fresh insights and enlarge our understanding, brings greater comprehension and sometimes even resolves the doubt. We must not let the fact that some things cannot be known with certainty block our progression toward the conquest of a little more knowledge and, possibly, a little more certainty.

Is It Necessary For an Ethical, Believing Jew to Attend Services?

Yes. What we feel in our hearts we should unashamedly wish to express, and make a habit of communicating with our lips. Awareness of God should permeate our lives with warmth and the happy confidence associated with feelings of love. Love which does not constantly express itself in words and deeds is taken-for-granted and deteriorates into indifference. Such "love" is meaningless both to the "lover" and to the "beloved." The "love" kept in one's heart, unexpressed, is cold, dead and buried. If our religion, like love, is to exert a strong and constructive influence in our lives, it must express itself in ritual and prayer as well as in moral living. This is what our sages were trying to communicate when they said: "The world of Judaism rests on three pillars: on Torah, on good deeds, and on *worship*."

The whole religious structure of life is shaky if one of the foundations is neglected or improperly maintained. For example, we meet people who observe the ritual of religion punctiliously and worship regularly with great outward fervor but are "sharp" and immoral in their dealings with other men. We are also familiar with the man who studies Torah in great earnestness yet does not perform good deeds. The sages of our religion were highly critical of both such types. By omitting from their lives one of the essentials, they are deluding themselves even when they are not deliberately trying to fool others. It is wrong to speak words that are not really in our hearts or that are not reflected in our deeds. It is equally hypocritical to insist we have feelings in our hearts which we refuse to express. This may be cover-up for the vacuum that actually exists in our hearts, or a fear of intense self-exploration, or a defense for evading an important area of responsibility.

If we do not understand the value of prayer and, therefore, question the value of attendance at services, it is still incumbent upon us to support with our presence the institutions that keep alive the moral and spiritual values which are our heritage. The intelligent and energetic individual will explore approaches to his religion and openmindedly seek to understand that which he has so lightly rejected. It may be too late for some of us to cultivate appreciation for our religion or for art or literature, but let us not, on that account, remove our support or mock those who do possess sensitivity. Every effort in the right direction is worthwhile and a little is better than nothing. With humility we can open the door to our senses and mind.

Is Private Devotion as Good as Formal Public Worship?

The individual may, and indeed is encouraged to, pray in solitude—in his home, under the open sky—wherever and whenever his heart prompts him. Public worship is not intended as a substitute for private prayer. However, Jewish piety is considered incomplete without participation in the local congregation and without sharing the fellowship of the Universal Congregation of Israel. The exhortation of the sage Hillel, "Separate not thyself from the community," (Abot 2:4 and Ber. 29b-30a) refers, among other things, to communal worship. Rabbi Simeon b. Lakish takes the extreme view that "whoever has a synagogue in his city and does not enter into it to worship is called a bad neighbor." (Ber. 8a) The architects of our religion stressed the importance of public worship because they recognized that it has values that cannot be obtained from private prayer.

Why Does Judaism Believe in Public Formal Worship?

Public worship, in a synagogue, unites individual Jews into a community and, eventually, binds them to catholic Israel. When Jews in a neighborhood organize for the purpose of collective worship, they soon find other common interests such as education, charity, improvement of the general community, and the welfare of the Holy Land. The synagogue, primarily a spiritual center, is also a social center where friendships are formed and individuals fulfil themselves in and through community service. The individual Jew is united with *Knesset Yisroel* (Congregation of Israel) and its common heritage of faith and responsibility.

Wherever the individual Jew travels, no matter what his race, his nationality, language, station in life, or appearance, he finds himself welcomed and at home in the established Jewish service of the synagogue. Common elements in the service bring him a sense of brotherhood with fellow Jews so that he is never a complete stranger anywhere. The impact of "Hear, O Israel, the Lord our God the Lord is One" recited in unison in public worship is quite different from that of a private repetition in solitude.

Public worship is also a medium for expressing loyalty to the people and religion of Israel. Prayer is undeniably a private matter of conscience between man and his Maker, a deeply personal experience. However, religion in the Jewish sense is also a sociological relationship involving the individual with the community, the Jew with the Jewish community, and the Jewish people with God. In the words of the Talmudic sage Rabbi Isaac, "In a synagogue at worship God is found. Indeed, wherever ten men (a *minyan*) unite in prayer, God's Presence (the *Schechinah*) is with them." According to the Rabbis, "the hour of congregational worship is considered a time of God's favor." The individual Jew who cannot join a *minyan* is enjoined to say his private prayers at the set time for normal public worship so he can identify himself with the worshipping community. Public worship has always fostered Jewish group-consciousness and communal unity.

The subject matter of Jewish prayer emphasizes the problems and aspirations of the Jewish people as a whole even though it takes cognizance of the situation of the individual. In the final analysis, the function of prayer is to make and keep life meaningful. Public worship links the individual to the noble concerns and spiritual aspirations of collective Israel, and detaches him from excessive self-centeredness. Generations of Jews have poured out their hearts to God in the midst of fellow-worshippers in a synagogue with a fervor that could never be approximated in privacy. Therefore, the Jew who says, "Why go to the synagogue? If I want to pray, I can pray just as well at home," is mistaken. He really does not pray just as well, if at all, except in extreme situations which tear from all of us spontaneous, desperation-tinged petition.

An incidental value of public worship has been the sublime inspiration for creative arts. To meet the needs of public worship, poets have produced a vast literature and composers have created a multitude of soul-stirring compositions. Artists and architects have united the beauty of holiness to the holiness of beauty in the structure of the synagogue, the place for public worship. Public worship has brought together the aesthetic and the spiritual for the common purpose of glorifying God.

What is the Purpose of the Various Types of Prayer?

The prayers of the Jewish service were meant to reflect the various moods which normally evoke, or should evoke, spontaneous prayer and to give them poetic expression.

PRAYERS OF THANKSGIVING

The measure of man's happiness is limited only by his capacity for gratitude and appreciation. Prayers of thanksgiving are meant to guard us against a form of spiritual poverty. They sensitize us to appreciation and remind us to concentrate on what we have and not on what we have not.

1. They make us conscious of the blessings which surround us and from which we benefit daily. This is good and necessary, for only through our consciousness of them do blessings exist for us and bring us benefits.

2. They make us appreciate our blessings. Appreciation

adds to our happiness. Happiness depends not so much on what we have but on how well we appreciate what is ours.

3. They make us give expression to our thankfulness. Only a boor receives but does not acknowledge. Our characters are refined by the habit of acknowledging with graciousness.

4. They encourage us to rejoice in our portion even while we strive to improve it. We should look with gratitude upon what we do possess instead of fruitlessly and bitterly complaining about what we do not possess.

5. They remind us that our blessings come from God. Therefore, in all humility, we are obligated to use our blessings prudently and for moral purposes. What we receive, with God's help, we should be willing to share and use for God's purposes.

6. They encourage a reverential attitude toward life. By a simple prayer of thanksgiving the commonplace becomes holy. Appreciation sanctifies life. For example, the simple act of opening one's eyes each morning to a new day of life and opportunity becomes a joyful privilege through a prayer of thanksgiving.

7. They make us aware of God's love. Every blessing is an expression of God's love for us. Those who do not appreciate the gifts of love simply take them for granted. Those who fail to express gratitude for them do not truly experience the love of the Giver.

PRAYERS OF PETITION

Our religion encourages us to be content with our lot but it does not ask us to consider our lot a petrified condition. Living requires that we pursue material and spiritual improvement. Prayers of petition express the desire for such improvement.

In Greek, the word to pray means "to wish"; in German, "to beg"; in Hebrew, "to judge one's self" or "to evaluate one's needs." Thus, prayers of petition, accor...ng to Judaism, become an exercise in evaluating our material needs. Material blessings are also gifts of God and the desire to enjoy them has been implanted by the Creator. To strive for material achievement and progress is normal and virtuous; to strive *only* for them is sinful. Judaism maintains that even the needs of the body must be met in a spiritually and aesthetically satisfying manner. Man's spiritual needs should be neither denied nor neglected in the process of material attainment.

PRAYERS OF CONTEMPLATION

Thinking and reasoning engage us in a process of analysis involving provable qualities and quantities. Meditation, on the other hand, elevates us above the confines and limitations of our reasoning powers. In prayers of contemplation, we meditate on the meaning of God, God's Will, man's relationship with Him, the purpose of life and its values. They are warm and gentle musings that widen our spiritual horizons.

We live in an age that encourages and respects scientific reason. Our materialistic society places a high premium on calculation and manipulation directed toward practical gain. The ulterior motive for this largely mathematical type of thinking is to find out how much there is in it for us. Most of us, however, are too busy, too rushed, too preoccupied with self, too empty, to engage very much even in this kind of thinking. Who has time to think at all? The art of contemplation is practically lost. Who has the time to waste on such "useless" matters as the meaning of life, God, love. Prayers of meditation make us cultivate the art of contemplation. In the House of God, with a prayer book in hand, we are already meditating.

PRAYERS OF ADORATION

In prayers of adoration, we consider the power and

majesty, the greatness and mystery of God. God does not need our adoration but we need to adore Him. How do we benefit from singing God's praises?

There is a need to love as well as to be loved. It is essential to man's well-being to find an object of supreme worship. Unless we direct our worship to the Highest, to God, we are in danger of worshipping that which is unworthy and adoring that which is corrupting. Prayers of adoration protect men from becoming enamored with the false, the debasing. The purpose of prayer is to find our relationship with a living God. That relationship is expressed in words singing God's praises. Praise of God is a response to His majesty and glory. As we utter these praises, we are elevated to a higher plane of feeling and thinking. Our own concerns are temporarily put aside so we can turn back to them later with clearer perspective, a better sense of proportion, and a nobler purpose.

PRAYERS OF AFFIRMATION

Daily disappointments and frustrations tend to tarnish our faith. We need, therefore, to turn to God as often as possible. In His presence, we restore and reaffirm our faith in the abiding and indispensable values of the good life. In prayers of affirmation, we restate our ideals and strengthen our determination to live by them. We address our conscience and reassure God the Father that we will not fail Him. This type of prayer keeps us from forgetting altogether, or conceding to expediency, our highest loyalties and values.

PRAYERS OF RESIGNATION

There are times when things are just too much for us and we cast the full burden of our sense of defeat on the Lord. In resigning ourselves to God, we recognize our need for help from a Higher Power. Confidence that such help is forthcoming inspires us with renewed strength and with fresh devices with which to meet our problems. A prayer of resignation is an expression of hope and a source of strength. It is an affirmation that what we alone cannot do, God will help us do if it ought to be done.

PRAYERS OF PENITENCE

The very same conscience that man denies, so that he may sin freely, comes to extricate him with its proddings. Defeated conscience rises and helps raise the fallen. It draws its strength from the Source that planted conscience in us for a purpose. In a prayer of penitence, man confesses his guilt and appeals for purification from it. He prays for God's help so that he may overcome his own evil desires in spite of himself. He appeals for another chance when he repents and trusts in God's merciful forgiveness.

PRAYERS OF INQUIRY

When we are lost, we seek direction and guidance; when we are confused, we look for clarification. The soul refuses to accept darkness and bewilderment as the final end of man's efforts. At such times, we pray to One Who Knows: we pray to God for Divine guidance. In times of crisis and confusion, we are able to find new resources within ourselves: it is the light of God brightening the vision of man. Prayers of inquiry are the plea for light and direction.

CHAPTER V

Revelation

Where Did Society Get Its Basic Moral and Spiritual Values?

Three possibilities suggest themselves in answer to this question.

1. *Man is the source and inventor of values.*

Man establishes all moral ideas and ideals, and he alone is final judge of their validity. All values are subjective, relative, and temporary. Their status and endurance depend on human opinion. Man creates and experiments with them: he rejects them when they do not serve his purpose, clings to them when he considers them beneficial, modifies them as he sees fit.

Judaism *rejects* this conception of the origin of moral values because it reduces them to human contrivances and denies their objective validity. It sets up man as a sort of god who creates values "ex nihilo" and ascribes to him the highest moral authority. It enables man to accept or reject these values according to the dictates of human "reason."

2. *God creates and man discovers.*

God has invested the universe with purpose, meaning, and moral order. These aspects of the structure of the universe are as real as its physio-chemical aspects. Moral law, like natural law, is imbedded in reality. Man does not create these laws; he discovers them. Moral and spiritual propositions, like scientific principles, are human formulations descriptive of an objective reality. Values are the discoveries of man "breaking through" to the cosmic meaning of life. Although the pathfinders in the realm of values are men of acute moral sensitivity and special spiritual endowment, all men are endowed with the ability to discern the fundamental values and laws of life. Only the psychologically disoriented are unable to subscribe to their reality because they cannot face reality. Man's power of perception is limited; he sees only a little way and that not too clearly. Therefore, faith as well as reason is needed to help him in his search for moral and spiritual truth.

3. *God reveals when man's need exists and he himself cannot discover.*

God has never abandoned man to his limited resources. What man needed to know but could not discover, God revealed to him. God has broken through to man by revealing supernaturally what man could not know naturally. Certain knowledge about the moral and spiritual reality of the universe, not accessible to man nor even verifiable by reason and experience but nonetheless essential for him to possess, was revealed by God.

What Is The Jewish Conception of the Origin of Man's Moral and Spiritual Values?

Moral values are not the product of ingenious speculation, or transitory conventions for expressing man's hopes and better impulses. They are divinely ordained laws of life which are written into the very structure of the universe. They are absolute, permanent, valid and unquestionable commands of God. God is their Creator, Guardian and Guarantor.

How Are the Moral and Spiritual Values, Which Emanate From God, Communicated to Man?

These values, which have been incorporated in the very structure of the universe, are part of the reality in which man lives. The moral and spiritual truths enter into the conscious life of man and become part of the social heritage by two means: discovery and revelation.

1. *Discovery*—Man Breaks Through to God.

The entire creation reflects and communicates the Will of the Creator. As the Psalmist says, "Heaven and earth declare the glory of God." Man, who is part of this creation, has the power to hear, if he listens; to grasp, if he reaches forth; to comprehend, if he tries to understand the "Voice of God" as it is recorded in the creation.

Prior to the unique Revelation at Mt. Sinai, certain universal postulates and basic moral laws were recognized: idolatry, adultery, murder, theft, cruelty and blasphemy were forbidden. Courts of justice were established to uphold them. Man had been able to discover truth from his own experience of the universe. Every human discovery is, at the same time, a Divine revelation and part of the never-ending process of communication between God and man. Primitive man had this power of communication, and so does modern man.

2. *Revelation*—God Breaks Through to Man.

According to Judaism, every human discovery of truth is a Divine revelation and Revelation was a human discovery. What, then, is the difference between the continual discovery-disclosure process of the human-divine dialogue and the special Revelation at Sinai?

The Torah Revelation was unique because God broke through to man in a direct and sudden Self-disclosure. The powers of man played only a minor role in this experience: reason, intuition, insight, moral and spiritual vision were *not* the decisive factors. Here was the only instance of the whole, complete and vast body of moral and spiritual truth breaking through to man in one great thrust. Man's discovery of truth, his break-through to God is, on the other hand, gradual and evolutionary. The Revelation at Sinai was inexplicably and miraculously direct, overwhelming and convincing to a whole people simultaneously. Moses and all the children of Israel assembled at Mt. Sinai received from God laws reflecting His Will.

What is the Biblical Account of the Revelation at Mt. Sinai?

In Exodus, the second book of the Bible, chapters 19 and 20, we are told that the children of Israel came to Mt. Sinai in the third month after their flight from Egypt. There, amid thunder and lightning, blasts of the shofar, and flames of fire, God "spoke" to the children of Israel and gave them the Ten Commandments.

How Was the Biblical Account of the Revelation Interpreted In the Jewish Tradition?

How can we grasp the rabbinic mind on any subject of belief, especially on one so complex as the belief in Revelation? The builders of our tradition expressed their inner thoughts, to a degree, in their statements, and in the practical application of the Law. We can examine those.

According to some of the sages, God gave the Ten Commandments at Sinai and revealed the rest of the Torah (Pentateuch or Five Books of Moses, which contain 613 biblical laws) to Moses at intervals during the 40-year sojourn in the desert. According to others, the whole Torah was revealed at Sinai. But all were agreed that the Torah was from Heaven; "that God had dictated it and Moses written it down," that it was the "complete, final and perfect" Revelation of God; that, therefore, "nothing could ever be subtracted from or added to it." The belief that the Torah was Divine Revelation was accepted by all Jews. Beyond this point, the first serious break in the unity of the Jewish religion occurred. Two lines of thinking in reference to Revelation resulted in a debate that continues into our own day. Below are indicated briefly the history and implications of these two lines of thought:

1. *The static concept*

Historically, this has received only minority endorsement, and is best exemplified by the position of the Sadducees and the Karaites. Acording to their view, God had dictated the

Torah to Moses, who wrote it down. God's laws are perfect so no changes, interpretations or expansions are possible. They fought against the efforts of the Talmudic rabbis to interpret and expand the body of Torah law because they considered them sinful, presumptuous attempts to "improve" on God's Revelation. The Karaites, in particular, rejected all the innovations of the Talmud, resisted vigorously the expansion and development of Jewish law, and repudiated the whole process of interpretation as alien to the written, literal Word of God. By taking this extreme position, they read themselves out of the mainstream of Jewish religious development.

The early Christian sects in Judaism isolated themselves from the main road of Judaism by taking another extreme position. Under the influence of Paul, whose Jewish name was Saul, they viewed the Torah as the literal word of God, its purpose to foretell the Messiah and prepare the people of Israel for His coming. The appearance of the Messiah would be the fulfillment of and, therefore, the "end" of the Law. The early Christians, like the Karaites, did not view the Torah as "a tree of life" bearing new fruits in every age.

On the Jewish scene today, there are some who do not countenance adjustment of Jewish law to the conditions and needs of contemporary Jewish life. They are to be found in the Orthodox, Conservative and Reform movements. But their attitudes and conclusions differ.

Among the Orthodox there are some who sincerely regard innovation as heresy, and adjustment as unworthy compromise. In their passion to remain Torah-true, they deny Torah's need for interpretation, application and adjustment. Among Conservatives are some who are intellectually convinced of, and committed to, the principles of change and relevance. However, they fear the risks involved in making changes, and the criticism of the guardians of the static condition of Jewish law. Among the Reform there is general reluctance to accept the idea of a need for a uniform standard or code of Jewish observance. Instead of careful modification of Jewish law in line with their own principle of reform, and systematic selection of those aspects of Jewish law which, by their own standards, were still relevant, they allow each individual to choose for himself what he wishes to observe.

A number of individual Jews completely disassociate themselves from the Jewish religion because they consider the Torah Revelation static and obsolete. They refuse to recognize that it is subject to rational inquiry and interpretation, growth and development, and reject the entire Torah as a result. Their dynamic and progressive pattern of thinking in other areas of living by-passes the Torah altogether and they remain outside of the Jewish religion.

2. *The dynamic concept*

The mainstream of Jewish Rabbinic thinking, transmitted through the Pharisees, who opposed the Sadducee way of thinking, also held to the view that the Torah was the miraculous, final and complete Revelation of God's law.

However, they held that its text possesses intrinsic potential for further clarification and realization of God's Will. Adjustments and changes within the framework of the Law are not negations of Revelation, or "necessary evils," or lapses inferior to the original literal provisions of the Torah.

For example, after the Temple was destroyed, all biblical laws pertaining to sacrifices and Temple ritual became inapplicable. The Rabbis suspended these laws and substituted for them laws of prayer. Sacrificial rites are part of the 613 "revealed" laws of the Torah; prayers are not. Yet, the Rabbis declared prayer, "service of the heart," more important than sacrifices (Ber. 32b).

The Rabbis found scriptural justification for prayer just as they did for all readjustments that became essential. Prayer became a religious law on the basis of Hosea 14:2: "We will render for calves the offering of our lips." They drew the same inference from a verse in Deuteronomy 11:13:

"To love the Lord your God and serve Him with all your heart." "What is the service of the heart?" they ask. And they answer: "Prayer." (Taanit 2b) Conclusions of this kind, far from detracting from Torah, enhanced the grandeur and power of God's Word. In the unlimited treasury of truth to be found in it, in its flexibility, and in its powers for infinite expansion, lie Torah's dynamic, living perfection.

It was rabbinic dogma that the entire Bible was *inspired*, but every word of the Pentateuch was verbally "dictated by God and written down by Moses." God's law *is* perfect and unchanging but the ability of mortal, imperfect man to grasp and *fully* comprehend it is limited. Consequently, constant interpretation of the written word was considered necessary and desirable. The Rabbis of the talmudic period cultivated reinterpretation as a deliberate process and referred to many of their deductions, quite frankly, as "mountains hanging by a hair." No check was imposed on the ingenuity which read into or out of the text meanings which appear poles apart from the literal *intention*. It was held possible for two students of the Torah to draw seemingly opposite conclusions from the same scriptural text on the ground that both contained an aspect of the underlying biblical truth; "Both points of view are the word of the Living God."

The Sages denounced as irreverent anyone who challenged the Divine origin of even a single letter of the Torah. However, they made a distinction between God's Revelation and how it was understood by the generation that first received it. "The Torah was spoken in the language of man" so man must constantly study, interpret and apply the original Revelation in order to maintain its relevance in the evolving history of the Jewish people, and as a living, fruitful force for the individual. This "continuous revelation," they held, is inherent in the original Revelation. "Turn it and turn it and you will always discover new truths in it." The verse: "Thou shalt not add or subtract," was interpreted to mean that nothing extraneous or contrary to the Torah should be added and nothing vital and basic to it should be subtracted. Thus, God revealed to Moses, in addition to the 613 laws in the Torah and additional laws which do not appear in the Torah, certain principles of logic by which the revealed laws could be applied to any situation that might arise in later ages. The Rabbis said that Moses himself would hardly recognize the Torah of Akiba as the same Torah he himself received from God.

How Can the Word Revealed to One Generation be Meaningful to Another?

The Rabbis firmly believed that whatever truth or insight might be required by subsequent generations could be drawn out of the inexhaustible wells of the Torah by trained and devout minds. On this they based their conviction that nothing spoken by a later prophet or scholar could in any way be in conflict with, add to or subtract from, the original Revelation. Scholars of the Law in every generation applied the Torah to their times, continuing to harmonize Jewish life with the meaning of God's Word. They interpreted and legislated for contemporary circumstance in conformity with God's Will as they read it in the Holy Scriptures. The verse from Jeremiah, "Is not My Word like a hammer that breaketh rocks in pieces?" was construed to mean that just as a hammer causes numerous sparks to flash forth in all directions so is the Word of God in the Scriptures capable of yielding many interpretations.

The sacred text was read in the light of contemporary knowledge and need, but justification for *every* rabbinic thought and utterance was sought and found in it. Laws instituted by the sages had to be based on a verse in the Torah, and they could always find in the Torah what they were looking for. The revealed Word of God was *the* only source for justification, but the stimulus for their insights and orientation was life itself. First they experienced the need in their environment, then they found the scriptural rationale. It would appear that this has always been the order: first came the need, then the Revelation. Was not this the meaning and way of God's Revelation at Sinai?

Both the Written Law and the Oral Law reveal their intentions when the need arises. Stimulated by the challenge of other systems of thought, the Rabbis introduced modifications in line with advancing religious ideas and developing ethical concepts. That they were influenced by social, economic and other environmental conditions is clear. For example, they developed the daily, Sabbath and Holy Day disciplines from only sketchy references in the Torah; they virtually eliminated capital punishment for first-degree murder by a novel interpretation of the biblical demand that there be two witnesses to the crime; they discouraged and eventually forbade polygamy which was permitted in the Bible; they interpreted the principle of "an eye for an eye and a tooth for a tooth" to mean monetary compensation in proportion to the damage done, thereby reading it out of Jewish jurisprudence altogether; they interpreted as "warnings to sinners" rather than as actual punishments biblical references to putting to death "the rebellious son" and destroying the "idolatrous city." In every instance, the Rabbis used the Scriptures to justify their conclusions.

The Rabbis believed that the purpose of God's Revelation was to sustain His creatures and to protect life. Therefore, in an extreme emergency, they could even set aside temporarily all laws (except adultery, blasphemy and murder) in order to save a life.

Revelation was declared to be a Divine paradox containing all the essentials for a dynamic religion: stability and flexibility, permanence and progress, the absolute and the relative, the eternal and the temporal, the fixed and the fluid. The written law contains the immutable qualities; the oral law, provided for in the written law and emerging out of it, the expanding qualities.

What Is the Oral Law?

The Rabbis insisted on the dual character of the Revelation: written law (the Torah) and oral law (the Torah tradition). Both bodies of law go back to the Revelation at Sinai. The Talmud describes forty-two laws to which there is no reference in the written Torah as oral "laws given to Moses at Sinai." The rest of the oral Torah is implied in the written Torah and deducible from it by certain rules of exegesis. The oral law was counted on to provide the flexibility necessary to adapt written law to the changing conditions of life itself. "If the Torah had been given in a fixed form, the foot would have had no standing (our position would have been intolerable)."

The Rabbis pictured Moses saying to God: "Sovereign of the Universe! Cause me to know what the final decision is on each matter of law." And God replied, "The majority must be followed. When the majority declares a thing permitted, it is permissible; when they declare it forbidden, it is not permitted." (Sanhedrin 22a). The religious leaders and the people of each generation were thus empowered by the authority of the oral law to legislate for their own time in the light of contemporary circumstance.

Because the Torah is the result of an encounter between God and Israel, it is both Divine and human. The written Torah has eternal validity; the oral law cannot be eternally valid because it is human. Operating with this point in view, the tradition was able to resolve areas of conflict between the heritage and the Jews of each age without resorting to futile debate, or artificially contrived compartmentalization.

Today some Jews stress the unchanging and eternal qualities of the Bible; some the changing and temporal. To some it is almost completely Divine; to others, almost completely human. Some oppose almost completely any change in Jewish law; others advocate decisive but cautious change. Still others call for sweeping modification of the law in order to deal with the contemporary needs of Jewish life.

What Are the Different Views of Revelation to be Found In Judaism Today?

THE ORTHODOX VIEW

According to the Orthodox view, there was only one Revelation, a completely Divine act, sudden, miraculous and supernatural. The event was unique. Never before or since the Revelation has anything comparable occurred: The God of the universe addressed an entire people, over 600,000 souls. How God spoke and how the people heard is, and will remain, a mystery. There is mystery in every miracle, and especially in the one of Revelation. Although we cannot understand the mystery, we must and should know its meaning: The Torah was *given to* man and not *made by* him. The Torah is subject to man's interpretation but its validity cannot be argued. The truths of the Bible, unlike truths which are products of history or human discovery, came into the world from beyond history, through an act of God and, only incidentally, through the people of Israel who served as the instrument of God's Self-disclosure. No other legitimate source of knowledge, such as sense-perception, intuition, reason or inspiration, is so perfect as the knowledge that was given through the direct communication of Revelation.

THE REFORM VIEW

According to the Reform view, the Bible is not the result of a sudden, miraculous, and supernatural revelation. The product of a gradual process of discovery and interpretation, it is a human work telling the story of Israel's effort to understand God, her duties and her destiny. To be sure, God does reveal Himself in the Bible but His revelations continue to be expressed in the language of Israel's experience and through Israel's gropings. Thus, revelation is not so much an event as a never-ending cultural process analogous to the creative process experienced by poet, artist or composer. In brief, moral and spiritual revelations, like all truths, come from God as progressive, evolutionary and continuous revelations of the Divine Will. This interpretation of revelation is expressed in the Union Prayer Book: "Open our eyes that we may see and welcome all truth, whether shining from the annals of ancient revelations or reaching us through the seers of our own time, for Thou hidest not Thy light from any generation of Thy children who feel after Thee and seek Thy guidance."

The Orthodox and Reform definitions are clear and definite. Orthodoxy views Revelation as a thrust into the human consciousness from a Source external to and beyond man, leaving no doubt that the Lord has, in truth, spoken. Reform views Revelation as a divinely inspired human process evolving from man's inner consciousness, his inductive reasoning, and from his experience with God. Conservatism Judaism has not defined categorically its conception of Revelation, so views range from total acceptance of the Orthodox position to total acceptance of the Reform.

CONSERVATIVE VIEWS

Between the two extreme positions of Conservative Jews, lie three middle-of-the-road views.

One of them regards the Torah *subjectively* as a direct and literal Revelation, an historic event at Sinai where God spoke to Moses and the children of Israel. A miracle occurred there: all the people heard God. The account in Exodus 19 and 20 is authentic. The wisdom heard at Sinai was not the discovery of inadequate and limited man but Divine Revelation. Therefore, the Torah is the binding Word of God and requires our reverence and obedience. However, the Torah is a body of truth in man's expanding experience. *Objectively*, it is a cultural product of the Jewish people subject to evaluation and judgment. This subjective-objective approach serves its adherents as a control and as a means of avoiding the— as they regard them—extremes of Orthodoxy and Reform. It satisfies their emotional attachment to Torah as sacred

Revelation and answers, to some degree, their need for certainty. At the same time, it satisfies the rational requirements demanded as a result of the impact of modern thinking.

A second middle-of-the-road view defines Revelation as a unique spiritual event, a meeting of God and a receptive Israel, out of which came Torah. Torah is what Israel learned from her encounter with God: Israel's interpretation of what God revealed. It is both divine and human. The divine element in the Torah is universal, eternal, ever-valid; the human elements are temporal, transient, subject to eclectic evaluation. The interpretation of the Torah is a continuing process of applying scripture in every age to changing historical settings. Torah is the "revealed" Bible and also the Bible as it is interpreted by the collective conscience of the Jewish people in every age.

According to a third view that enjoys some popularity among middle-of-the-road Conservatives, Revelation is essentially a process. Thus, the "revealed" Torah is itself the result of a gradual and evolutionary Divine-human process. Israel's encounter with God is not to be limited to a one-time meeting at Sinai, in a single act of Revelation; the relationship between the Living God and living man brings continuing revelation and discovery. The revelation of God's Will and man's understanding of the Will of God take on new forms and new expressions as man's relationship with God develops. The Torah of man, or God's Will as understood and interpreted by man, can never be perfect: God's revelations and man's discoveries are conveyed through imperfect vehicles, the human mind and heart. Consequently, the insights man gains from God's continuing revelation depend largely on man's effort to understand and respond to the Divine Will.

All three branches of Judaism approach the Bible both as *mattanah*, gift of God, and as *kabbalah*, acquisition on the part of Israel—as Revelation and as Heritage. Therefore, they all consider themselves within the dynamic Sinaitic tradition. The basic difference is one of degree rather than of principle. The Orthodox are most reluctant to admit that any portion of the Bible is temporal or relative; the Conservatives do consign parts of the Bible to the historical experience of Israel; the Reform tend to reject anything in the Bible which conflicts with modern theories of reality.

Does the Scientific Study of the Bible Challenge Belief in Divine Revelation?

Biblical criticism, the scientific study of the Bible, has come up with suggestions which run counter to the traditional conception of the origin of the Bible. Some critics state that the Torah could not have been written by Moses or any single individual; it was compiled from many sources at various times and pieced together into one book at a later date. The following evidence is used to prove their point:

1. Differing literary styles in the Torah point to many authors.

2. Marked ideological contradiction within the Torah indicates that sources at variance with each other were included in the compilation.

3. The same event is described in more than one way and, in some instances, the descriptions differ greatly.

4. Events in the history of Israel that took place after the biblical period are referred to in the Bible.

5. Some crude moral and primitive spiritual notions found in the Bible can hardly be the Word of God. These lower forms are found side by side with much higher conceptions which reflect a later stage of Israel's moral and spiritual development.

Does Modern Science Challenge Belief in Divine Revelation?

Modern science tends to shake belief in Revelation by

contradicting some of the "unscientific" facts in the Bible, thereby casting doubt on the reliability of the whole. Scientists find it difficult or impossible to accept the biblical account of:

1. the origin of man,
2. the age of the earth and the manner of creation,
3. the miracles, e.g., receiving manna from heaven, splitting the Red Sea, making the sun stand still.

How Have Jews Responded to the Challenge of Science and Bible Criticism?

1. *Rejection*

Out and out rejection of the challenge is the reaction of the extreme Orthodox. The Torah, containing the objective and final truth, is above human reason and cannot be questioned, much less abrogated, by human wisdom. Revelation is divine, all-powerful, perfect, and unchanging; reason is human, limited, fallible, and incomplete. Revelation is God's instrument for communication; reason is man's means of discovering. Revelation soars above reason's resources: theories, criticisms, doubts, and philosophies. Revelation should not be adapted to the latest worldly theories; times and theories must adapt themselves to it. Only to the extent to which human knowledge reflects and is in harmony with the Divine Revelation is it reliable and correct. Reason cannot be the judge of God's Word.

2. *Compartmentalization*

Another Orthodox approach is to think of religion and science as two distinct and unrelated views of reality, each valid for its own purpose. Religion should not contradict the theories and conclusions of science; science, for its part, has no authority in the field of religion. Religion is concerned with the structure of the moral and spiritual order; science with the psycho-physical world. Religion interprets and applies revealed truth verifiable only through faith and *mitz-*

vah; science operates with phenomena verified by measurement and experiment. Scientific theories concerning the origin, emergence, or development of life must be formulated solely in naturalistic terms; science is not competent to pass judgment on the biblical, supernatural account of the Creation. It can explain the miracles of the Bible in terms of nature or it may declare that there is no explanation at all for miracles. However, it may not assert that the miracle did not occur.

Biblical criticism, the scientific study of the Bible, is an effort to understand the Bible in purely human terms, as literature. From this standpoint it makes philological observations and linguistic parallels, suggests sources, dates and possible authorship. Such efforts to reduce Revelation to reason and explain the Bible in the human terms in which it cannot possibly be explained is, according to the compartmentalists, both pointless and misleading.

3. *Evaluation*

Reform Judaism welcomes the theories and empirical conclusions of modern thought as an aid to contemporary evaluation of the Bible. The views and data of the biblical writers are considered subject to examination, appraisal and modification just as are the findings of the scientist or genius in any field where truth is sought. Biblical pronouncements and insights should, when necessary, be adapted and changed to harmonize with the spirit of every age. The historical narrative and scientific views set forth in the Bible are, assuredly, not unchallengeable. Reform Judaism insists that cultural influences have shaped the contour and content of Judaism in the past and should be reflected in its present and future development. Thus, Reform rejects in the Bible that which is not in harmony with the highest conceptions of truth being revealed wherever men are groping to describe truth. Most adherents of Reform Judaism consider the moral laws of the Bible as perfect Revelation, yet others insist that even the *specific* forms expressing the timeless moral truths are subject to revision and improvement in order to make them more relevant and meaningful in our own age.

4. *Harmonization*

Conservative Judaism attempts to conserve the tradition and to harmonize it with modern thought. The enormous difficulties involved in such synthesis are undeniable but Conservative Jews insist that this is the way tradition has always functioned. There is need and justification for evaluation of the biblical tradition, as well as for the entire tradition of Jewish moral and spiritual thought, but the latest scientific theories need not be the measuring stick. Evaluation should be made on the basis of the tradition alone and methods of growth and change must be inherent to the system of Judaism as it has functioned in the past.

Conservatism stresses the fact that the Bible was never considered to be a history book or a science book: it functioned in the Jewish tradition as a source of religious instruction and moral-spiritual guidance. The Holy Bible was never the Jewish catechism for incontrovertible scientific information so why should Judaism feel challenged by the views of modern science? Was the world created in six days? Are all men descended from Adam and Eve? Such questions are not the concern of Judaism. For Jews, the questions have always been: What is the moral and spiritual significance of the biblical narrative? What do the biblical statements teach us about God and man? About man's relation to his fellow man? Along such lines the Conservatives seek to harmonize the heritage with the times. The heritage never was or should be rigid and fixed; it absorbs what is valid for continued growth. It can and should be harmonized with the needs and aspirations of each age, not merely recast in the spirit and intellectual categories of their times.

Why Do Many Jews Believe That God Literally Revealed The Torah?

1. Not once in the entire tradition, in the literature and

records available, is there a suggestion of denial or even doubt that Revelation took place. The Revelation at Sinai was witnessed by a whole people, 600,000 adults.

2. Moses' teachings were profoundly moral and his personal life exhibited remarkable spiritual sensitivity. It is, therefore, not possible that he took the name of the Lord in vain. It strains credulity to believe he could have fabricated his account of the Lord speaking to him.

3. If the Bible were the product of Moses, there would have been more self-glorification and less self-criticism contained in it. The Bible related that on several occasions God rebuked Moses for his unwillingness to accept responsibility, for his impatience and, at times, for his folly and lack of faith. Moses was not even privileged to enter the Holy Land because of his disobedience to God. Moses did not seek nor did he accept special honors or titles.

4. If the Bible were a hoax, the people would never have accepted as Divine Revelation its many unflattering condemnations. In it are to be found numerous reminders that Israel has been cowardly, ungrateful, morally blind and faithless, all very human failings.

5. No people accepts a burden unless it is convinced of the authenticity of the authority behind it. And the Bible imposes tremendous responsibilities on the people of Israel.

6. The *content* of the Torah is really the best proof of its Divine character. No human mind could possibly have invented the sublime ideas of the Bible in the cultural and religious atmosphere that prevailed at the time of its writing. The moral and intellectual condition of the world at that time was not conducive to and can hardly serve as an explanation for the emergence of the Torah.

7. Ancient writings and modern archeological findings tend, increasingly, to confirm the Bible's accuracy and validity.

8. Christians and Mohammedans not only acknowledge but base their religions on the genuineness of the Revelation and refer to the Jews as the People of Revelation.

9. Bible criticism is tentative and highly speculative. Varying theories and a host of contradictory conclusions drawn from the "scientific" study of the Bible are evidence of its unreliability as a test of truth.

Must a Jew Who Wishes to Remain Within the Mainstream Of Traditional Judaism Believe that the Bible is Literally True?

We have already noted that those who treated the Bible as the absolute, complete and literal truth read themselves out of the growing, evolving tradition of Judaism. The dynamic tradition recognized levels of meaning beyond the literal and even considered certain literal interpretations inapplicable and irrelevant under changing conditions. The sages found many Biblical statements *literally* untenable but reinterpreted them, finding in the familiar words fresh and vigorous insights.

Torah study, the chief prerequisite for living in the spirit of Judaism, is not merely "reading the Bible." It is intelligent study of the text of the Revelation in the light of all the brilliant spiritual insights and interpretations which have been accumulated by scholars and students throughout the ages. They read it reverently, as invaluable heritage from the past, and faithfully, in the context of contemporary needs.

The true Torah is "a tree of life" rooted in the written law, which is understood and continually nourished by interpretations of a dynamic oral law. The tradition never succumbed to the error of assuming that words are rigid, with fixed, unchanging meanings. Words, like life itself, were not considered to be static. That is why, in Judaism, Torah did not stop with the Bible; the literal text of the Revelation was the beginning, not the end of God's communication with Israel and of the Jewish search for the meaning of His Will. Interpretations and reinterpretations are living evidence of that undying search for meaning.

CHAPTER VI

Judaism and Science

As Scientific Knowledge Increases, Will Men Outgrow Their Need for God?

The assumption underlying the question is that the need for and belief in God spring from human weakness and ignorance. The more capable man becomes of doing things for himself, the less his need for God. When man becomes master of his destiny, he will not need the Master. As his knowledge increases and the unknown recedes, man will not require the mental prop of God. Faith is inversely proportionate to facts. As man discovers more about the world in which we live, he will discover that he needs God less.

This is a false assumption, based upon a misunderstanding both of science and religion. The scientific search for truth is endless, constantly expanding. The more we learn about our world, the more fully we realize how much more there is yet to learn. After all his achievements in science, Isaac Newton said that he felt like a boy playing with pebbles on the shore of truth. This is just as true for scientists today except that they are playing with atomic pebbles on the brink of outer-space disaster.

Advances in science do not make the world simpler to understand. They expose increasingly its infinite complexity. The elements of wonder and mystery will never cease. As we outgrow some mysteries and wonders, we climb higher to behold ever greater mysteries and wonders. To the astronomer with his high-powered telescope and to the space man in his rocket vehicle—even more so than to the Psalmist who beheld with his naked eye—the Heavens declare the glory of God and the firmaments show His handiwork. No scientist says that we will ever know everything. The religionist, too, recognizes that the more we learn, the more we come to appreciate the limitless and exciting possibilities of the world in which we live and of the God Who fashioned it. As science grows, so grows our belief in God. The sages taught: "The seal of God is truth!" The more we discover of truth, the closer we come to God.

When man learns to overcome his weaknesses and to use scientific tools to control his environment, he will feel closer to God. Man performs *mitzvos* when he *knows* he *should* and when he *thinks* he *can*, and not when he is feeling worthless and impotent. Man serves God, according to Judaism, when he is feeling strong, not when he is overwhelmed by thoughts of his own weaknesses. Children who are strong and independent can love their parents more deeply and give far more satisfaction to them than those who are frightened and insecure. Similarly, in our relationship with God, our strength and knowledge of our own worth make us capable of deeper, healthier love than our dependence on God in times of stress and weakness. Men will never solve all their problems nor should they want to—a life without problems is a life that is blind to the challenges of a remarkable world. The solution of simple problems makes us more capable of recognizing and dealing with more complex ones. We may overcome fears only to discover new fears in other areas of experience; by our very nature we will always be dependent on God. Our attempts to conquer poverty, disease, ignorance, and many other social evils; our increased mastery of mind and emotion; and our effective use of free will to fashion a destiny in closer harmony with the Divine Will, will bring us nearer to God in gratitude for the marvelous powers with which He has endowed us.

The great advances in science and technology have put unprecedented power in the hands of man. As our knowledge and power grow, we develop greater capacity for destruction as well as for creativity. Because increased power implies the need for greater moral responsibility and spiritual wisdom, man's need for God will also increase. Science does not set itself up as the ultimate judge of right and wrong. It gives us no standard to live by. The children of earth can never outgrow the moral and spiritual need for their Heavenly Father.

How Does Tradition Look Upon Science?

1. *Does it reject science?*

The average layman today thinks science and religion are in conflict. Judaism never took this view. To the Jew, science and religion are both truths of the One God: science tries to describe the work of God in nature, religion tries to understand how God functions in the life of man. A natural law, like a moral or spiritual law, is a divine commandment. It has been ordained by God to govern nature and cannot be in conflict with a *mitzvah* governing man's behavior.

2. *Is it neutral toward science?*

This is the view that science and religion are separate and unique and neither contradict nor support each other. Judaism has not espoused this approach either. The great talmudic teachers and medieval philosophers of Judaism displayed a lively interest in the sciences of their day and regarded the truths of science as the truths of God. The words of science and the words of religion support each other, both being the words of the Living God.

3. *Does it encourage the study of science?*

It was an axiom of rabbinic thinking that what is false in science cannot be true in religion and what is true in religion cannot be false in science: all truth is from God, one and indivisible. In his *Emunah Rama* ("Exalted Faith"), written in the 12th Century, Ibn Daud said: "There are many who dabbled a little in science and . . . since in such men the light of investigation has extinguished the light of belief, the multitude think it dangerous and shrink from it. In Judaism, however, knowledge is a duty and it is wrong to reject it." Even before Ibn Daud, the Rabbis of the Talmud and the great medieval philosopher-scientist Maimonides commended the sciences to our attention. Saadiah in his book *Emunot V'deot* ("Beliefs and Opinions") said: "The only reason why the love of physical science has been implanted in man is that it might support the science of religion and its laws, both together making an excellent combination." There never was a hot war or cold co-existence between science and religion in Judaism. As the 18th-century Elijah, the Vilna Gaon, put it: "If man is ignorant of secular sciences, he will be a hundredfold more ignorant of Torah . . . for both Torah and science go together." Albert Einstein of the 20th century is in accord with this view: "Science without religion is lame, religion without science is blind." Together they are whole.

How Does Tradition Explain Discrepancies Between the Teachings of Science and Religion?

Discrepancies indicate an error in interpretation:

1. *Interpretation of the scientific law or fact may be wrong.*

Scientific knowledge has its limitations: measuring instruments, our powers of analysis, the experimental method and our ability to draw conclusions are not infallible. The history of science demonstrates convincingly that scientific theories of one generation are either refined or replaced in another generation. The efforts of scientists have disclosed only partial and relative truths. Scientific explanations and supports for moral-spiritual laws can be helpful only insofar as we make a distinction between the divine commandment which is binding, whether we understand it or not, and the human interpretation which may be wrong.

2. *Interpretation of the religious law or fact may be incorrect.*

The sages regarded the Torah as infallible but they did not consider their explanations of the laws and facts of the Torah beyond human error. Their interpretations of the Torah did not possess the same validity as the Torah itself and they would admit a possible misinterpretation of a moral-spiritual law if it conflicted with an incontrovertible scientific *fact*.

3. *Interpretation of both the scientific and religious law may be faulty.*

When a religious law is reinterpreted to harmonize with the latest scientific theory, the reinterpretation proves faulty when the scientific theory on which it was based is superseded.

Guided by Tradition's View of Science, What Should Our Own Approach Be?

We must be ever mindful of the fact that there can be no conflict between one truth of God and another, only between one interpretation and another. We must make a distinction between God's laws, which are absolute and perfect, and our human interpretations of them, which can only be partial and transient. All definitions of the natural laws (science) and of the moral and spiritual laws (religion) are interpretations and, therefore, subject to human error. Should a discrepancy arise between a scientific and a religious interpretation, a misinterpretation of a law should be suspected. The law itself is not a human creation but a Divine one and, therefore correct. The human element is our own perceptions and deductions, which must remain open to re-examination.

Does the Theory of Evolution Contradict the Biblical Story of Creation?

The biblical story of creation and the theory of evolution can be compared on several levels:

THE ORIGINAL SUBSTANCE

The theory of evolution posits that lifeless substance gradually evolved into complex living matter. It does *not* explain how the original matter came into existence. The biblical story starts with God Who created the original matter out of nothing. No scientific theory explains, or indeed can explain, original matter. Thus, without God, there is no explanation. There is no conflict between the Bible which accounts for the beginning and science which explains later developments.

THE PURPOSE

The theory of evolution does not explain *why* there was an original substance and *why* it evolved. Science simply notes that there was an original substance and concludes, on the basis of observation, that an original substance evolved. It explains the "how," or the objective physical facts and mechanics of the evolutionary process but does not attempt to interpret or assign a reason and purpose underlying the process. On the other hand, the biblical story explains the *purpose* of the original creation and its evolution: God's Will. The Bible and science do not deal with the same problems so they are not in conflict.

THE ORDER

According to the theory of evolution, lifeless matter produced living matter; in the next stage, living matter without feeling endowed itself with feeling; then, feeling and perceptive life brought forth mind. A speck of motionless matter began to move; a one-celled amoeba was the starting point in a process that resulted in rational, moral and spiritual man. In the beginning, was lifeless matter; in the end, a living man. In every stage of development a lower form produced a higher; out of something lesser emerged something greater. In the biblical story of creation, the world is also traced back to its inanimate beginnings and living things appear in the same general sequence as that discerned by science. There is no conflict here but rather remarkable correspondence.

THE METHOD

The theory of evolution tries to explain *how* inert matter began to move, *how* plant life became animal life, *how* simple animal life became human, endowed with powers of mind, heart and spirit. It tries to explain how x becomes y even though y possesses qualities nonexistent in x. New qualities are explained in terms of adjustment to environment and of changes resulting from such adjustments. A plausible theory, but not convincing—scientists still cannot produce a living thing from inert matter or a man out of an ape. At best, man sometimes makes a monkey out of himself, a reversal of process! However, should science one day succeed in demonstrating the process in the laboratory, there would still be no conflict between science which describes *how* and the Bible which explains *why*—God said, "Let there be."

COMMON SOURCE

According to evolution, man evolved from the lower animals and is a high-animal form. This view does not conflict with the Bible. According to the story of creation, man and all animals were created out of the dust of the earth. Religion and science agree that man and the rest of the creatures share common characteristics. This implies a common source. Religion starts with a First Source, the Life-Giver; science has no First Source.

The theory of evolution tries to explain how man's moral, rational and spiritual qualities evolved from his biological nature. It wants to describe how something that was not present in man's predecessors emerged in man. Science seeks an answer to the question of *how* man became human. Religion, on the other hand, is interested in the *why*. The two neither overlap nor conflict.

TIME

According to the theory of evolution, it has taken countless ages for the universe to reach its present form. The Bible says the creation was completed in six days. As we have noted elsewhere, the Torah is not designed as a textbook to teach physical science or even historical facts. The narrative is essentially a vehicle for instruction in morality and spirituality. Why, then, does the Bible state that God completed creation in six days and rested on the seventh? Many great sages and teachers of our religion said or implied that we have no more reason to insist that the days are days, literally, than that we should suppose that God literally speaks as man does. The Psalmist who said, "A thousand years are as one day in Thine eyes," was not contradicting or explaining creation. The real importance of the biblical story lies in its emphasis on the sacredness of the Sabbath: God rested on the seventh day, therefore man should rest on that day. This neither conflicts with the theory of evolution nor with the traditional Jewish view that God created an unfinished universe, for God renews the work of creation, and man is a partner with God in the continuing work of creation.

MANNER OF CREATION

The evolutionary description of creation differs from that found in the opening chapters of the Bible. There are, however, within the Bible itself and in rabbinic literature also, several differing accounts of creation. That God created the universe is a basic and unchallenged article of Jewish belief; the manner of creation has no definite, authorized or binding version. How the universe came into being is presented in Jewish literature in varying forms and is expressed in different ways. The Bible itself contains at least three different descriptions:

The first chapters of Genesis give us the creation story in the form of a Divine drama unfolding in six momentous acts in the course of six days; 2. Psalm 104 presents a poetic description; and 3. Proverbs 8 gives still another picture of the birth of nature.

In the writings of the Rabbis, there is considerable speculation as to the manner of creation. Some expressed the view of "successive creations," i.e., God experimented with and destroyed many worlds before this world was finally established. Others held to the view of "continuing recreation," i.e., God renews each day the work of creation.

Great scholars and commentators of the medieval period did not consider the details of the biblical account theologically binding. Maimonides declared that it was not to be taken literally. Joseph Albo, in his great classic on Jewish religion called "Principles," states that the science of the first four chapters of Genesis was not intended to be taken literally. Rav Kook, a contemporary sage, takes the same position.

Judaism did not combat a theory of creation unless it *denied* the basic moral and spiritual principles of the Torah. The tradition held that there could be no contradiction between the teachings of the Torah and the truths of science, and modern Judaism in all its forms, Orthodox, Reform and Conservative, concurs. Evolution need not be considered a contradiction of any of the moral and spiritual views of the biblical story of creation.

Can Scientific Theories Ever Negate the Story of Creation?

Something cannot come out of nothing. The theory of evolution starts with the inert, the inorganic, but cannot account for this original substance. The belief that God created the "initial something" does not contradict the view that the world evolved from an initial something, an initial something with built-in possibilities for evolving life.

The evolutionary process, or mechanism whereby the potential becomes actual, and the inert alive, lends itself to the interpretation that the potential for life was inherent from the beginning. There is no conflict between this theory and biblical faith that God is the source of the creative process in a dynamic universe, that by a willful and purposeful act He created something out of nothing.

The evolution of man may have taken millions of calendar years but the creation of man was willed by God in the beginning. The galaxies of the heavens may have required billions of years to evolve to their present form but it all began when God said, "Let there be light!" It may take a millenium for the world to achieve what God had in mind when He looked upon His creation and said, "Behold, it is good." From the beginning, when God willed it into being, the cosmos held the seeds of its own future development. The scientists can only explain how the potential became actual. The "why" falls into the province of religion. Science cannot and does not deny the belief that the universe is God's creation.

What Does the Story of Creation Teach Us, Which We Cannot Learn From Science?

1. God is Supernatural Lord of the Universe. He created it and He sustains it. Although He transcends and is distinct from it, His Will is expressed in and made manifest through nature.

2. The universe has a purpose in God's plan. It was conceived in the "mind" of God and fashioned by the Divine Will for a reason. It is still evolving according to the "Word" of God.

3. The sanctity of the Sabbath is divinely established. It is the Will of God that the seventh day of the week be a day of rest and recreation.

4. The dignity of man is divinely ordained. Man, made of the dust of the earth, shares the same elements as all other living things. Biologically, man is an animal. Created

in God's image, and "but little lower than the angels," man is unique because of his spiritual endowments:

A. *Faculty of reason*—man's power to deduce new truths from given or assumed truths, to proceed from the known to the unknown, to produce creatively something new out of old materials.

B. *Gift of freedom*— the ability to mold and change his environment as well as to adjust to it, to master as well as to be subject to forces that determine the lives of all other creatures.

C. *Moral character*—the power to choose, deny himself and transcend himself, to do what is right even when it means going counter to his normal desires, to distinguish between right and wrong.

D. *Spiritual nature*—sensitive awareness of God. Man's ability to experience awe, reverence, faith and a sense of obligation enables him to reach up to God and out to his fellowmen in a common kinship of humanity.

5. Men are united in brotherhood by a common Father in Heaven.

Can Science Prove That God Does Not Exist?

In man are qualities of both heaven and earth. Some evolutionists do deny the transcendent God and His ultimate purpose but their denial does not follow from the major premises of their scientific analyses. No scientific theory, including evolution, can contradict the Biblical view unless it makes the following unprovable assumptions:

There is no God.

There was never a moral-spiritual purpose to the creation.

Life, mind, conscience, values, goals and all other characteristics that suggest the moral-spiritual quality of reality are accidents, mechanical products of a purposeless, unthinking nature.

The universe has no destination; life has no purpose or ultimate objective.

As we have already seen, it is impossible to prove the existence of God. We might now add that it is even more impossible to prove that God does *not* exist.

How Do Jews Today React to the Challenge of the Theory of Evolution?

1. Very Orthodox Jews generally find the theory aesthetically repugnant and intellectually inadmissible. To them it is an unattractive, unconvincing, and unedifying effort to explain what the Bible already explains in a superior manner. Any valid scientific theory can be reconciled to the truth of the Bible, but why ascribe to evolution "undeserved validity" simply because it is popular in scientific circles? They think largely in moral and spiritual terms and are secure in their convictions; therefore, they prefer the simple, beautiful biblical statement to the "uninspiring" theory of materialistic, mechanical evolution. They prefer the picture of a dynamic God creating with broad, sweeping, decisive action, to a slow process of gradual emergence.

2. Some modern traditionalists try to harmonize the biblical version of creation with the theory of evolution. They see in the biblical order of creation an evolutionary sequence. They point to the Psalmist's declaration that in God's sight a thousand years are but as yesterday when it is passed, and call attention to rabbinic statements which suggest grounds for harmonizing the religious and scientific views. The Midrash expounds various conceptions of creation and different versions of man's origin, some akin to the Darwinian view. Statements in the Midrash describe early man as appearing more animal than human and in one place

Adam is pictured as a hairy animal having a tail. They make every effort to show that biblical statements anticipate modern scientific theories. The adherents of this approach are motivated by a desire to uphold the infallibility of the Torah and to accept modern assumptions at the same time.

3. Some modernists resolve the challenge by distinguishing between the eternal moral-spiritual messages and the temporal frames of reference in which the messages are expressed. The creation story is intended to teach certain essential moral and spiritual truths: that the universe and all it holds are not the result of blind, mechanical necessity but rather the result of a deliberate act of God; that there is a Divine purpose behind creation and man must live in harmony with that purpose; that Torah guides man to the knowledge of what the Lord God requires of Him. These truths are held to be self-evident and incontrovertible. The age of the world, how it came into being, the origin of man, etc., are purely scientific problems. Whether God created the universe in six days or employed the method of evolution is not a religious problem. From this standpoint, the scientific adequacy or inadequacy of the biblical statement is no problem. God made His Revelation in the scientific jargon comprehensible to the generation that received the Revelation. If the best scientists in the world today were to rewrite the creation story in terms of valid contemporary scientific propositions, that revised statement would probably be obsolete one generation from now. In any event, God did not intend that the Revelation should bring man ultimate scientific principles but rather enduring moral and spiritual truths by which to live.

4. Modernists who feel liberated from the tradition think largely in terms of contemporary conceptions and are enthusiastic in their endorsement of the theory of evolution. They reject the "unscientific" portions of the Bible and apply the evolutionary principle also to moral and spiritual messages

of the Bible. The Torah as a cultural expression is itself an evolutionary product, according to them. They interpret the Bible as the product of several generations of Jewish life and distinguish in it lower and higher stages of Jewish civilization. This interpretation of the Bible, according to them, does not detract from its moral and spiritual worth. God does not reveal His Will in sudden and "miraculous" thrusts but through the orderly evolution of history. Evolutionary though the Torah is, it contains God's Revelation to Israel.

Does Judaism Retreat in the Face of Advancing Scientific Knowledge?

We have already noted that the tradition did not regard the order, chronology, and method of creation as matters of religious significance. Torah was never conceived of as a final pronouncement on scientific subjects. Similarly, science does not challenge the moral and spiritual truths revealed in the Torah.

As a result of advances made in the sciences and other branches of knowledge, the significance and grandeur of Judaism have, if anything, been greatly enhanced. Jewish tradition rejoices in all forms of progress, including scientific discovery, confident that it will clarify and heighten, rather than undermine, appreciation of religious truth. Judaism has a special blessing, in a set formula, which must be pronounced when one sees even a non-Jewish sage who discovers God's truth in some branch of learning. "Blessed be God Who hath imparted His wisdom to His creatures." Every scientific discovery calls for moral and spiritual advance, not retreat.

How Does Judaism Define a Miracle?

Judaism distinguishes between the "hidden miracle" and the "revealing miracle."

THE "HIDDEN MIRACLE"

In rabbinic thinking, a "hidden miracle" is an event or effect so common-place and ordinary that the marvel of it is overlooked. We take it for granted as a normal event and natural thing, and not as an occasion for amazement or wonder. The popular definition of a miracle, is "an event or effect that apparently contradicts known scientific laws and is, hence, thought to be due to supernatural causes or an act of God." The occasional inexplicable event that seems to contradict the normal order of nature, however, has never been the major preoccupation of the Jewish mind. Judaism has been far more fascinated by the miracles that are daily with us: the heavens and the earth, the sun, moon, and stars, the planets in their set courses, the air we breathe, the water and food that sustain us, even the common blade of grass. Everything in the universe is a miracle. In the tradition, God, the Giver of Life, is viewed as renewing constantly the miracle of creation, making repeated decisions affecting the destiny of nature and of man. The daily *Amidah*, the prayer which every Jew is enjoined to recite morning, noon and night, keeps us mindful of the "hidden miracle" and grateful for it: "We give thanks to Thee for Thy [hidden] miracles which are daily with us and for Thy wonders and Thy benefits which are wrought at all times."

THE "REVEALING MIRACLES"

The "revealing miracle" is the extraordinary, sudden, mysterious event or effect that contradicts the normal order of nature. This is commonly thought of as a miracle wrought by supernatural intervention, and in which God reveals Himself. Judaism says that God can perform such miracles also. However, Judaism discourages man's desire for God to interrupt the sublime, miraculous constancy of natural law. The hankering after proofs of God's omnipotence by His reversal of nature, in order for us to be impressed, marks a feeble faith and immature mind. Why should we not be content with, and grateful for, the countless miracles that are always with us? How can we fail to see the power and presence of God at work in these? By asking for a "revealing miracle," we imply that either God's power is not manifest in the natural order or that He has failed to make adequate provision for us in that natural order.

How Did the Tradition Discourage the Yearning for "Revealing Miracles?"

A basic principle of rabbinic thought is: "We must not rely on miracles." We do not build our lives and our faith on miracles. God can and does perform miracles of which we are unaware. He could feed us, just as the raven fed Elijah, if we made no effort to cultivate the earth. But we are morally responsible for our own life and destiny.

In Jewish theology, miracles are not indispensable prerequisites for the validity of the faith. We do not believe in Moses because of the miracles he performed; we do believe in the intrinsic value of the Torah message. Some religious faiths are based on a particular miracle that allegedly occurred, and the entire structure of that religion would topple if the miracle were disproved or even doubted by its adherents. Judaism is not one of them.

Our Prayer Book does contain prayers of petition in which we invoke Divine aid. We ask God to guide the course of nature to meet our needs, to heal us when we are sick, to bring rain when drought threatens, to sustain us, to comfort us in bereavement, to give us strength to meet the special trials of life. But our tradition instructs us not to ask God to alter events which have already taken place or to act contrary to His own laws of nature. Nothing is impossible for God, but it is presumptuous to expect Him to perform miracles for us.

Tradition was aware that reliance on miracles weakens man's independence, and divests him of responsibility for his own destiny. A quaint story in the Talmud illustrates rabbinic concern lest man's reliance on reason be undermined by his reliance on miracles: Rabbi Eliezer was heatedly disputing a point of law with his colleagues. Finally he shouted, "If the law is according to my view, may this tree prove it!" Whereupon, the tree did indeed move from its place. His colleagues remained unconvinced, "No proof can be brought from a tree." Whereupon, Rabbi Eliezer said, "If the law is according to my view, may the water in this channel flow backward." And it did! Said the rabbis, "No proof can be brought from a water channel." "If the law is according to my view, let the walls of the House of Study prove it." And the walls started to cave in so the entire structure almost collapsed. The rabbis remained unconvinced. When Rabbi Eliezer said, "If the law is according to my view, let it be proved from Heaven," a Voice from Heaven was heard, "Decision is according to Rabbi Eliezer's views." At this, Rabbi Joshua arose and said, "The Torah is *from* Heaven but it is not *in* Heaven." Rabbi Jeremiah arose and said, "The Torah, having already been given at Sinai, is now our responsibility to understand. We pay no attention to a Voice from Heaven but must rely on our own reason to decide the correct interpretation of the Torah."

Can God Break His Own Laws of Nature to Perform a Revealing Miracle?

The miracles recorded in the Bible were explained as being preordained from the beginning of the universe; they were not sudden, belatedly necessary departures from the natural order. "At the Creation, God made a condition with the Sea that it should make a passage for the children of Israel; with the sun and moon, that they should stand still at Joshua's bidding . . ." (B'reshit Rabbah 5:5) The Rabbis of the Midrash were trying to make the point that miracles were not arbitrary or sudden, indicating God's failure to anticipate the needs of His creatures or to provide adequately for the proper functioning of the natural order. God, who foresaw the need for certain exceptions to the rules, ordained that such exceptions (miracles) be part of the natural order.

On the other hand, some of the great commentators on the Torah tradition do not hesitate to explain a number of the miracles of the Bible in terms of *natural causes* in order to impress on us the fact that the natural order is the best proof of the wonderful Will of God. For example, the Red Sea was parted by a tidal wave at a fortuitous moment; the manna of the 40-year period of wandering in the desert was a kind of vegetation natural to the environment at that time; the revival of a child after death, recovery from a cataleptic state; the appearance of angels, dream sequences in which spiritual truths suddenly became clear.

Nachmanides, a very conservative commentator, interprets the verse Deut. 6:16, "Ye shall not try the Lord as ye tried Him at Massah," to mean: at Massah the Israelites sinned by asking for a miracle to prove God's presence and power as a condition for obeying His Law. Moses warned the people not to put the Torah to the test of miracles and extended this caution to all future generations. Sforno comments on Exodus 3:2, "And the angel of the Lord appeared unto him in a flame of fire out of the midst of a bush," that Moses did not see the angel with his physical eyes but in a prophetic vision.

Maimonides declared that the account of the Revelation at Sinai must not be taken literally, that the Divine Voice at Sinai was "not an actual voice but a simple, rational, prophetic comprehension." Like his master Maimonides, the great Talmudist, physician and mathematician Gersonides, insisting that nothing in the Torah can be contrary to reason, declared that Joshua's stopping of the sun's movement is to be interpreted rhetorically, and that Jacob's wrestling with an angel occurred in a dream.

Do Jews Today Believe in the Miracles of the Bible?

Most people in the past accepted the miracles of the

Bible literally. Nothing in our religion discourages such belief; nothing is impossible for an omnipotent God.

In the past thousand years or so of Jewish religious development, the literal interpretation has been supplemented by or has given way to interpretations that seemed more in harmony with our conception of the laws of nature. In the Jewish tradition there is no *one* authoritative interpretation of the miracles of the Bible. We are free 1) to accept them literally, as supernatural phenomena, acts of God which are contrary to nature; or 2) to interpret them as hidden miracles which may be explained in terms of natural law, God acting in and through natural law. Whether or not we interpret the narrative literally, we should have no trouble recognizing the essential moral and spiritual truths expressed, and the "Hand of God" directing the miraculous events recorded. For example, to accept the fact that Lot's wife literally turned into a pillar of salt when she glanced back toward the burning cities of Sodom and Gomorrah, is not so important as recognition that by concentrating on the irrevocable past and failing to move forward to the promise of the future we become as unable to go forward as though we ourselves are turned to stone.

Many Jews today find it difficult to believe in miracles that are contrary to natural law. Some of the talmudic Rabbis, as we have noted elsewhere, had the same difficulty. They arrived at the view that miracles were not interruptions of nature's law: God provided for them as part of the cosmic plan. This rabbinic view is remarkably similar to the views of modern science which, in its efforts to explain deviations from the laws of nature, has come to the conclusion that exceptions to uniformity are as characteristic of nature as uniformity.

Can a Jew Today Believe in God Without Believing in Miracles?

No. If a Jew does not believe that the orderly and regular

operation of natural law in the universe is a miracle of God, he has read himself out of the tradition. In the Jewish religion, God is the God of Nature. To deny that God is the author of nature is to deny a basic Jewish belief.

If a Jew says that the irregularities of nature, the exceptions to the rules of nature's uniformity, are not the work of God, he too has read himself out of the tradition.

Within the tradition, the miracles of the Bible may be interpreted as natural or as supernatural phenomena. We may accept them literally or explain them logically. But we must not deny that God *can* perform miracles: He established the laws of nature and He may suspend them. To deny that God *can* make a miracle come to pass is to limit God's power and, according to the tradition, to deny God.

How Do the Three Major Branches of Judaism Treat the Belief in Miracles?

Many Orthodox Jews regard the rationalist's attempt to explain the revealed miracles in naturalistic terms as blasphemous distortion. Miracles, they contend, are literally the work of an Omnipotent God, and humans, with their limited powers of reason, cannot fully understand them. Only faith, which goes beyond reason, can deal with miracles. The validity of the Torah and the whole structure of Jewish faith is found in, and based upon, the miracles of Revelation and Prophecy. Some of the extremists among the Orthodox attach great importance to the literal meaning of the miracles of the past and also to the miracles promised for the future. For example, they reject the possible interpretation of the miraculous coming of the Messiah in naturalistic or historical terms. They do not recognize the re-establishment of the State of Israel because the miraculous coming of the Messiah did not precede it. The liberal Orthodox accept the rational interpretation of miracles given in the works of the Rambam, the Ralbag, and others who attempted to reconcile miracles with the scientific conception of the orderly processes of nature.

REFORM

Reform Jews also believe in the power of God to perform miracles. However, they understand the miracles as acts of God working through nature and history, according to the orderly processes and laws He established. Just as the laws of nature can be understood in terms of reason, so can miracles. Thus, all revealed miracles recorded in the Bible are interpreted in naturalistic terms.

CONSERVATISM

Very few Conservative Jews believe literally in the miraculous stories of the Bible; very few reject them altogether. Most Conservative Jews strain to avoid surrendering all reason to faith or all faith to reason. By and large, the approach is rationalistic but there is strong reluctance to treat anything in Holy Writ with cold objectivity. They do not challenge or reject the possibility of the miracles nor do they hotly defend their probability. They stress the moral and spiritual value of the narrative. The miracle may or may not be a literal fact but, assuredly, it reveals a great truth.

CHAPTER VII

The Problem of Suffering

How Shall We Understand Pain and Suffering?

A Jewish sage once said, "It is not *why* I suffer that I wish to know but only whether I suffer for Thy sake!" Senseless suffering *is* unbearably painful. Although the Jewish people has suffered perhaps more than any other, its suffering was endurable and ennobling: it suffered for God. Of course, the greatness of the people lies not in its endurance but rather in the wisdom it has learned from its travail. The tradition has sought to capture the meaning of suffering and to explain pain in the following ways:

1. *Pain as Punishment*

This explanation is common in biblical and rabbinic literature. "If you are visited by pain, examine your conduct." (Talmud Berechot 5a) Man must be taught the difference between right and wrong; he must learn to discipline himself to choose to do good; he must distinguish between good and evil, morality and immorality. Pain and suffering come to those who have sinned: wrong-doing must be punished and punishment must be painful in order to bring the sinner to repentance.

2. *Pain as Warning*

Violation of the laws of nature brings pain. If we were protected from pain, we could never establish what is good for us and what is bad. There would be no incentive to learn and explore possibilities if we could not distinguish between danger and security, health and illness. In the physical realm, pain is an effective teacher: when we do the wrong thing, wittingly or unwittingly, our error causes pain, so we hasten to eliminate the error. Pain is a necessary warning that we are heading in the wrong direction, and indicates the need for caution and corrective action.

3. *Pain as a Test*

God devised pain in order to test our faith, our integrity, and our love to our fellowmen as well as to Him. An omniscient God knows the quality of each man's endurance and willingness to sacrifice for convictions that make life meaningful. God does not need to test man to prove anything. Man, however, needs the test: he learns the true quality of his convictions only when he is called upon to suffer for them. Passing these trials is an achievement in self-knowledge, and man extracts values from life in direct proportion to the degree to which he is able to cope with his trials.

4. *Pain as a Challenge*

Pain is man's reaction when his enjoyment of health and happiness is blocked. It has motivated many of his most salutary and creative efforts to ease the lot of mankind. The challenge of pain has stimulated man's ingenuity and lead to important preventive and remedial findings. Technological advances have roots in the profitable effort to reduce or wipe out poverty. The desire to alleviate pain has spurred investigations in the field of medicine.

5. *Pain as a Contrast to Pleasure*

Experience with pain helps us appreciate pleasure. If there were no pain as we know it, there would only be lesser or greater pleasures, and lesser pleasure would be painful to bear when a greater pleasure was frustrated.

6. *Pain as Prerequisite for Sympathy*

The sight of suffering evokes sympathy. Sensitivity to human suffering releases in men their noblest impulses. Suffering, more than anything else, reminds men of their brotherhood and moves them to extend a helping hand. Our sympathy and a desire to help may even be selfishly motivated—we may feel threatened personally or we may identify ourselves with the victim—but our response to the needs of others binds us to them. Pain may be the price we have to pay to achieve brotherhood.

7. *Pain as Sacrifice*

Much pain springs from the sacrifice man makes for love—love of family, of fellowman, of ideals which he cherishes, and of God. The sages of Israel called it *Yesurim shel ahavah,* suffering for love. Such suffering ennobles the sufferer and lifts him to great spiritual heights. All the achievements of humanity required sacrifice, and all sacrifice is painful. It is the price man pays for the privilege of being human, his opportunity to perform good works as a purposeful creature of God.

8. *Pain as Testimony to the Glory of God*

Commentators on the verse, "And God tested (*nissah*) Abraham," in the story of the sacrifice of Isaac, tell us that the test was not an experiment by which God intended to gain some new knowledge: God is omniscient. They suggest that the translation of *nissah* is "miracle" rather than "tested." God gave Abraham a chance to demonstrate the miraculous extent of human suffering and sacrifice for love of God. Still another interpretation for *nissah* is "banner." God gave Abraham a chance to unfurl a lofty banner for all nations to behold. The pain involved in our sacrifices for worthwhile objectives sets a shining example for other men to emulate and testifies to the glory of God, the Creator of so heroic a creature as man can be.

9. *Pain as the Price for Rationality*

We live in a universe which is essentially law-abiding, governed by cause and effect. The very same natural laws which work for us may also work against us. The benefits of water are innumerable—without it life would not be possible. It quenches our thirst, causes the earth to bring forth its fruits, and cuts great rivers through the mountains. Yet water can effect great destruction, as in floods, and inflict great suffering. The same biological laws that produce a normal, healthy child sometimes produce a child imperfectly formed physically, mentally, or both. Wherever conditions can work out right, we must accept the possibility of their working out wrong.

Two divinely ordained consequences, one beneficial and one obnoxious, can follow from a natural law, a phenomenon, or a system of logical and moral propositions. It follows that we cannot have the one without the other. As Job said to his wife, "Can we accept the good and refuse to accept the bad?" If life did not follow certain natural laws, even though the laws sometimes inflict great pain, rationality would be impossible. Because the natural order is law-abiding, probabilities, predictions, the accumulation of ordered data and dependable experience are able to serve as guides. Along with the advantages of a law-abiding natural order we must accept its causally and logically necessary disadvantages.

10. *Pain as a By-product of Progress*

The Jew of faith always regarded pain as essential to some desirable end. It helps to fulfill some providential purpose and is subservient to some benign purpose. Pain is a by-product of birth. We experience pain when life-giving ideas and values struggle to emerge into the world. Whenever there is birth or rebirth, there is pain: the unborn child tearing free from the womb, the child breaking out of childhood into adolescence, adolescence struggling toward maturity. Thus, we might think of pain as a necessary concomitant of progress and growth. As one Talmudic sage put it, "Pain and suffering should lead to liberty" (Berachot 5a) ; and another, "If you want life, expect pain" (Midrash Psalms 16:11). Pain can lead to more abundant life. The sages called pain, the "birthpangs of the Messiah."

How Shall We Face Suffering?

As part of God's creation, suffering must have some meaning even when that meaning is hidden from us. We start with the premise that suffering has purpose, then proceed to try to understand it, capture its message for us, and make the most of it. The pain of life must not be borne with resignation. The attitude that "since you can't do anything about it, why try?" is alien to Judaism.

The sages call upon us to face some types of suffering gladly, to endure martyrdom, to find expiation for transgression, and partial atonement in suffering. However, the suffering in itself is neither noble nor desirable. To suffer joyously is vastly different from enjoying suffering. Even while Judaism maintains that suffering can be made a spiritual discipline and a source of increased power for good, suffering is never desirable in itself even when it brings about a desirable end. God weeps when His children suffer. According to rabbinic legend, God rebuked the angels for singing joyfully at the sight of the Egyptians drowning in the Red Sea: "My handiwork is drowning in the sea and you dare sing?" Judaism insists that suffering must be combatted and its elimination attempted in all areas of living.

It is a paradox commonly noted that those who sacrifice the least complain the most and consider themselves the greatest sufferers. Those who make the greatest sacrifices to assuage the pain of others are too busy tackling constructively the problems underlying suffering to indulge in complaints. How we face our trials determines victory or defeat in the face of suffering. Jews have had considerable experience with suffering and Judaism, their accumulated wisdom, prescribes how to understand and face suffering.

1. *Find its meaning.*

When we deafen our ears with loud cries of bitterness and shouts of protest, we fail to hear the message of the meaning of suffering. More beneficial than raising an angry fist to heaven and demanding that God justify Himself, or denying completely His existence, is to ask ourselves. "Why? Wherein have we failed? What is God trying to teach us? What can we learn?" In many a sigh is to be found an insight, in pain wisdom, in sobs a lesson, in shock a jolt out of complacency and a call to action. In every loss, there is a gain; the loss we know, the gain we must find. In the experience of searching, we garner some wisdom.

2. *Extract from it a blessing.*

Suffering is a calamity, but when it is regarded also as a challenge, a blessing may be extracted from it. Jacob wrestled with the angel, and Israel was born. Good comes out of suffering when it leads to enlarged sympathy, to a determination to do something constructive, to social service.

3. *Accept it with faith.*

Our healthy impulse and our moral duty is to prevent suffering, but some aspects of destiny are in God's hands. What is already done and cannot be changed we must accept with trust and confidence in God's judgment. Through the miraculous power of faith, we discern the meaning of life even when it is beyond our understanding. Like the Psalmist we must say, "I found trouble and sorrow but I called upon the name of the Lord." Out of faith spring strength, comfort, healing and courageous acceptance. Faith is no invitation to inactivity, surrender and resignation; passive acceptance is synonymous with neglect and irresponsibility. We are called upon to do everything possible to ease the suffering we cannot prevent.

4. *Accept responsibility.*

The Talmud's prescription for human suffering is given in *The Sayings of the Fathers*: "Repentance and good deeds are a shield in front of suffering." Most of us part with cheap sympathy, alas, then loudly proclaim our disillusionment with God. A case in point is the extermination of six million Jews by the Nazis. Had we been more responsive to Jewish—indeed, human—needs, willing to think with courage and act with greater responsibility and risk of sacrifice; had we even consented sooner to part with greater sums of money, we could have saved many lives. Our own guilt, folly, irresponsibility and perversity are quietly excused or completely overlooked as we rush to bring God to judgment.

By divorcing ourselves from responsibility for mitigating and eliminating human suffering we make possible fresh instances of Jewish pain and failure.

Suffering caused by our own sins must be faced honestly. After proclaiming, "We have sinned," we can go on to build a shield of good deeds to protect Jewish life from future unnecessary suffering. Only fools and cowards excuse themselves by crying loudly against God's injustice or impotence. We are not helpless puppets in the hands of God; we are free men capable of making decisions. A man selects what he wants to buy but he must be willing to pay the price.

5. *Ask why, but listen for the answer.*

The tradition pictures God as saying to the sufferer, "Ask Me, but understand in silence." We must question suffering for we learn in the process of seeking answers. In a vision, Moses beheld the last moments of Akiba, that saintly teacher of God's Law. As Akiba was being flayed alive, Moses cried out, "Is this a just reward for such learning and virtue?" God replied, "Be silent for such is My decree." (Talmud Menachot 29b). If we raise the question humbly, in prayerful silence, an answer will be forthcoming. Akiba himself asked, "Why?" and he found God's reply in his own prayers: "All my life I have repeated the verse, 'And thou shalt love the Lord thy God with all thy heart and with all thy soul and with all thy might.' Now at last I know its meaning—Thou shalt love the Lord God even when it requires the sacrifice of your life." Love of God makes even supreme suffering intelligible. Love infuses suffering with meaning.

6. *Thank God for ill fortune as well as for good fortune.*

In a chasidic story, Schmelke and his brother approach their teacher: "Our rabbis have a saying which troubles us. They have written that man ought to praise God for ill fortune as much as for good fortune, for suffering as well as for joy, and should welcome both with equal gladness.

How are we to understand this rabbinic statement?" Their teacher advised them to seek out Rabbi Sussya in the House of Study. When Rabbi Sussya heard the question, he laughed: "You have asked the wrong person. In all my life, I have never experienced misfortune. You must seek the answer elsewhere." The brothers understood this was really the answer itself. To others, Rabbi Sussya's life appeared to be one long stretch of pain. His faith in God and joy in study, however, made life so meaningful that they neutralized suffering.

Far fetched as it may sound, some people do manage to maintain an amazing perspective in the face of adversity. If some can achieve it, all of us are capable of trying for it. In any case, Judaism holds that we can and should make it a habit to thank God for ill fortune as well as for good. By cultivating the habit, we may eventually develop the faith.

7. *Alleviate and combat suffering.*

Judaism does not attempt to achieve uniformity of belief. It says to the Jew, "Here are the best opinions we have been able to find. Take one or take all; take some or take none. What you believe is not nearly so important as what you do." It does not say what a man must believe but it *does* say decisively how a man must act. Thus, no matter what a man thinks about suffering, Judaism expects him to care for its victims—to comfort mourners, to help heal the sick, to feed the hungry, to clothe the naked, to house the homeless, to defend the oppressed, to liberate the enslaved and to root out the causes of suffering from nature, from man's mind, and from society. And concerning the suffering that is beyond all human control, Judaism says to man: endure it with courage and, above all, with faith. All the *mitzvos* were given for the purpose of alleviating and controlling suffering. All the ritual laws of our religion may be set aside to prevent suffering.

Why Do the Wicked Prosper and the Righteous Suffer?

Explanations for the presence of suffering in a world

created by a good God are difficult enough. But these difficulties are as nothing compared to the paradoxical phenomenon of the happiness of the wicked and the suffering of the righteous. The question is as old as Judaism itself and many have wrestled with it. Although the Jewish tradition affirms the belief in the righteous Judge and in the righteousness of His judgment, it finds no one completely satisfactory answer. The tradition records differing responses, some of which are listed below.

1. *There is no Divine justice.*

The Talmud relates that Elisha ben Abuya once saw a young man climb a tree in response to his father's request to bring down some birds. Before removing the young from the nest, the young man released the mother bird, for the Bible says that such conduct would insure "that it may be well with thee and that thou mayest prolong thy days." (Deut. 22:7) Climbing down, he lost his footing, fell, and was killed. To Elisha this seemed to prove that there is no Divine justice, and he became an unbeliever. His colleagues, on the other hand, interpreted the verse, "that it may be well with thee" as a reference to the world where all is well, namely, the hereafter; and "that thou mayest prolong thy days," in the world of endless days. The choice was between a denial of God, which meant acceptance of the view that all of life is accidental, and between faith in God, which meant confidence that ultimately even the accidental may have meaning. Elisha made the former choice. Of course, the sages rejected this conclusion because it would have destroyed the foundation of morality.

2. *Only God knows the answer.*

Some of the Rabbis held that "it is not in our power to explain either the prosperity of the wicked or the afflictions of the righteous." Some experiences and events which man cannot explain were ordained by God and must simply be accepted with faith in the ultimate wisdom and goodness of God's Will. Man is, after all, a creature of nature who can judge the universe and life's experiences only by his own human, rational standards, and within the framework of his own human limitations.

Man's mind is finite, therefore, he cannot comprehend the Divine plan in its entirely. However, man is endowed with enough of the Divine to enable him to interpret experience in terms of faith in God and with humble recognition that he can never find all the answers. The teachers of our tradition adopted the conclusion of the Book of Job, "Who can understand the thunder of God's mighty deeds?" If man could see all the concealed factors involved in the ultimate relations of things, then the seemingly unjust would be recognized as infinitely wise and just. That is what the Jewish prophet meant by "the righteous shall live by his faith." Without faith in God's justice, the structure of moral life is doomed. Judaism counsels man to contemplate, to try to understand and, when he has reached the limitation set by the human mind, to believe that events have meaning. "Despite everything, abandon not belief," said a rabbi.

3. *The scales of justice have to be balanced.*

The Rabbis did not view life on earth as complete in itself: life extends beyond the grave. Only by combining the two stages of life, the here and the hereafter, can God's providence be fully understood. Some held that God punishes the righteous for transgressions in this life so they may inherit the world to come; conversely, the wicked prosper for their virtues in this life because they will not enjoy the world to come. Some of the Rabbis suggested that a good man suffers because he is not completely good and a wicked man prospers because he is not wholly bad: ultimately no virtue will be unrewarded and none will escape deserved punishment. With the Psalmist, the Rabbis said that "those who sow in tears will reap in joy." One Rabbi put it thus, "He who labors before the Sabbath (in this world) will eat on the Sabbath (the world to come): but, if a man does not labor (suffer) before the Sabbath, how can he eat (enjoy happiness) when the Sabbath comes?" (Avodah Zorah 3b)

4. *The good suffer for the wicked.*

In the simple, moral thinking of man, only those who sin should suffer its consequences. In the Divine moral order of the universe, the righteous, who are morally strong and capable of extracting positive values from suffering, should be willing to suffer for the morally weak. Men's reason rebels against this unthinkable jurisprudence but, through faith, man can appreciate the need for charity in the moral order. Suffering comes into the world because of human wickedness and the righteous must endure the consequences because they have the moral strength and capacity to interpret it constructively. Also, in a sense the righteous bear some responsibility for those who err because they have within themselves resources which must be used to prevent circumstances conducive to the spread of evil.

5. *Love sprouts out of the seed of pain.*

Some of the sages looked upon suffering of the righteous as proof of God's love, not as punishment. In the Talmud and Midrash, this view is expressed as follows: "Should a man see suffering come upon him, let him scrutinize his conduct. If he does not discover the reason for his suffering, let him attribute it to his failure to study Torah. If he has studied Torah, then it is certain that his suffering is a manifestation of God's love." Suffering is good, according to this viewpoint, because it leads to the world to come. Some of these sages even went so far as to say, "Whoever rejoices in suffering that comes upon him in this life brings salvation to the world." In more modern terms, it means that suffering should be viewed as a challenge. As we meet successive challenges, we gain in strength and insight and in ability to meet other problems as they arrive. The challenges of life lend it zest, and are to be welcomed—at least in retrospect, if not at the time when they are painful crises.

CHAPTER VIII

The Problem of Evil

Since God Is Good and All-Powerful, How Can We Account For Evil?

Why does an all-powerful God allow evil to prevail in the world? Is God's power limited or is God not even concerned with good and evil? If God is benevolent, why do we have evil? Is evil the creation of some power in the universe opposed to God? If God is the Creator of everything, is He not the Creator of evil? Five main positions have been taken to answer this complex of questions:

1. There is no God.
2. There are two Gods—a God of good and a God of evil.
3. God is all-powerful but not all-good; or, He is all-good but not all-powerful. In other words, God is limited.
4. God is all-good and all-powerful but is concerned with the welfare and fulfillment of the entire creation, not with the opinions of men concerning good and evil.
5. God is all-good and all-powerful, and evil is part of a benevolent Divine purpose.

1. *There is no God.*

No moral power stands behind the universe. There is no plan, providence, purpose, or goal. These are illusions springing from apprehensions in the minds of men. Thus, there is no ground for disappointment over evil because there never was real hope for good. There is no God who is "good to all." The original reality is matter and physiochemical reaction. Everything in the universe, including mind, imagination, hope, courage, faith, vision, good and evil, happiness and suffering, right and wrong, is the accidental result of a simple cause-and-effect physio-chemical reaction. Everything evolved and developed by chance, over a period of billions of years, into the highly complex structure of life.

2. *There are two Gods—a God of good and a God of evil.*

In one of the great religions of the Orient, there are two Gods, one all-good, the other all-evil. The world is the scene of a struggle between these great powers. In some religions of the West there is a similar tendency to become enmeshed in dualism. God is good, loving and creative; Satan is evil, hateful and destructive. God and the Devil (Satan) are engaged in a match to win the world and are competing for men's souls. God will surely win but the Devil prevents it from being an easy victory. These two forces are called by various names in different religions but all religions assert the ultimate triumph of the power of good. In the end, Satan will be conquered and all peoples will worship the true God. But, until that eventuality, Satan will tempt man to do evil.

Jewish thought maintains that God is all-powerful; it cannot accept the idea that there is a cosmic power competing with God to control the universe. That is why Jewish philosophers have insisted on the biblical view that God created the universe out of nothing. Everything was created by, and is under the control of, God. Consequently, there can be no principle of power in contest with God. The One God formed light and also darkness; He made peace and created the possibility of its opposite; He creates possibilities for both good and evil, for happiness and suffering; He gave life its meaning and challenge by leaving the choice to man.

3. *God is all-powerful but not all-good or He is all-good but not all-powerful.*

Because God is not all-good, He permits evil and suffering. In Greek mythology the gods, at times, even enjoyed the miseries of man and sported with human lives. Others have interpreted a limited-God idea to mean that God simply cannot prevent evil because He is not all-powerful. This latter approach is illustrated by the tendency of some modern theologies to reduce God to a Power. Judaism rejects any suggestion that the One God is limited morally or in any other way.

4. *God is concerned with the over-all welfare and ultimate fulfillment of the total creation and not with the opinions of men concerning good and evil.*

According to this view, God is absolutely perfect and powerful but His cosmic purpose transcends the well-being of any one of His creatures. He has created out of an infinite intelligence; His nature is perfect so there are no imperfections in nature. Men have deluded themselves into thinking that everything was created solely for their benefit. They evaluate everything by their limited and imperfect human yardstick. That which they believe to be beneficial, they call good; that which is not to their taste, comfort or convenience, they call evil. But things are not good or bad according as they delight or offend human sensibilities. This delusion leads man to attempt to influence the Infinite God through his prayers and by his will. It sets human will above cosmic necessity, thereby challenging the wisdom and sovereignty of God. Petition and persuasion become decisive factors in the relationship between God and man, an unworthy and unashamed form of bargaining. It is an expression of hope that "my will be done, not Thine." Why should God be concerned with that arrogant worm called man?

Judaism's position is that God is indeed concerned with the ultimate fulfillment of total creation but, at the same time, He is mindful of the needs of every living soul. The transcendent God concerned with the order of the universe is also concerned with the need for order and intelligibility in the life of man. He is a compassionate God, accessible to man. God is a Father of Mercy who, in love, remembers His children. "He is good to all and His tender mercies are over all His works." "He openeth His hand and satisfieth every living thing with favor." "He listens to prayers, hearkens to cries," and "is near to all who call upon Him in truth." Prayer is not construed in Judaism as a device for influencing and controlling God. Man is not presumptuous when he desires to understand the will of God but he must recognize that some things are beyond his comprehension, and must accept the fact of his own limitations. The question of how to explain evil and suffering is accepted as the human need for inquiring and understanding. The question of why evil and suffering exist is a normal expression of the desire for reassurance that the burden of suffering and evil is being borne in the service of God. This questioning is neither complaint against God nor a slogan of rebellion. It is the normal reaction of thinking, feeling beings.

5. *Evil is part of a benevolent Divine purpose.*

Since evil is God's creation, it is a Divine instrument serving His purpose in the world. Determined to find the meaning and purpose of evil, Judaism discovered good coming out of evil and some good hidden in evil.

In the Light of Jewish Tradition, How Shall Evil Be Understood?

Here are some of the ways in which the tradition tries to understand evil.

1. *Evil is the price of moral freedom.*

Moral freedom is based upon free choice between good and evil. If there were no alternatives, human decision would be impossible: man could be neither free nor moral. There must be liberty to sin if there is to be freedom to do good; there must be opportunity to shun *averah* (sin) if *mitzvah* is to be a positive, intelligent and devoted act of goodness.

2. *Evil is a challenge.*

Evil is a challenge in man's heart and in his environment. He cannot shut his eyes to it or turn away from it. He is compelled to face it, then yield to or conquer it. It provides the contest without which there can be no moral victory. If there were no evil to overcome, there would be no goodness to achieve. Goodness is the triumph over evil. A modern sage interpreted the verse, "And the Lord said: 'It is not good that man should be alone; I will make him a help-mate'" (Gen 2:18) as follows: "And God said: 'There can be no goodness in man while he is alone without an evil impulse within him. I will endow him with the ability to do evil, and it will be as a help-meet to him to enable him to do good if he masters the evil nature within him. Without the evil impulse, man could do no evil; but, neither could he do good.'"

3. *Evil is a test.*

Evil is the work of the "Satan" of the Book of Job. He constantly tries to prove to God, his Master, that man is unworthy of God's love and beneficence. It is the test out of which real good emerges—out of evil, despite evil, triumphing over evil.

4. *Evil is explained by the Fatherhood of God.*

God rules His creatures as a human father should desire to raise his children. Insulating or isolating them from all possibilities of harm would render them incapable of making decisions and leave them ignorant of cause and effect. God is raising children, not robots; thinking men capable of decision, not puppets. The Heavenly Father says, "Behold, I set before you this day good and evil. Choose the good and live."

5. *Evil as a necessary contrast with goodness.*

Goodness would be unrecognized if there were no evil. Without vice there is no virtue, only innocence. Without evil there would be no moral standards, no moral distinctions, only moral indifference. We would not know and benefit from good if we did not know evil. We can only appreciate how well off we are if we recognize that life could be worse.

Contrast is essential to our enjoyment of life's blessings. Artists create beauty, poets extol it, and people enjoy it because of the manifold gradations of ugliness as well as loveliness that are possible. If there were never a cloud and no night, if life held the monotony of perpetual flawlessness and predictability, the human heart and mind would not be moved to celebrate in joy and thankfulness the bright warmth of a sun which creates changing shadows.

Water becomes more than water when it quenches a great thirst. Goodness is more profoundly cherished when attained by resisting temptations to evil. In brief, God created evil for the benefit of His creatures so they might discern between good and evil, and learn to turn from evil in order to enjoy what is good.

6. *Evil is a protection against greater evils and disasters.*

Often what we call evil is only a semblance of evil because we are unable to see its far-reaching influence for good. What appears as an evil may be good in terms of larger historical scope and the ultimate unfolding of God's purposes. Our judgments are limited by our restricted vision; we must, of necessity, stand too close to what are really transient moments in human experience. Time and distance lend perspective, but, as humans, time is not long and we have not far to go. What looks like evil to us may be the birthpangs of some divinely perceived good; being a lesser evil than might have overtaken us, it may actually be a good. When man passes judgment on God and cries out bitterly against the evil of the moment (anything incurring his displeasure or seeming to interfere with his self-interest) he fails to reckon with the possibility that the real evil in the situation is his own presumption and misjudgment. "My thoughts are not your thoughts, neither are your ways My ways, saith the Lord." (Isaiah 55:8)

7. *Evil is a blessing.*

Rabbi Akiba recounts how a whole series of unfortunate mishaps befell him one night while he was on a journey. Being patient, wise and a man of faith, he accepted each catastrophe of the night with the expression, "Whatever God does is for the best." In the morning he learned that the misfortunes which forced him to spend the night in the dark on a lonely road really saved his life. The inn which he had been trying to reach was ransacked in the night by marauders who murdered everyone in the inn. Thus, what appears as evil is sometimes a blessing in disguise, preserving us from greater evil. Sometimes evil jolts us into remembering a truth which had begun to fade from our consciousness, and compels us to recapture a blessing that might have been lost.

8. *Evil is an instrument for moral correction.*

God uses evil to rebuke, to chastise, to goad man to action when he sinks into complacency and self-satisfaction, to keep man sensitive to the need for continuing moral growth. God uses evil forces as His instrument to arouse moral awareness in nations and men. The prophets and sages of Judaism interpreted the military victories of other nations against the Jewish people in this light. The destruction of the Temple in Jerusalem taught the Jews that they had grown unworthy to possess a temple; the massacre of six million Jews by the Nazis, made Jews everywhere aware of their moral responsibilities toward their brothers and of the need to support the rebuilding of Israel; the threat of Communist domination and the havoc it would create are awakening the American conscience in our own day. Unfortunately, we require the shocking power of evil, real or potential, as a vivid reminder of our moral failure and spiritual apathy.

9. *Evil is a potential good which has gone astray.*

Judaism teaches that we can serve God with our *yetzer hara* (evil inclinations) as well as with our *yetzer tov* (good inclinations) ; that the power for evil in man can serve as a power for good. Evil is frequently a power for good which is misunderstood, misapplied and misused; it is "an angel, fallen and turned Satan." Self-concern, which should lead to self-realization, can lead to ruthless self-centeredness. Ambition, which is the wholesome drive behind man's search for knowledge, becomes ugly when man misuses it to exploit his fellowman, to squander natural resources, for, in the process, he blunts his own sensibilities. Sex, which should be the wholesome urge for man to marry, build a home, raise a family and find spiritual security, can lead to corruption and destruction. Love of country, which is a positive loyalty, can become chauvinism and imperialism.

10. *Evil is self-imposed suffering that can be avoided.*
We have only ourselves to blame for evil consequences which follow from our indulgence in activities injurious to our psychological, moral, spiritual and physical health. We pursue personal pleasures of the moment without regard to how they affect others and ourselves; and we organize social destruction in order to enlarge ourselves at the expense of others. This kind of evil, men can and must learn to shun.

What Is the Nature of Evil?

The mainstream of Jewish tradition takes the following stand on evil:

1. Evil is God's creation and is subject to God's Will. It is real but relative, not absolute.

2. The reasons for God's creation of evil are many. All point to its usefulness.

3. God's plan for the world includes the reality of evil, the constant struggle against it, and, eventually, the complete conquest of it.

4. Man is morally bound to understand, to combat and to repel evil because he is a free agent.

5. The Bible anticipated modern thought by recognizing the existence of natural causes responsible for evil results. Rabbinic legislation also took into account the existence of such factors and tried to reckon with them. The scientific analysis and treatment of a problem in terms of its causes, became part of the rabbinic way of thinking about evil and, particularly, about suffering. This approach may be traced in many of the health laws and in the social legislation

promulgated by the talmudic Sages who displayed a marked interest in the sciences of their times. This technological approach to evil and suffering led to the reproach of Judaism as a materialistic religion, too involved in the affairs of this world. Such criticism is acceptable. Judaism considers the application of technology to the problem of suffering to be a methodical approach to the mitigation of evil, in accordance with the Will of God.

6. The existence of evil cannot be accounted for fully. It will always hold an element of mystery.

Why Do Men Do Evil?

Tradition offers some reasons for man's evil behavior. It may arise because of lack of faith in God, the sins of the parents, the influence of wicked companions, the influence of community or society, or faulty education and lack of Torah.

Tradition recognizes that many factors influence human decision. However, man possesses the power to choose between good and evil. Why do men do evil? Because they choose to, not because they have to.

How Should We React to Evil?

Many religions preach nonresistance to evil because:

1. The world is irremediably evil. Try to improve it and you become involved with and contaminated by the very evil you are attempting to resist.

2. The elimination of evil is God's work. When man makes efforts to fight evil, he is presumptuously 'playing the god.'

3. The nature of man is evil. He pits evil against evil when he fights against evil. The outcome can only be more evil.

4. Resistance is evil in itself.

Judaism rejects such reasoning. It constantly insists that we must:

"Know evil and avoid it," Remove the evil from our midst," "Resist evil and destroy it."

Judaism says to man, "Most of the evils that blight the world can be controlled; control yourself and you will control them: anger, arrogance, blasphemy, brutality, carelessness, cheating, disobedience, disorder, disrespect, drunkenness, envy, evil-tongue, extravagance, falsehood, forgetfulness, greed, hatred, haughtiness, idolatry, ignorance, injustice, irreligion, jealousy, laziness, lust, melancholy, miserliness, indecency, pride, presumptuousness, quarrelsomeness, rivalry, selfishness, slander, talebearing, temper, unfaithfulness, vanity, vulgarity, worry, xenophobia, yammer, misplaced zeal."

Do Jews Believe in Satan?

This is actually a restatement of the basic questions, "Why do men do evil? Where does evil come from?" There was an irresistible temptation to yield to a belief in a Satan or devil, a force independent of God and outside His control, to explain the abundance of evil in the world and in man. However, this belief never became part of serious Jewish theology nor did it enter into the sober and realistic moral and legal discussions of the Talmud. Jewish folklore and popular thought made reference to a Satan with greater or lesser frequency, depending on the period in Jewish history, but always as a figure of speech. Belief in any power rivaling God was inconsistent with Jewish monotheism. The great teachers and authorities of the Jewish religion were able to prevent folk beliefs from gaining ascendancy over the sober, rational views of the tradition.

In the early biblical period there was no reference at all to a devil. Although the idea of a Satan must be very ancient and was surely prevalent at the time, the Bible ignores it almost completely. The Hebrew word *Satan* appears in the Bible, but it means an obstacle or adversary and has implications neither divine nor demonic. In only three late biblical passages does Satan become personalized:

1. In Zechariah 3:1-2, Satan appears as man's enemy and accuser before God's Judgment Seat. God reproves Satan for his false testimony.

2. In Psalms 109:6, Satan again appears as a malicious, false accuser of the innocent, pious man.

3. In the book of Job, chapters 1 and 2, Satan appears as a celestial being in the service of God. He disagrees with God's estimation of Job and claims that man's loyalty is limited to his own self-interest. God consents to let Satan test Job's loyalty to God.

Thus, in the Bible Satan never appears as God's rival or as the Creator of Evil. He is neither the adversary of God nor the perpetual tempter and seducer of mankind. He is in the employment of God and subordinate to Him, and acts only with His permission. He plays the role of prosecuting attorney in the trial of man by God.

Later, the personality of Satan underwent marked change. In post-biblical folklore and in the legendary sections of the Talmud, he appears as chief of the angels who rebelled against God when he created man on the sixth day. He becomes supreme head of the evil spirits, a rival of God, a demon who influences man to do evil, so that God's dominion in the world should be overthrown and His purpose frustrated.

It has been correctly pointed out that all authentic beliefs of Judaism have found expression in our prayer books. In the entire liturgy of the Jewish people there occurs not a single serious reference to a literal Satan. None of the branches of Judaism today retains any trace of a belief in Satan.

CHAPTER IX

The Chosen People

Why Did Jews Believe Themselves To Be the Chosen People?

One of the dominating themes expressed in the Bible is that the Jews are God's chosen people. The first mention of the election of Israel occurs when God chose the first patriarch of Israel. In Genesis 12:1-3, God says to Abraham: "Get thee out of thy country . . . and go into the land that I will show thee, and I will make of thee a great nation and I will bless thee, and make thy name great and be thou a blessing. And I will bless them that bless thee, and him that curseth thee will I curse and in thee shall all the families of the earth be blessed."

According to another story in the Bible, God chose Israel to be His people when He led them out of Egypt and gave them the Torah at Mt. Sinai. In Exodus 19:4-6, we read: "Ye have seen what I did unto the Egyptians and how I bore you on eagles' wings and brought you unto Myself. Now therefore if ye will hearken unto My voice indeed and keep my covenant, then ye shall be Mine own treasure from among among all peoples; for all the earth is Mine. And ye shall be unto Me a kingdom of priests and a holy nation."

In biblical verses too numerous to quote, the *meaning* of the doctrine of Israel's election by God to be His people is spelled out.

What Did the Belief Mean?

To arrive at a clearer statement of the meaning of chosenness, let us set down some of the popular misconceptions which have grown up around the term. Chosenness *did not* mean any of the following:

It did not mean that God chose to love Israel exclusively or that He loved the rest of mankind less.

It did not mean that Israel was granted special privileges withheld from the rest of mankind.

It did not mean racial or any other kind of superiority. It implied no inequality or favoritism.

It did not mean exclusiveness, that only those born into the people of Israel were God's elect. From the time of the first patriarch, anyone sincerely desiring to do so might enter the Jewish fold and become an integral part of the chosen people. And Israel continues to pray that one day all people will choose God and be God's elect.

It did not mean that salvation was the exclusive possession of those who belonged to Israel.

It did not mean that Israel was to dominate the world or enjoy a privileged position of power among nations.

It did not mean that Israel chose God and, in that sense, God chose Israel. The Living God of the Bible chose Israel. Israel only chose to accept and to comply, to welcome and to rejoice in being chosen, and to return God's love with its own love. There is no concept of a chosen God in the Bible, only the idea of a chosen people.

Having eliminated what chosenness did not mean, we can now attempt to state what it *did* mean:

It meant being chosen to perform a special task or mission in the world: to serve as the vehicle of God's Revelation; to receive the Torah, God's law; to live by that law; to be the example of a holy people dedicated to God; to be a priest-people bringing the knowledge of the Lord to the peoples of the earth both by precept and example; to be His servant and messenger, a teacher and a light to the nations, so that they might be brought to the Godly life of universal righteousness and peace; to be an instrument of the Divine purpose and to lead men and nations to the convictions which would make possible the establishment of God's Kingdom on earth.

It meant acceptance of a regimen of service to God and to mankind and, more than that, the readiness to sacrifice. As guardians of the Torah and as God's stewards in the world, the Jewish people had to be willing to sacrifice and suffer in the fulfillment of its appointed role. Assumption of so noble a commitment and so solemn a trust entailed very exacting training. Every Jew had to fulfill the whole law, the 613 commandments of the Torah, and the innumerable moral and spiritual requirements based on them, in order to merit God's grace. To serve as an example, every Jew's conduct had to be above reproach; to be a teacher, he had first to be a dedicated student; to become a light unto the nations, he had to run the risk of being burned by the wrath of those who hate God. Israel's election was intended for the exaltation of God and for the uplift of mankind. Therefore, the Jew had to be prepared to live primarily for others, not for his own elevation.

It meant severer judgment and punishment for failure to live up to its holy responsibility. The Jewish people was taught by its religious teachers to attribute all national misfortunes to its own sins and backsliding. When calamity struck, they said, "Because of our sins" and "Thou hast dealt faithfully but we have acted wickedly." Instead of wasting themselves en blaming other people or God and sinking into self-pity and self-justification, they were forced to look back and evaluate their own behavior with severity, then to take vigorous and positive steps to improve themselves and the situation.

It meant accepting a host of restrictions. Geographical boundaries for the land of Israel were fixed by God in the Torah so efforts to increase the land would run counter to God's law. The exploitation of the land's natural resources was restricted by the law of the Torah. Special moral obligations and ritual prohibitions protected the sanctity of the land. Acceptance of the sovereignty of God placed moral and political restraints on the people and its rulers.

It meant understanding and accepting Israel's dispersion among the nations as God's attempt to spread His word. And it meant keeping apart from the other peoples among whom they lived in order to preserve their morality and way of life. "Ye shall not do as they do in the land of Egypt where you dwelt, and ye shall not do as they do in the land of Canaan to which I am bringing you. Ye shall not walk in their statutes." (Leviticus 18:3) Election for a moral and spiritual task required the Jews to lead a unique and exemplary life. By standing alone, Israel had to pay a terrible price in suffering and persecution. To remain faithful in a world that is frequently intolerant and hostile is a challenge possible only for the strong and the dedicated.

Why Have The Unsympathetic Attacked The Concept Of A Chosen People?

The idea of a chosen people as expressed in the Bible has been compared with the *Herrenvolk* concept of the Nazis, a chauvinistic assertion of racial superiority and snobbishness. Some have called it an obnoxious expression of Jewish national pride, and an arrogant claim to a monopoly on salvation. It has also been cited by anti-Semites as evidence of a Jewish conspiracy to dominate the world. Some biased theologians infer from it that Jews believe in a "tribal God" who plays favorites, and contrast it unfavorably with the "Universal God of Christianity."

Do Jews Today Consider Themselves the Chosen People?

Secularism and scientism on the one hand, and anti-Semitism on the other, have combined to undermine belief in the doctrine of the divine election of Israel. Honest soul-searching on the part of morally sensitive and intellectually honest Jews has made further inroads.

To some secularists, belief in God, let alone a choosing

God, is sheer nonsense. Satisfied with an explanation of Jewish history in exclusively scientific and sociological terms, they have come to look upon Jewish belief in a chosen people as naive myth or even dangerous self-delusion.

Some morally sensitive, perhaps oversensitive, Jews have found certain expressions of the belief unacceptable. They regard the assumption by any group that it is "the chosen and indispensable vehicle of God's grace to others" as unaesthetic, offensive, and smacking of national conceit. They feel that prayers in which Jews give thanks to God "for not having made us like the gentiles" are unworthy of inclusion in our liturgy because they are insulting to non-Jews.

Some Jews have simply had their fill of the fruitless, acrimonious dialogue with Christianity concerning this belief. Since the time of Paul, the Christian claim has been that the Jews *were* God's chosen people but became God's rejected for refusing to accept the "Son of God"; that Christians became the elect, the true Israel. Jews who are weary of the "sterile and often malicious" debate have declared a plague on both houses: "We are not chosen and we are not rejected."

Those who take the naturalistic view of Jewish history and religion further weakened the belief in chosenness because they could not harmonize it with a modern conception of God. They cannot believe, as our forefathers obviously did, that God revealed Himself and His law exclusively to the children of Israel, that God made a "personal" promise to our forefathers thereby committing Himself to us, their descendants. Unable to accept the idea of a supernatural and anthropomorphic God who chooses in such fashion, they reject also the belief that the Jews are God's chosen people.

What Are the Viewpoints of the Three Branches of Judaism?

Orthodox, Reform and Conservative Judaism continue

to subscribe to the belief in Israel's election. But there are differences in emphasis and even in interpretation.

ORTHODOX JUDAISM

Orthodox Judaism retains all traditional prayers referring to the chosen people concept in both its particular and its universal aspects. In teaching and in practice, however, emphasis is confined to the particular: the importance of Israel's faithfulness to the covenant, of the observance of the law, of the preservation of its uniqueness. Israel's election to be a priest-and-Torah people in the present, rather than its eventual missionary function to the nations of the world, is their chief concern. Orthodoxy has been vigorously and almost exclusively halachic-minded (legalistic), and there has been little emphasis on the universal ethical aspects of the chosen people idea. At different times strong *musar* (ethical) movements arise in Orthodox Judaism but their concern is with the moral quality of the Jewish people itself and not with the Jewish people's mission to carry the word of God to non-Jews or with promoting universal social justice.

Orthodox Jewry prays for the nations of the world and for the establishment of God's Kingdom on earth but does very little to promote that Kingdom among the gentiles. It has been decidedly *not* mission-minded in practice.

REFORM JUDAISM

Reform Judaism has stressed the prophetic message of Israel's world mission. From their prayer books were eliminated those expressions of belief which appear to exalt Israel above other peoples and which might, therefore, give offense. They have retained expression of the belief that Israel has been invested with a special mission "to bear witness to the power and truth of God and to endeavor to unite all peoples in a covenant of brotherhood and peace." At one point, they modified the traditional phraseology in order to emphasize further the idea of election for a mission. "Thou hast chosen us" became "Thou hast called us."

Most theoreticians of Reform Judaism recognize the importance of preserving the distinctive identity of the Jewish people. However, the particularistic aspects of the chosen people concept were almost lost in the preoccupation with the ethical universalism of Jewish belief. Now it is coming to recognize more and more that both aspects are essential to the survival of the Jewish people and to its effectiveness as a spiritual force in the world.

CONSERVATIVE JUDAISM

Conservative Judaism considers *both* aspects of the chosen people concept important. In this respect it hews to the tradition which declared the Jewish people to be a priest-people and a people with a prophetic mission. It identifies itself with the Reform enthusiasm for a universal mission but decries the fact that this zeal for the universal was resulting in the elimination of the essentially unique character of the Jewish religion and of the Jewish people. To Conservative Judaism, the universal mission calls for preservation and even intensification of the specifically *Jewish* character of the Jewish people and its religion.

What Do the Reconstructionists Say About This Concept?

An association of like-minded men in the Conservative and Reform movements, the Reconstructionists, have completely eliminated the "election of Israel" idea from their Prayer Book. They assert that "every people that has contributed to enlightenment and progress is, in a sense, chosen by God. The doctrine of election is inconsistent with our premise that a religion is a natural process. The need for salvation being inherent in all peoples and the quest for salvation being a natural process evident among all human societies, we must assume that the way of salvation is available to all men and peoples everywhere and *on the same terms*."

The Reconstructionists extract and stress what they regard as the sensible elements of the belief: the need for the preservation of distinctive Jewish peoplehood; and for the Jewish people, like any other people, to think of itself, and to act as, an instrument of service to humanity.

Do Jews Believe that Israel Is the Holy Land?

The Bible tells us that God chose the children of Israel to be a holy people, gave them Holy Writ, and commanded them to live a holy life in accordance with His sacred law. The land where this life of holiness was to be lived was selected, promised, and given to the children of Israel by the Holy One, praised be He: "And ye shall inherit it and dwell in it and take heed to do all my statutes." It was to serve as a shining example to the nations of the world.

In the past, the Jews considered the land of Israel to be their homeland and the Holy Land. Yet, the grip of the land of Israel on the Jewish people cannot be explained in terms of anthropology, sociology or patriotism. Since the destruction of the Holy Land in the year 70 C.E., Jews all over the world have offered up daily prayers for the coming of the Messiah, the rebuilding of the land, and the restoration of God's Holy Temple. These prayers were not motivated by patriotism and did not involve political loyalty. They cannot even be considered the natural longing for an ancestral land. They were and are a nostalgic acknowledgment of the position of Israel in their spiritual life. To Jews, Israel was the *Promised Land*: "Unto you and your seed do I give this land as an eternal inheritance." It was the *Land of the Bible*: "For out of Zion shall go forth the Torah and the Word of God from Jerusalem." It was the *Land of Messianic Vision*, of ultimate and universal redemption: "When the Temple shall be rebuilt and all people come up to Jerusalem to worship the One God of all mankind."

The Jewish people never forgot its spiritual attachment to Zion: the Hebrew Bible was born there; the prophets appeared there; the psalmists sang their songs there; the great sages of our faith taught the Word of God there; and the hills of Jerusalem were once crowned by the mighty fortress of Israel's spiritual life.

It is normal for emigrants to preserve a sentimental attachment for the land of their origin. The first and second generations, born on the soil of the adopted land, may still retain traces of the culture, sing some of the songs, and share some of the aspirations of the old country. Beyond that, only a faint echo of the old family background survives. Sometimes the desire to assimilate is so strong that a deliberate effort is made to disown and to forget the ancestral land of their antecedents. The Jewish people never forgot. Its attachment was spiritual.

CHAPTER X

Jews and Non-Jews

Do Jews Believe that Judaism Is the Only True Religion?

When adherents of any religion are asked, "How do other religions compare with yours?" they might in all honesty answer:

"There is one truth. There can only be one true religion. My religion is the true one; yours must be wrong."

But there are other ways—equally honest—of answering the question without being disloyal to one's own religion or offensive to other religions. Jews have at least three possible answers.

The Jew who believes literally in supernatural Revelation of the Torah might say that Judaism is the only true religion but he might add that other religions are also true to the extent that they approximate Judaism. No Jew would say that all religions, except Judaism alone, are false.

Many Jews, on the other hand, take the position that no religion has the whole truth so it is misleading to speak of the "one true religion." They think of religious truth as discovery rather than revelation, and all religions have discovered some truth. They add that the Jewish people has had a special genius for religious discovery and that, therefore, Judaism is the best religion.

Another group of Jews maintains that it is childishly absurd to talk of best and better religions since religious truth cannot be measured or weighed or compared. All religions are different. Differences need no defense; there is no need to "prove" superiority. The civilization or culture of a living group has a religious component. If our society, which contains various religious groups, is to function demo-

149

cratically, religious groups must live under the pluralistic principle of unity in diversity. The Jew who reasons along such lines produces an answer like this: "The Jewish religion is my way of expressing the truth about God and the world. Your religion is your way. Comparisons are odious and debate over relative merits is endless and sterile. Judaism is the best religion for me; yours is just as good for you. I will live by my religion; you live by yours. I can love only mine but I can and do respect yours; do you likewise."

What Do Jews Believe About Christianity?

No study of the beliefs of Judaism is complete without some discussion of the Jewish attitude toward other religions, particularly Christianity. Within the Jewish tradition may be found ideas such as the following:

1. Christians believe, in common with us, that the Bible is of Divine origin and was given through Moses, our teacher. (Their interpretations, however, frequently differ.) A daughter-religion of Judaism, Christianity shares with us the great spiritual enterprise of making known the glory of God for the salvation of mankind. When all Christians live up to the teachings of Christianity, the coming of the Messianic Era will be advanced.

2. Christianity is spreading the worship of God and the knowledge of Scripture to those places and peoples that have not come in contact with these blessings. Through Christianity, the Torah, the law of God, is reaching people everywhere.

3. For non-Jews, Christianity is a monotheistic and true religion. Its non-monotheistic elements make it unacceptable, and therefore wrong, for a Jew. The trinity is *not* an expression of idolatry but the personification of the Divine attributes of Being, Power, and Knowledge. However, the expression of the unique Oneness of God as a trinity clouds the clarity of the concept of Oneness.

4. Christianity has many admirable traits and righteous principles. These are all to be found in Judaism. All the great values, the essentials of a desirable civilization—love, pity, patience, insight, restraint, etc.—are Jewish values. When the adherents of Christianity act according to their faith, happy are they and happy are we. As Nathan the Wise said to his Christian friend, "That which makes me a Christian in your eyes, makes you a Jew in mine."

5. The morals of Christianity are the morals of Judaism. The great commandments of Christianity—"Thou shalt love the Lord thy God with all thy heart, soul and might," and, "Thou shalt love thy neighbor as thyself"—are taken verbatim from the text and spirit of Judaism. The Christian doctrines of Creation, Revelation and Redemption originated in and are the great themes of the Jewish religion.

6. Christianity is not the fulfillment of Judaism. Rather, it is the acceptance of much of Judaism, the adaptation of part of it, and the adoption of other elements alien to it. It is a unique development of an offshoot of Judaism.

Why Did Christianity Change From a Jewish Sect to a Separate Religion?

At the beginning of the first century, there was no difference between Judaism and Christianity. The Christians were one of several sects among the Jews and their teachings either paralleled, paraphrased, or quoted verbatim beliefs or opinions current among the Jews of that time: Jesus' Sermon on the Mount was a Jewish sermon containing nothing contrary or new to the Jewish tradition; the golden rule, "peace on earth, good will toward men," "Thou shalt love the Lord thy God" and your fellowman, were basic Jewish teachings then as now.

Christianity, like other Jewish sects, could have remained a Jewish sect. It was Paul, originally a pious traditional Jew, who brought about the separation of Christianity from Judaism. In his overwhelming ambition to win

over the vast non-Jewish population of the world, he
created an independent Christian Church. Almost everything Paul taught had some basis in the Jewish tradition—
he even built the Christian theology out of Jewish teachings—but he welded them into a system of belief that became as un-Jewish in theory as it was in consequence.

In the course of time, in the process of absorbing multitudes of pagans, Christianity absorbed and assimilated
some of the ideas and practices of their cultures. Doctrines
such as the Virgin Birth, the mystery of a dying God, the
Trinity, transubstantiation and the adoration of saints and
images, widened the gap between Judaism and Christianity
until a total separation resulted.

Diversity of opinion always existed and has always been
tolerated in Judaism. Before the advent of Jesus and the
beginning of Christianity, there were Jews who believed
(as some still do today) in original sin, Satan, Heaven and
Hell, a supernatural and angelic Messiah, and other teachings which are today predominant in Christianity and un-
popular in Judaism. Like the disciples of Jesus who believed
they could drive out demons with the name of
their Master, other Jews who remained Jews did demon-
driving of their own. Some Jews living before Jesus believed, as did Jesus, that salvation was only for the Jews;
like Paul, other Jews of his period and earlier, believed that
man had to be "saved" from original sin and that conversion
of gentiles was necessary for their salvation. Similarly, belief in the sinful nature of man, the powerlessness and presumptuousness of the human will, the futility and meaninglessness of this life was not Christian innovation—Jews held
and expressed such beliefs before Jesus and Christianity.

A Jew today who professes to believe in any of the above
reads himself out of the mainstream of Jewish belief but not
out of Judaism. There is no one, single answer to any human
problem in life, according to Judaism. This was particularly
true during the period when Jesus came on the scene, and is
true today. The world of Jewish belief is wide enough to em-

brace many differences. Christianity took for its central teachings the mystical, apocalyptic, other-worldly, anti-rational, and highly speculative elements of Judaism which did not become part of its mainstream. In stating the general differences and points of agreement below, we have considered only entrenched opinions of Judaism and predominant views of Christianity.

What Elements are Common to Both Judaism and Christianity?

1. *Monotheism*
Despite the triune interpretation of monotheism in Christian theology, Christianity, like Judaism, holds to the principle that God is One and Universal. From the doctrine of the Fatherhood of God follows the belief in the brotherhood of man and the universality of ethical principles.

2. *Torah*
Both accept Jewish Scripture as sacred literature even though Christianity insists that it has fulfilled and superseded Judaism.

3. *Ethical and Moral Principles*
The moral goals and moral codes of both are essentially in agreement.

4. *Universal Mission*
Both consider it their God-given mission to spread belief in God throughout the world. They differ in method. Judaism does not hold that it is necessary to become a Jew in order to become a believer. Christianity's mission is conversion.

5. *Messianic Age*
Both religions believe in a Messiah.

6. *Immortality*
Both believe that every human being has a soul and that that soul is deathless.

7. *Prayer*

Both believe that God is concerned for each individual and that he can be reached through prayer.

What Are Some Important Differences Between Judaism And Christianity?

1. *Doctrine of Divinity*

According to Christianity, divinity is a trinity; to Judaism, a unity.

2. *Divinity of Jesus*

This is unique to Christianity alone. Both Judaism and Christianity believe that God is spirit. In Christianity, Jesus is really the God of Spirit who took on flesh so He could *reveal* Himself to man and offer Himself as a sacrifice for man's *redemption*. Both Judaism and Christianity believe in revelation and redemption but the concepts differ: in the Jewish view, God reveals His Will but not Himself, and certainly not in the flesh; in the Jewish view, redemption requires sacrifice on the part of man but not the sacrifice of God's self.

3. *Original Sin*

Christianity says man is fallen; Judaism says man has simply not risen high enough, certainly not to the full potential of his capability. Christianity says that since man is fallen and cannot save himself, he needs miraculous redemption that comes only from God through acceptance of the Risen Christ; Judaism holds that man assuredly needs God's help in all his endeavors but his redemption comes through greater and wiser acceptance of moral responsbility, not through vicarious atonement.

4. *Dogma*

There was very little dogma in traditional Judaism and there is even less today. Belief in God is it. And even belief in God is not absolutely necessary to achieve salvation. A righteous heathen is as worthy of salvation as a righteous

High Priest of Israel. Salvation depends on our conduct rather than on a fixed formula of belief. Christianity, on the other hand, believes that *believing correctly* is essential to salvation. Judaism stresses deed; Christianity creed. Judaism is largely humanistic, Christianity predominantly theological; Judaism stresses the role of man and the way of life; Christianity stresses the role of God and the way of faith.

5. *Sacraments*

Judaism has none. In the Roman Catholic and in the Eastern Orthodox churches, there are seven sacraments; baptism, confirmation, eucharist, penance, extreme unction, holy orders, and matrimony. Protestants generally acknowledge two sacraments: baptism and the Lord's Supper or Holy Communion. Sacraments are holy rites of mysterious meaning which are necessary to man's salvation. Some writers of Judaism have suggested that, in the Jewish view, the only sacrament is the saving power of the moral laws. In the Talmud God is pictured as saying: "I call heaven and earth to witness that whether it be Gentile or Israelite, man or woman, slave or handmaid, according to the *deeds* which he does, so will the Holy Spirit rest on him."

6. *Clergy*

In Judaism, the Rabbi is simply a teacher and preacher. In some segments of Christianity, the clergy has power to administer sacraments and give absolution for sins, etc. In segments of Christianity where this is not true, the clergy still has preeminence as agents of God: when they speak from the pulpit, they bring God's message to the people. The rabbi speaks about God, but not as His representative.

7. *The New Testament*

Christianity still considers the Old Testament sacred but has an additional revelation contained in the New Testament. Judaism clings to its idea of one, and only one, Revelation.

8. *Ultimate Purpose*

According to Christianity, man's ultimate purpose is to enter the Kingdom of God in Heaven; in Jewish teaching, the ultimate goal of all human striving is establishment of the Kingdom of God on earth. Therefore, Christianity is tinged with the rejection of the pleasures and values of this world, and Judaism emphasizes the importance of progress in the here-and-now.

9. *Social Values*

Judaism emerged as the spiritual product of the historic experience of a *community;* Christianity, on the other hand, was founded by *individuals* and its primary concern was with the salvation of the individual. The historical development of the two faiths accounts for the emphasis in Judaism on saving society, or social progress, and in Christianity on the salvation of the individual.

In our day, both religions are approaching better understanding of each other's principles and problems, increased appreciation of each other's merits, and greater recognition of their common goals.

10. *Salvation—"Beliefs that Save"*

Some Jews believed that salvation was only for the Jews. Some Jews today still believe that the Jew who keeps the whole Torah attains a much higher degree of salvation than the non-Jew whose good conduct alone entitles him to salvation. This idea is voiced in extreme-Orthodox circles. Moderate Orthodox, Conservative and Reform Jews, on the whole, believe that in the eyes of God a man's worth is determined by his character and conduct. The widely accepted view is expressed in the tradition thus: "The righteous of all peoples have their share in the world to come."

In other words, Judaism recognizes that the non-Jew can possess moral and spiritual merit sufficient for salvation even though he does not even know or accept the beliefs of Judaism. Jews, generally, have believed that their spiritual conceptions are superior but they have never asserted that their ideas and beliefs are indispensable for salvation. This is in sharp contrast to the austere Christian view that only those who believe in Christ are saved; all others, no matter how truth-loving and virtuous, are damned. In the words of St. Paul, the original expounder of this belief, "He that disbelieveth shall be condemned."

What Does the Tradition Say About Jesus?

The Jewish tradition is mute in reference to Jesus. Modern scholars have tried to explain this silence in various ways: Jesus was not an outstanding personality in Jewish history; there never was a Jesus—he was the composite invention of a group that fabricated an ideal man out of its wishful thinking; the early Christian Church did not permit the Jews to "blaspheme" Jesus by treating him other than as the official Christian hero; Jews acquired a fear and distaste for the very name Jesus as a result of their vilification and merciless destruction at the hands of Christians who called them "Christ Killers."

The fundamental Christian theory is that silence of the Jewish sources is no enigma. It is a deliberate effort to obliterate Jewish guilt for the crucifixion and it is proof of the continuing sin of the Jews in refusing to accept Jesus as the Christ. Individual non-Jews have been kinder to the Jews on this point. In a speech in the House of Commons, the English statesman Peel said, "If the Jews did commit an inexplicable crime nearly 2000 years ago, we have had no authority given to us—even if we could determine who were the descendants of the persons guilty of that crime—to visit the sins of the fathers upon the children . . . unto the 300th or 400th generation. That awful power is not ours." Voltaire puts the following argument into the mouth of Rabbi Akiba: "You Christians confess that Jesus publicly called our Pharisee rabbis and priests 'races of vipers, whited sepulchres.' If any one of us should run incessantly through the streets of Rome calling the

Pope and Cardinals vipers and sepulchres, would he not be punished?"

In the chapter on the Messiah, we will point out why Judaism and Jews can have no belief *in* Jesus, but Jews today do have and do express various beliefs *about* Jesus.

What Do Jews Believe About Jesus?

1. Generally speaking, Jews believe that Jesus was a Jew born of Jewish parents. In addition, he was scrupulously pious, living and dying as a Jew. Like many other sensitive Jews, he was critical of the formality of the Temple worship and of the immorality of his age. None of his teachings was contrary to the great simplicities of essential Judaism and none was new to the Jewish tradition. He influenced a small yet dynamic group of dedicated followers but had no impact on the broad masses of Jewry. Had he been a well-known scholar and teacher, his name would have appeared among the great masters of the Talmud. Pallière, the French student for the priesthood who converted to Judaism, states it thus in *The Unknown Sanctuary*: "It is a historic fact that he (Jesus) instituted no rite, no sacrament, no church. Born a Jew, he wished to live and to die a Jew and, from the swaddling clothes of circumcision to the embalmed shroud of sepulchre, followed only the rites of his religion. Jesus was not converted to Christianity until long after his death." Jews adhering to this view believe in the religion of Jesus only in the sense that Jesus believed in the Jewish religion.

2. Some Jews believe that Jesus was a great teacher and would have been given recognition in the tradition if some of his followers had not misinterpreted His teachings and made a Messiah out of Him. Klausner in *Jesus of Nazareth* expresses the view of this group, "Jesus is, for the Jewish nation, a great teacher of morality and an artist in parable . . . If ever the day should come and his ethical code be stripped of its wrappings of miracles and mysticism, the Book of the Ethics of Jesus will be one of the choicest treasures in the literature of Israel for all time."

3. As pointed out elsewhere, the Jewish tradition never overglorified any of its great personalities—they were represented as men possessing human weaknesses in addition to their nobler endowments. Some commentators have suggested that the grave of Moses was unmarked lest the man should become an object of worship. Just as Judaism opposes the tendency to make God too human, it combats the universal desire to turn a human into a god. Intensive hero worship is regarded as a moral and spiritual danger. And yet there are a few who are carried away by a great enthusiasm for Jesus.

A modern rabbi, dedicated to Judaism, expresses this view thus: "Jesus was not a being come down from heaven but one who attained to heavenly heights. He was not a god who walked on earth like man but a man who walked with God on earth. He was not a god who lived humanly but a man who lived divinely . . . to US he belongs—not his Church, but he—the man, the Jew, the PROPHET." A few individual Jews, like Sholom Asch, have gone to even greater extremes in their interpretation of Jesus and in their insistence that he be reclaimed as our own. Norman Cousins, in a recent article in *American Judaism,* advocated that Jews and Christians set aside their reluctance to see Jesus as a Jew. He stated that "no other figure has had a greater impact on human history and that to belong to a people that produced Jesus is to share in a distinction of vast dimension and meaning . . . The modern synagogue can live openly and fully with Jesus. And the rediscovery of Jesus can help Jews to forgive their tormentors—including those who have done evil to them in Jesus' name. . . . It will also help the Christians to come to terms with the fact of Jesus as Jew." Mr. Cousins concluded: "For twenty centuries two branches of the same religion have lived without harmony and understanding. Both have a common origin and can come together in a new attitude toward the figure of Jesus, the Jew. The common reluctance can give way to common knowledge and respect based on the reality of the connecting figure of Jesus. Such an amity speaks to the spiritual condition of both Christian and Jew. And out of this amity can come the nourishment of reconciliation."

This view is *not* popular among Jews. Although they do seek amity and understanding, the price cannot be the "upgrading of Jesus by the Jews and his downgrading by the Christians." Ideologies should never be compromised for the sake of expediency.

Further, Jews have always recognized Jesus as a Jew. They have rejected non-Jewish ideas about Jesus but not Jesus the God-fearing and Torah-loving Jew. Jews resent the New Testament representation of Pontius Pilate, the ruthless Roman governor of Palestine who crucified thousands of Jews, as helplessly washing his hands and saying of the blood of Jesus, "This blood has not been shed by my hands." Jews regard with abhorrence the transfer of guilt from the Romans to the Jews, who are pictured as saying boastfully and cruelly, "His blood be upon us and upon our children." (Matthew 27:25) In order to make Christianity acceptable to the Romans, the Romans were whitewashed and millions of Jews, in consequence, were submitted to bloodbaths throughout the ages whenever the cry of "Christ Killer" was let loose. The attitude of Christians toward Jews requires change but that is a spiritual problem for Christians, not Jews. Jews have another task: they must learn to overcome their anxiety and resentment whenever anti-Semites invoke the name of Jesus to justify their words and deeds.

The proposal to glorify Jesus as a prophet or as the greatest spiritual figure of history cannot be taken seriously. Jewish tradition was not enhanced by the teachings of Jesus; Christianity, which speaks of itself as the fulfilment of Judaism, has nothing to offer the Jews except their dissolution.

Should Jews Become Missionaries?

This question is under discussion today. The debate is

not new: even in the pre-Christian era some were in favor of it, some opposed. Some talmudic sages felt we should seek proselytes to join the ranks of the Jewish people. There is undoubtedly some truth in the New Testament sarcasm, "Ye (Pharisees) compass sea and land to make one proselyte." (Matthew 32:15) On the other hand, other talmudists agreed with Helbo, who said, "Proselytes are hard on Israel, like a sore on the skin," and were opposed to accepting them. In Tractate Yevomot 47b, the talmudic view toward the potential, or would-be, proselyte was expressed thus, "He is neither persuaded nor dissuaded. With one hand we discourage him and with the other we draw him closer."

The sages always had a healthy reluctance to engage in aggressive missionary activity on a large scale. But if a would-be proselyte persisted in his intention to accept the faith and was able to prove his sincerity, the traditional view was: "If one wishes to adopt Judaism in the name of God and for the sake of Heaven welcome and befriend him, do not repel him." (Mechilta to Exodus 18:6) An even more positive statement has been attributed to both Rabbi Simeon ben Yohai and Rabbi Simeon ben Lakish: "A proselyte is dearer to God than Jewish saints, or than was Israel at Sinai, for he accepts Heaven's yoke without having witnessed the thunders and trumpet blasts which attended the Revelation."

The arguments for an active, organized effort to win converts to Judaism may be summarized as follows:

The insights of Judaism must be brought into the mainstream of modern thought. Judaism can contribute much to the moral and spiritual welfare of large segments of the world's population. There is a crying need for the concepts and beliefs of the Jewish religion.

The missionary effort of Christianity has not been successful. Moreover, many nominal Christians even here in the United States no longer subscribe to the tenets of their religion: they are seeking a religion like Judaism, with its strong rational appeal and emphasis on morality, to meet the requirements of a spiritual life in a scientific age.

Proponents of the mission to non-Jews claim that Judaism was always a proselytizing religion until Jewish missionary activity was forbidden. Jews accepting converts, as well as the converts themselves, were severely punished by the powerful medieval church. In our day, Jews are not persecuted or handicapped by their religion. Ergo, we should renew our missionary activity.

Arguments opposing an organized missionary effort run along the following lines:

All of us, Jew and Christian alike, have drifted too far from our spiritual moorings. The greatest need today is not to search for some anchorage in an alien berth but for each of us to seek diligently the way back to his own. The competition today is not between one religion and another but between meaningful religion and hollow religion. Instead of dissipating our strength and resources on combatting each other, we should face our common dangers—the forces of skepticism and materialism that undermine man's faith, dignity and fundamental decency—and prepare to do something about them.

There is need for Jewish dialogue with Christianity. There is undoubtedly mutual feeling that each has something vital to offer the other. In our conversation, we may each discover what we both need by opening our minds to what the other has to say instead of concentrating on what we want to say. Missionary effort, Jewish or Christian, is not dialogue. The conversion motive places such concentrated effort on forcing something on someone else that it blinds and deafens us to values and possibilities that might be drawn from that someone else. We may find a market for members and build up our numbers, but little, if any, good can come of attempts to convert Christians. On the contrary, such activity would arouse much antagonism, thereby hurting chances for joint efforts to improve society. What we really want is a society of better people; it is the problem of good people rather than big numbers that should engage us.

Judaism was never a proselytizing religion. It was never part of our belief that the non-Jew had to become a Jew in order "to be saved." What we have to offer to the non-Jew, out of the vast treasury of Jewish mind and spirit, is an enrichment that can be freely received without detaching him from his own religious faith.

Our real challenge is to make Judaism meaningful to Jews, to convert Jews to Judaism. If we can get Jews to understand and accept their religious, intellectual, cultural and spiritual heritage, and to live an exemplary life, we will be accomplishing by example what precept alone can never do. This has always been the Jewish way of teaching and helping others.

Not fear or clannishness but our religious teachings have restrained us from proselytizing. We have been taught to respect our fellowman and uphold his dignity. Missionary activity, despite the high-minded spiritual quality of its rationalized motivation, is basically disrespectful and offensive to the religious expression of others. In effect, the missionary says, "My religion is better than yours; mine is true, yours is false; you are lost and I can save you." The absence of aggressive proselytizing is unique to Judaism and we should preserve that uniqueness.

Did the Jews Ever Seek, Actively, to Spread their Ideas to Non-Jews?

Yes! Possession of a great faith, or important truth of universal significance, imposes a moral obligation upon those who possess it to share it with all. The Jews felt very keenly their duty to share their spiritual blessings with all mankind. According to the Midrash, Abraham wandered from land to land to spread belief in God; for this very purpose was Israel exiled and dispersed. Some of the prophets addressed their messages to non-Jews; some of the sages of the Roman period crossed seas and continents to preach and teach the Word of God to gentiles. Jewish teachers prepared the pagan world and paved the way for Christianity. Mohammed, too, learned from the Jews and was inspired by their teachings to found Mohammedanism. One of the few beliefs of our religion over which there has been no disagreement is that one day all the nations and peoples of the world will unite in the worship of the One God. Jewish teachers wrote, taught and entered into discussions with non-Jews in order to present the God-faith to the people of the world. However, they regarded example as more powerful and more persuasive than precept; they insisted that Jews everywhere must maintain a high standard of moral and spiritual living so that non-Jews might be influenced to emulate them.

Every act of a Jew which brought a non-Jew closer to God was considered a *Kiddush Hashem,* sanctification of God's name; any infraction of the moral law which alienated a non-Jew from God was denounced as a *Chillul Hashem,* profanation of God's name. This doctrine of *Kiddush Hashem* became a supreme ideal and obligation of the Jewish people. As servants of God, they were His witnesses; their conduct had to reflect credit on their Master. "The Lord of Hosts is exalted through justice and the Holy One is sanctified through righteousness . . . Through them that are near unto Me will I be sanctified and before all people will I be glorified." The Commandment, "Thou shalt love the Lord," was interpreted to mean that we must behave in such a way as to make Him beloved of our fellowmen. *Kiddush Hashem,* or setting the right example, became the chief method of attracting non-Jews to God.

Did Jews Ever Organize Missionary Groups for the Purpose of Proselytizing?

No! The organization of missionary efforts designed to promote large-scale organic affiliation of non-Jews with the Jewish people was never undertaken, nor even encouraged. At no time did there exist in Judaism anything at all comparable to the Christian doctrine of salvation through the body of the church; nowhere in Judaism is to be found the suggestion that special salvation or miraculous spiritual advantages accrues to anyone affiliated with the body of the Jewish people. It is not part of Jewish thinking that non-Jews have to convert to Judaism "for their own sake" in order "to be saved." This is purely Christian doctrine.

It is true that, at some periods, an element among the Jews became ambitious to enlarge the household of Israel; they resorted to energetic efforts to convert non-Jews to Judaism. For example, John Hyrcanus, a Jewish King, and several of his successors in the royal line forcibly converted the Idumeans and other people they conquered. However, they were inspired more by political expediency than by religious zeal. In any event, such aggressive proselytizing was severely condemned by the Rabbis as being totally out of harmony with the spirit of Judaism.

Do Jews Accept Converts?

Yes! Jews have always accepted converts and always will. Throughout the ages, many non-Jews have been attracted by the reasonableness of the Jewish religion, by the strong emphasis on moral conduct, and by the piety and purity of Jewish family life. Before the rise of Christianity, many non-Jews accepted Jewish monotheism and ethical standards without converting; others sought admission and were made welcome. It was an occasion for great rejoicing when a sincere convert was admitted to the fold. Regardless of race, color or former creed, anyone who can sincerely say as did Ruth of the Bible, "Let your people be my people and your God my God," is gladly accepted into the Jewish faith.

Today, despite the fact that Judaism does not seek proselytes, conversions to Judaism are not uncommon. Judaism makes no distinction between Jews born into Judaism and those who choose to adopt it.

What Is the Jewish Attitude Toward Christians?

The Jewish attitude toward non-Jews is set forth in the Biblical injunctions, "Thou shalt love thy neighbor as thyself," and "Love ye therefore the stranger." A Christian is more than a neighbor and a stranger to the Jew—he is a brother who worships the same God as the Jew's. Love is the only word we have to express the attitude of the Jew toward the Christian.

A vast religious literature, setting forth the Jewish attitude towards Christians, has accumulated through the ages and further additions are being made today. A multitude of detail, governing every aspect of the Jewish-Christian relationship, adds up to a basic principle: "Jews must treat all human beings, Jew and non-Jew, alike." Some antipathy toward Christians does exist among Jews, but no doctrine or tenet of Judaism itself encourages anything but respect and love for all.

Does Judaism Teach That We Should Love Our Enemy?

Judaism demands of the Jew that he love his neighbor and the stranger within his gates. Love is a moral necessity. However, nowhere does the tradition say explicitly that we must love the enemy. Rather, it makes other, perhaps more difficult, but certainly more practical, moral demands:

Judaism urges us not to hate the enemy.

The Bible says, "Thou shalt not hate thy brother in thy heart." A Jewish philosopher said, "If hate you must, then hate falsehood, violence, and selfishness." The Talmud says: "May not hatred of us rise in any heart and no hatred of *any* man in our heart"; "To hate a man, even an enemy, is to hate his Creator"; "A hater is like a murderer"; "Hatred upsets the social order."

Judaism urges us not to seek vengeance of the enemy.

The Bible says, "Rejoice not when your enemy falls" (Prov. 24:17) ; "Thou shalt not take vengeance nor bear a grudge" (Lev. 19:18) ; "And say not, 'I will do to him as he has done to me'." (Prov. 24:29). The Talmud says, "Let not your heart be glad when your enemy stumbles lest the Lord see it and it displease Him" (Aboth 4:24) ; "Say not, 'Since I have been humiliated, let my neighbor be humiliated.' Know it is the image of God you would thus humiliate." (Ben Azazi) ; "Who takes vengeance or bears a grudge acts like one who, having cut one hand while handling a knife, avenges himself by stabbing the other hand." (Yerushalmi Nedarim 9:4)

Judaism urges us to help our enemy.

The Bible says: "If your enemy is hungry, give him bread to eat" (Proverbs 25:21) ; and "Help your enemy when he is in need." (Exodus 23:4-5) The Midrash says: "If you refuse help to a neighbor because he has been unkind to you, you are guilty of revenge." The Talmud says: "Aid an enemy even before you aid a friend, to subdue hatred." (Tosefta Baba Metzia 2:26)

Judaism urges us to pray for the enemy.

The Baal Shem Tov said, "Pray for an enemy as for yourself." The *Orhat Tsadikkim* 15C says: "Pray for your enemy that he serve God."

Judaism urges us to befriend the enemy.

This is our moral duty and challenge: to make a friend of an enemy. Only thus can we fulfill the commandment to love one's neighbor. "Who is a hero?" ask the sages. "He who converts an enemy into a friend." Judaism asks us to forgive but not to forget; to befriend but not to turn the other cheek; to demand restitution but not vengeance; and to require vindication but not retaliation. Friendship must be based on justice. We are ready for love—the highest rung in the ladder of interhuman relationship—only after we have achieved friendship based on mutual and reasonable respect. In Judaism, to love the enemy is a goal; in Christianity, to love him is a commandment. An important difference.

CHAPTER XI

The Messiah and the Messianic Age

What Does the Word Messiah Mean?

When we hear the word Messiah, we immediately associate it with the idea of the expected redeemer who will usher in the Messianic Age. However, the term Messiah does not have this connotation at all in the Bible.

Messiah is from the Hebrew word *Mashiach*, anointed. The Aramaic term is *Meshicha*; the Greek, *Messias* or *Christos*. Originally, the term was a reference to the High Priest, *ha-Kohen ha-Mashiach*, who had oil poured upon his head when he was consecrated to his spiritual office as teacher and leader of the community (Lev. 4:3, 5:16, and 6:16). The Messiah was one whom God had invested with special spiritual responsibility.

The King of Israel was called *Mashiach Adonoy*, anointed of the Lord (I Samuel 24:7). The ritual of anointment symbolized the high office of kingship and dramatized the idea that authority vested in the king came from God and must be exercised in accordance with God's Will. The Messiah thus came to mean one to whom God delegated regal responsibility. Cyrus, King of Persia, and not a Jew, was called Messiah also: "Thus saith the Lord to His anointed, to Cyrus." (Isaiah 45:1)

In some books of the Bible—Isaiah, Daniel, Amos, Ezekiel and Obediah—the term refers to a collective Messiah, the anointed people of Israel. These prophets envisioned all Israel as the priest-people and the suffering servant of the Lord designated by God for a special role in carrying out His spiritual purpose in the world.

In the Book of Psalms, 105:15, and in I Chronicles 16:22,

168

"touch not mine anointed," is clearly a reference to the Patriarchs. In Isaiah 61:1, "the Lord hath anointed me to preach," the prophet is referring to himself!

It is quite clear that the Messiah meant "anointed with oil." It referred to one whom God invested with special spiritual responsibility or chose for an important role in the affairs of Israel and of the world.

In some of the prophetic books of the Bible—Isaiah, Hosea, Micah, Jeremiah, Zechariah—there is described an ideal future leader who will rule over Israel "in the end of days," an age of great redemption. In no instance, however, is this ideal leader called the Messiah.

How Did the Prophets Envision the Ideal Future Leader?

The ideal future leader was envisioned as a human being, a Jew, descended from the House of David, of the seed of Jesse, a man of lofty moral and spiritual quality, wise and understanding, inspired and courageous. Appointed by God and armed by Him with power and authority, this triumphant leader will throw off the yoke of Israel's oppressors, re-establish the land of Israel, and restore the liberated people of Israel to the land. He will rule with wisdom and justice. The people will enjoy peace, prosperity, freedom and righteousness. "Every man shall dwell under his own fig tree unafraid." This future King of Israel will win the respect and confidence of all the rulers of the world. As they come to him for advice, he will show them the way to an ideal world order of universal peace and righteousness. "Out of Zion will come forth the Law and the Word of God from Jerusalem . . . Nation shall not lift up sword against nation, neither shall men learn war anymore . . . Justice will well up like a mighty stream . . . All the earth will be filled with the knowledge of the Lord." The nations will come up to the House of the Lord in the rebuilt Temple of Jerusalem and all will worship the One God.

1. All the prophets speak of the glorious future or the ideal life on earth in the future.

2. Only few of the prophets mention the ideal future leader who will become King of Israel and establish the reign of righteousness and peace.

3. Even these few prophets lay far greater stress on the new life of the future age than on the figure or personality of the leader.

4. This future leader and King of Israel is not called Messiah and he is not called a Redeemer. In the Bible there is only one Redeemer—God.

When, How and Why Did the Figure of a "Messiah-Redeemer" Become Part of the Jewish Belief?

The sober, realistic, vigorous, optimistic social and predominantly this-worldly Jewish religion assumed a heavy otherworldly and supernatural theological emphasis during the two centuries preceding and following the beginning of the Common Era. It was a period of successive crises for the Jews wherein the heart of the people began to fail. In their desperation, people sought to know why God's chosen suffered so unendurably while the really wicked nations, their oppressors, prospered. The prophetic vision of the future, wherein an ideal ruler would eventually bring justice and prosperity to the Jews and to all mankind, was not sufficiently satisfying to help raise the low morale of the people. The widespread disillusionment, hopelessness and bitterness that afflicted the Jews made them eager to follow anyone who offered them escape from reality.

It was natural for the Jewish people to turn to Scripture for help. Around each biblical phrase they spun exaggerated interpretations to fit their needs. The ideal future leader who, according to some of the prophets, would usher in the glorious age of the future began to be referred to as the Messiah and the age itself as the Messianic Age. The desire to escape their misery led the people to read into the prophetic references an all-powerful, mystical, superhuman being—a Messiah and Redeemer—who would save them. The wicked world and impious nations would not enjoy redemption. A new world would come into being after a terrible Day of Judgment.

These ideas inspired a whole new literature. It was called Apocalyptic (from "Apocalypse" which means "Revelation") because the authors of these books were supposedly setting down what was revealed to them either by direct vision, communion with the spirit of God, or through the medium of an angel. It was also called pseudepigraphic because authorship was also attributed to ancient saints or heroes in order to make them more authoritative.

The reasonable elements of the prophetic vision of the future were replaced in the popular mind by mystical, irrational, otherworldly conceptions. Some of the Rabbis were themselves infected by these apocalyptic visions and Messianic dreams. One of the great sages had to be rebuked by Rabbi Jose the Galilean for "profaning the Divine Presence" by making the Messiah as important as God. He had been teaching that the Messiah occupies a throne alongside of God (Hagigah 14a and Sanhedrin 38b).

The Rabbis of the Talmud withheld their approval from apocalyptic literature but their efforts to curb unreason were in vain. In several places in the Talmud, the people were exhorted and warned that "there is no difference between this age and the days of the Messiah except that there will be freedom from oppression and the restoration of Israel's independence." Cumulative misfortunes and exhausted patience twisted their emotional needs and inflamed the imagination of the people. They indulged in all kinds of mystical reckonings to determine the imminent arrival of the Messiah. One sage declared: "May the curse of heaven fall upon those who calculate the date of the advent of the Messiah thereby creating political and social unrest among the people." (Sanhedrin 97b). Another sage declared that there is no Messiah! As the misery of the Jews in Palestine increased, the Messiah concept assumed new, strange forms altogether contrary to the original beautiful ideal of the prophets: the Messiah emerged as a performer of supernatural feats, a worker of miracles.

It is understandable why the figure of such a Messiah fascinated the troubled, and how he became a symbol of hope to the despairing. The search in Holy Scripture for every possible clue about the "Messiah personality" was really a search for hope and reassurance by those who lacked both. Perhaps, this preoccupation with a miraculous Messiah preserved the Jews from utter hopelessness and spiritual extinction. Who knows? "God works in mysterious ways His wonders to perform."

How Did the Christian Messianic Belief Emerge Out of the Jewish Tradition?

First, let us examine the historical conditions that laid the groundwork for the belief. The period following Pompey's capture of Jerusalem in 63 B.C.E. was marked by disastrous Jewish rebellions against Rome, multitudinous crucifixions, and humiliations for the Jewish people. To escape the unendurable present, many people turned to the messianic hope of a miracle-working Messiah. Various sects sprang up. Some sought relief from the harshness of reality in asceticism and retreated to a quiet, monastic simplicity; others, by practicing mystic rites in preparation for the coming of the Messiah. The messianic hope stood at its zenith and many claimants arose who professed to be the Messiah. One of these was Jesus of Galilee who was put to death by the Romans as a rabble-rouser.

To the Jewish people as a whole, Jesus was just another Messiah that failed; he did not fulfill the messianic prophecy of the Jewish people. His name, unlike that of other martyred "Messiahs," was preserved through the zeal of his dedicated followers and their insistence that he rose from his tomb and ascended to heaven. Their devotion and missionary zeal resurrected a crucified preacher into a "glorious saviour," and transformed a small group into a world-wide religion.

To understand more clearly how the Christian messianic belief emerged from the Jewish tradition, let us examine briefly the main differences between the prophetic and the apocalyptic conceptions of the future.

The prophets saw in man and in society divine forces working for righteousness. The inherent potential goodness of man and the eventual establishment of a moral society would surely be realized. Man might become estranged from God but repentance leading to righteous conduct would bring him back to God. God would turn back to man, and both, united in a common moral purpose, would transform the chaotic present into a spiritual world order "in the end of days."

The apocalyptic writers, on the other hand, despaired of human nature and the world. They tended to equate this life with suffering and evil. How could the good society possibly emerge out of a world so corrupt? They foresaw the apocalyptic doom, the complete destruction of this sinful world. Some of them envisioned a new world built by God on the ruins of the old; others, wrote of a new life beyond this world.

Some Jews adhered to the prophetic, some to the apocalyptic world view. Those who put their trust in the Kingdom of God to be established on earth concentrated on the moral disciplines and spiritual requirements of a good society. Those who abandoned hope for this life concentrated on a Kingdom of God in heaven. This latter apocalyptic view was the one adopted by the first followers of Jesus, the Jewish-Christians who laid the foundations for Christianity. "My Kingdom is not of this world," attributed to Jesus in the Gospel of John (18:36), indicates the otherworldly stress of Christianity. Jesus himself was viewed as the supernatural, miracle-performing and god-like Messiah of apocalyptic literature.

Why Didn't the Jews Accept Jesus as the Messiah?

Jews, apart from a small group of Jesus' earliest adherents, did not believe that he fulfilled the traditional messianic hope articulated by the prophets and sages of Israel:

this Messiah did not save Israel from her enemies, bring about the restoration of glory to Israel, or inaugurate the Kingdom of God on earth in his lifetime. Many gentiles, on the other hand, did accept Jesus as the Messiah. Hopelessness hung over the world and they needed the belief in the Messiah to save them from crushing despair.

What made Jesus even less acceptable to the vast majority of the Jews was the interpretation of Jesus set forth by Paul and, still later, by the Greek Fathers of the Church. In Pauline Christianity Jesus, the man, became the Son of God. In the elaborations of the Church Fathers, he became God incarnate who assumed the flesh of man so he could die and, with his blood, wash away the original sin of man. Because Jesus was interpreted by his followers to be an object of faith, the mainstream of Jewish thought and faith ignored him. In Judaism, only God can be the supreme object of our faith. Our monotheistic religion never asked us to believe in the Messiah, only in his coming as a messenger and instrument of God's redemption of all mankind. The Jewish and Christian concepts of Messiah are very different.

In What Ways Are the Jewish and Christian Concepts of the Messiah Similar?

The early Jewish-Christians absorbed their ideas about the Messiah from Judaism. Even after estrangement and separation took place, similar elements remained. Both Jewish and Christian conceptions of the Messiah are dynamic, not static. We have already noted that the Jewish conception of the Messiah varied from period to period and that there were variations and differences in each period. The Christian belief also underwent evolution and change and differences of interpretation. For instance, Jesus himself understood his "messiahship" quite differently from the way in which it was understood by Paul. Later Church Fathers modified Paul's views very markedly. Catholics, Greek Orthodox and Protestants today differ among themselves in their understanding of the Messiah. At best, we can compare beliefs held by great numbers of Jews with beliefs generally accepted by many Christians. This we shall do below when we indicate the differences in the Jewish and Christian concepts of the Messiah.

How Do the Jewish and Christian Concepts of the Messiah Differ?

1. From the Jewish standpoint, history is still in the making and fulfillment is yet to be achieved. The Jewish Messiah is to come "in the end of days," when the purpose or goal of history is fulfilled. According to Christianity the Messiah has already come, and the purpose of history has already been fulfilled in him. From the Christian point of view, influenced by Greek and Roman thought that saw the Golden Age in the past, we are living in time, not in history. Those Christians who believe in the second coming of the Christ come closer to the Jewish view of a Golden Age in the future.

2. The Jewish Messiah is a mortal man, albeit a great personality endowed with remarkable spiritual and mental qualities as well as physical power, appointed by God to carry out an appointed task. He is human. The Christian Messiah is, in Pauline Christianity, the Son of God; in later Christianity, God incarnate in the flesh and form of man. He is divine.

3. The Jewish Messiah is envisioned as a dynamic and heroic personality who wins the respect of all nations by virtue of his wisdom, spirituality and prowess. He becomes the acknowledged leader of a world united to do the will of the One God. The Christian Messiah was crucified and, by his blood, atoned for and washed away the original sin contaminating man.

4. The Jewish Kingdom of Heaven which is to be ushered in by His Messenger, the Messiah, is an ideal society here on earth where the rule of God will be established. For the Jew today, as in the past, the word Messiah evokes pos-

sibilities for social progress, the coming of a better world, the achievement of political, economic and social as well as moral and spiritual goals. The Christian Kingdom of Heaven is an otherworldly salvation. "My Kingdom is not of this world," is attributed to Jesus in the Gospel of John (18:36).

5. The Jewish Messiah is only an instrument of God; only God Himself is our Rock and our Redeemer. According to Christianity, the Messiah himself is both Saviour and Redeemer.

6. The Jewish Messiah will concern himself with the political and economic, as well as with the spiritual, well-being of his people and the nations. He will lead Israel to political independence, and the world to peace. The Christian Messiah came only to redeem man from spiritual evil. "Salvation from evil in this world can be found only in salvation from this world itself."

7. The Jewish Messiah will be of the seed of David. Jews employ the term *Avinu she-bashamayim* ("our Father Who is in Heaven") in a poetic and spiritual sense only. According to Jewish belief, all men are children (sons) of God. The suggestion that the Messiah will be the physical, biological son of God is completely alien to Jewish thinking. The Christian Messiah is the Son of God, born of a human mother by an immaculate conception. According to some elements in Christianity, the term Son of God, applied to Jesus, is understood in an actual biological sense.

8. The Jewish Messiah is an instrument for bringing Divine redemption to society; the Christian Messiah brings redemption to the individual soul.

9. In Judaism, the Messianic Age is more important than the Messiah. Redemption comes from God and through God to a redeemed society. The Jewish Messiah is a member of that redeemed society. In Christianity, the Messiah is of supreme importance since redemption of the individual soul is impossible without him.

10. The structure of Jewish faith is not seriously affected by belief or disbelief in the Messiah. Jewish redemption is conceivable without a Messiah. Christianity is Christ-centered; it collapses completely without belief in Christ. In Judaism, the Messiah is God's man; in Christianity he became man's God.

11. Jewish prayer is addressed directly to God; the Jewish Messiah is a mortal. In Christianity, the Messiah is either the mediator between God and man, or God Himself; he is a Divinity. "We ask this in the name of our Lord, Jesus Christ," is the liturgical formula with which Christians conclude their prayers.

12. The "he" in Isaiah 53:12 ("Yet he bore the sin of many") is interpreted by Jews as a reference to the collective persecuted people of Israel some 700 years before Jesus. To Christians, the "he" is the Messiah who died, by God's will and his own, in order that humanity might be redeemed from sin, suffering and the power of satan. The concept of vicarious atonement is present in the Jewish tradition but was never part of essential doctrine. In this particular form —God offering His son as a sacrifice and vicarious atonement for the sins of all mankind—it is entirely alien to Judaism.

Do Jews Today Believe in the Coming of the Messiah?

The belief varies in the three main branches of Judaism and, indeed, within each branch. The extreme Orthodox believe that the Messiah is an indispensable figure in the divine drama of redemption. Until the Messiah comes, the people of Israel will not be restored to the land of Israel and society will not be redeemed: the coming of the Messiah must precede the fulfillment of the messianic promise. On the ground that the Messiah has not yet come, they even reject the spiritual legitimacy of the present State of Israel. They consider its present re-establishment an impertinence and defiance of God's will.

Moderate elements in Orthodoxy do not attach quite such importance to the person of the Messiah and do not regard belief in the coming of the Messiah as a major principle of Judaism. They do look forward to his coming but do not deny the spiritual legitimacy of the present re-establishment of the State of Israel.

Liberal Orthodox Jews interpret the re-establishment of Israel as partial fulfillment of the messianic promise and ignore the fact that the Messiah did not precede its restoration. They have not abandoned belief in the coming of the Messiah but sometimes speak of the rebuilding of the Holy Land as a sign of the Messiah.

Conservative Jews retain the figure of the Messiah in the vocabulary of the Jewish faith as a symbol of the conviction that men are capable of bringing Divine redemption into the world when they serve as instruments of God. The coming of the Messiah is not a theologically acceptable proposition but the Messiah figures prominently in the emotional content of the Jewish religion. The Messiah is not expected for one decisive visit which will transform the world, in the apocalyptic sense of the word. However, he is a distinguished and very precious being whose presence is intimately felt on many occasions in the religious calendar. The Messiah is ever-present in our songs, our literature, our liturgy and in the hushed expectancy of the solemn *Neilah* service of Yom Kippur. In a sense, man is God's Messiah: if man uses his God-given potentialities and creative efforts effectively, he has the power to forge ahead to his own redemption and make the messianic dream a reality.

Reform theology has completely rejected the belief that realization of an ideal society depends on an individual. No matter how remarkable and God-like, no one Messiah can singlehandedly accomplish the redemption of the world. Instead, they stress belief in the Messianic Age when a social order of peace, justice and freedom will be established. They hold firmly to the belief that the mission of the Jewish people is to assume a major role in the moral education of mankind, thereby promoting the attainment of a messianic social order.

Why Can We Believe in the Messianic Age Even if We Don't Believe in the Messiah?

Judaism *can* function without the Messiah; it *cannot* function without the messianic vision and without man's commitment to the moral effort that is indispensable to its realization. Not all Jews believe in and pray for a personal Messiah but no Jew who thinks or feels in the spirit of Jewish tradition would surrender belief in the Messianic Age.

The Messianic Age for which we constantly pray, and which all religious Jews accept as God's glorious promise, will be marked by the fulfillment of the following reasonable expectations:

1. The One God will be worshipped on all the earth.

2. All men will find their brotherhood in the Fatherhood of God.

3. Peace, justice and freedom will prevail throughout the world.

5. The historic role of the Jewish people as the suffering servant of God for humanity's sake will be vindicated and acknowledged.

The messianic promise is inherent in life. It will surely be fulfilled when man proves himself worthy of it and God so wills it.

CHAPTER XII

Life and Purpose

Does Life Have Purpose?

Some secular philosophies maintain that there is no convincing evidence for the belief that life has any purpose. They would have us believe that man is the product of natural causes which had no pre-vision of the ends they were achieving, and that purposeless nature begot a creature who thinks in terms of purpose. How different is this attitude from that of Judaism: "The Holy One created not a thing without a purpose." (Rab. T: Sabbath 77b) It is an axiom of Jewish faith that to deny purpose is to deny God. When we deny that life has purpose, we have denied God even though we may profess belief in Him; when we deny God but not His purpose, we have not really denied Him.

What Is the Purpose of Life as Judaism Understands It?

Life has *immediate* purposes which are obvious to everyone. But its *intermediate* and *ultimate* purposes must be discerned.

1. *Self-fulfillment*

The purpose of life, to begin with, is the wise, good and creative enjoyment by man of the material, intellectual, moral and spiritual blessings provided for him by his Creator. Judaism regards as sinful both *rejection* of the pleasures of life, which is in effect the denial of the wisdom and loving-kindness of a beneficent Provider, and *indulgence* in exclusively material satisfactions which desensitizes and makes us unconscious of our intellectual and/or moral-spiritual-aesthetic needs. Man is Body-Mind-Spirit. Denial of any aspect of the self, or failure to satisfy its legitimate needs, rules out maximum self-fulfillment. There is no tug of war among them: the Creator has provided for the gratification of the healthy wants and desires of the body, for the joys of the mind, and for the adventures of the spirit. Part of the purpose of life is the wholesome and harmonious fulfillment of the self, with none of its aspects neglected or improperly used.

2. Social Fulfillment

In the process of enjoying life, we discover that real pleasure involves giving as well as taking: enriching life through creative effort as well as extracting from and exploiting it for our own satisfaction. For example, the *mitzvos* of marriage and child-bearing require self-sacrifice and effort to provide for the security and well-being of those we love. The welfare of our marriage and of our children is bound up with the welfare of the society of which we are a part. To fulfil the purpose of life as God intends, we become involved in serving others, along with helping ourselves, by participating in affairs that affect the well-being of society. According to Jewish law, which sets forth the requirements of purposeful living, we are required to exert ourselves as creatively as possible for the entire community as well as for the health, education, and welfare of our own children.

As we contribute to the improvement of society, we help achieve fulfillment for others and for ourselves. In God's plan, there can be no society without individuals, no individuals without society. "Thou shalt love thy neighbor as thyself" is basic to fulfillment of the purpose of life. "A man's closest relative is his self" (Sanhedrin 9B) but he is not related at all until he discovers that others are his other self. As Hillel put it, "If I am not for myself, who is for me? And if I am only for myself, what am I?" (Abot 2:4) True harmony and social fulfillment do not require self-surrender. The self must be itself to love the others as itself.

Without being and remaining one's self, there can be neither self-fulfillment nor social fulfillment. Judaism affirms that true self-interest leads to self-transcendence and to social interest. Society is partly the product of the self fulfilling itself and partly the milieu in which the individual actualizes himself. It is the combined effort of men to help each other to greater self-realization.

3. *Ultimate Fulfillment*

The Jewish tradition defines the purpose of life in terms of man's obligations to himself, to his fellowmen and, finally, in terms of the highest vision of useful living—man's obligation to God. Mature comprehension that we are expected and able, through our own efforts, to serve the purposes of God brings us to a definition of the ultimate purpose of life. Jewish tradition defines it thus:

> To do the Will of God: to walk in His ways and to serve Him;
> To reveal His Glory; to be a co-worker with God;
> To sanctify His Name; to advance His Kingdom;
> To accept the yoke of the Kingdom of Heaven.

Man discovers the real purpose of life when he realizes that not only does he need God but that God needs him; when, without denying himself, he can transcend himself and enter the service of God; when he has progressed spiritually to the point where he can sincerely ask, "What doth the Lord God require of me?"; when he rises to the greatest challenge given to him—the sublime privilege of helping to fulfill the Divine purpose of life.

Why Does Judaism Place Such Strong Emphasis on Belief in the Good Life on Earth?

Belief in the good life is a corollary to the belief that there is One God, that the purpose for which He created the world is good, and that His purpose will be realized in the world. Good will triumph because God wills it: this is the essence of our faith, its main message and strong conviction. The will is a maker of truth. It follows that man's will *can* make the good life come true and *will* make it come true if it is coupled with God's Will.

Those who see the present in terms of an unsatisfactory past, see little possibility for the future; those who see the present in terms of a perfect past, see only decay in the present and no hope for the future. The presence of evil makes some reject the world and despair of the future; the presence of evil spurs Judaism to exert itself more energetically to alleviate the evil. The buoyant optimism of Judaism makes it see evidence for the good life in the present, and the present in terms of an ideal future. During the most desperate hours of history, our people conceived the great vision of a glorious future; in the events of their own times they found evidence for such belief. Today, the Jew who has lived through the black period of Nazi extermination, and even now sees freshly scrawled swastikas, also finds evidence of God in the events of the world. He sees good men striving in the right direction, social progress, and justification for the faith and hope that the good society will be realized. He sees promise in the present, and redemption and fulfillment in the future. "The Kingdom," said the Rabbis, "is not only in the future but in the present." Judaism's goals are difficult but not impossible: the end of war, international cooperation, eradication of poverty, security, freedom, the practice of compassion, decency, sobriety. The work toward these goals for the future must go on today.

We are not blind to the persistent moral failures of men and nations: corruption, passions and confusions abound. Our past failures point up the fact that we lacked a strong faith in man and in God, and we have not honestly translated our beliefs into the practices of daily living. Even religion has given little more than lip-service to the exalted and compelling vision of the good life. We have merely *preached* faith in men and faith in God. Some day the world will learn what Judaism learned long ago: religion is the service of the heart, the mind and the soul—the whole being of man. And the Torah of the good life will become the world's way of life.

Why does Judaism place such strong emphasis on belief in the good life? If we did *not* believe this, there would be very little else worth believing in.

Does History Have a Specific Destination Toward Which It Is Moving?

There are a number of ways in which this question may be answered. Below are some of the more well-known theories of history.

1. *History has no goal.*

History is unpredictable: it has neither purpose nor meaning, and follows no sensible pattern. Its direction is a matter of chance.

2. *History's destiny is pre-determined by nature.*

History is a sequence of causes and effects which evolves according to its own laws of logic. The passions and wills of men are subservient to these same laws of logic.

A. *Automatic progress theory*
History must inexorably evolve toward the realization of its potential: it must grow and mature increasingly toward the perfection of society. Man may postpone or accelerate the good society but, ultimately, the laws of nature are stronger than the wills of men. History is naturally and necessarily self-fulfilling.

B. *Automatic degeneration theory*
Civilizations rise and fall; advance, then deteriorate. Men build; nature tears down. History records that pattern.

C. *Cyclical theory*
History moves in cycles: men may think they are

progressing but they are engaged in an essentially
repetitious process, trapped in a cyclical historical
movement.

3. *History is man-made.*

Its values, purposes, goals, directions, control and final
destination are fashioned and determined by the motives
and behavior of men. Thus, the outcome of all historical
effort depends on whether men follow a reasonable and
moral, or an imprudent and destructive, course of action.
Some believe that man's reasonableness and virtue will win;
some believe man's irrationality and selfishness will prevail;
some believe that the ambivalence in man's nature will perpetuate the inescapable confusion of history.

Judaism rejects the theory that history has no goal for
the same reasons that it repudiates the view that life has
no purpose. Judaism rejects the theory that history follows
a pattern fixed by nature for the same reason that, historically, it repudiated idolatry and steered clear of any
form of fatalism or rigid determinism. Judaism rejects also
the view that history is man-made. To the Jewish mentality,
making man the Lord of History is as repugnant as making
nature the god of history.

What Is the Philosophy of History as Expressed in Jewish Tradition?

The Lord of History is God the Creator. The Will of God
determines the direction and ultimate destination of history
—the establishment of the good life (Kingdom of God) on
earth.

MAN'S ROLE IN HISTORY

God has set the goal or destination of history but man
is, nevertheless, the maker of his own destiny. The *realization* of the purpose of history depends on man as well as on
God: man, having been endowed with free will, is not entirely

a creature of necessity and nothing is inevitable until it has
actually happened. In every historical situation man is confronted with a choice between a good and an evil. God calls
upon man to take up the cause of the greater good, but the
choice itself is up to man.

THE CONTENT OF HISTORY

The Bible interprets history in terms of the tension between the will of man and the Will of God. There is a constant struggle of rebellious man against the commandments
of God. Upheaval and catastrophe are explained as Divine
judgment throughout the Bible, yet its pages pulsate with
optimism that man will ultimately accept God's Will.

The Prophets added nothing new to the older view of
history, but they formulated it in greater detail so that some
of its elements become clearer. The Vision of the End of
Days, the establishment of the Kingdom, has been set as
the destination and goal of history by God. Its realization
depends on man working in partnership with God. Morality
is a decisive factor in advancing man toward the good life,
moral corruption brings about the fall of nations. Idolatry
is the decisive sin: the worship of false values or false gods
brings about ruin. God judges in order to rehabilitate: afflic-
tion is intended to chasten men and nations. No mistake is
inevitable and no calamity is final; God forgives by opening
up new historical possibilities. The repeated prophetic demand for repentance is intended to bring man's will into
harmony with God's.

The rabbinic view of history is identical with that expressed in the Torah and by the prophets. History is a
partnership between God and man to effect the establishment of a good life on earth. In order that man may achieve
this ideal good life, or Kingdom of God, God has given him
laws of the good life, power, energy and resources for building the good society, and free will. Man often flouts God's
law and violates the moral foundations on which the King-

dom of God must be constructed. But no sin or error is totally catastrophic: man's failures can only delay the coming of the Kingdom.

The Talmudic tradition recognized two possibilities: either men can gradually progress toward the Kingdom, or they can bring about such disorder as to necessitate the miraculous intervention of God. Either way, the Kingdom of God, the purpose for which the world was created by God, must eventually be fulfilled. The goal of history, the establishment of the Kingdom of God, will be achieved when man will be at one with God, with himself, with his fellowman, and with all creation. The Kingdom of God is life as it should and will be.

What Is the Traditional Jewish Conception of the Good Society?

In the good society, the Jewish people will be a holy people, respected by all the nations of the world; the land of Israel will be restored and out of Zion will go forth the Law of God; the Temple will be rebuilt and serve as a House of God for all peoples.

Politically, morally and spiritually, the world will be blessed.

1. All men and nations will believe in God and accept His sovereignty.

2. Justice and peace will be established on earth. Harmony and brotherhood will prevail, for all nations will discover their essential oneness.

3. Nature will be at peace and in harmony with man.

4. Men will enjoy unprecedented material prosperity due to increased productivity and more equitable distribution of God's goods.

5. Fear and insecurity will be eliminated. Men will turn away from wickedness and violence, and war and oppression will cease entirely.

Can a 20th-Century Jew Accept the Traditional Concept of the Kingdom of God?

Challenges to the traditional Jewish concept of the future are to be found in three major contemporary sources: modern political thought, existentialism and naturalism.

1. *Modern political thought*

Modern political thinkers object to theocracy and monarchy as antiquated ideas. Therefore, the idea of the Kingdom of God appears to be neither relevant nor respectable. However, such offhand dismissal is a judgment of the term rather than of the ideas embodied in it.

Translated into modern, relevant idiom, the traditional Kingdom-of-God concept is both pertinent and valid. It pertains to a *social* order in which God's moral law will be universally upheld. It is an expression of high trust and confidence that man is capable of recognizing and living up to God's moral law. The establishment of such a social order will result in maximum self-realization and social fulfillment. It will be a poetic but forceful confirmation of the holiness, worthwhileness and redemptive promise of life. It is Judaism's optimism that views the character of life in terms of its latent possibilities rather than its current disabilities.

Modern political thinkers also object to the notion of an ultimate purpose in history, or historical direction and destiny. However, the evidence of history itself belies this view: the Biblical concept of the unity of mankind and the prophetic emphasis on international peace are confirmed by the growing interdependence of all nations, and the increasing recognition by men of all nations, races and creeds, of the unity of mankind. The study and writing of world history is taking precedence over purely national studies, e.g., nations are being viewed more frequently in their world context. The course of history has been steered and many social improvements effected by social planning on the basis of desired goals and by agreement on moral objectives.

Modern political thinkers, furthermore, object to the

Messianic tradition as a threat to survival. Groups that claim a monopoly on the right faith and values for achieving the millenium are intolerant. They are dangerously fanatic and ruthless in forwarding their ultimate purpose. Nazism and Communism are modern examples of such groups acting destructively under the spell of a belief in destiny. In modern political life, those who talk loudly in terms of a final goal for history are the very forces that threaten to bring history to its final destruction. However, there is no valid reason for society to fear social goals and moral political objectives simply because contemporary tyrants and maniacs have donned the prophetic mantle for their demoniacal ends. The Communists have eliminated the most important and *the* decisive element in the Jewish conception of history: they have rejected the Lord of History and fashioned their own "god." Communism will share the fate of all idolatries. But society needs guidance and direction for realizing the purpose of history as determined by God. Jewish philosophy of history points the way; without a sense of direction, we will indeed lose our way.

2. *Existentialism*

According to existentialists, the characteristics of life are pain, confusion, and defeat rather than happiness, harmony, and a promise of ultimate victory. Because man is torn between sinful self-centeredness and an idealistic desire for self-transcendence, his life is filled with anxiety and frustration. Man may strive heroically to be moral but society only offers choices between greater and lesser evils rather than a clear-cut choice between good and evil. Even his honest efforts to build a reasonable and decent life by solving his problems in the least evil way, lead to the emergence of other problems whose solutions are similarly infected with ambiguity and evil. Escape from this inherent-in-life predicament is possible only by a leap of faith to God Who, by His grace, may confer salvation. Man is powerless to save himself; only God can save.

In an age of crisis, frustration, and profound disillusionment, the existentialist analysis and diagnosis are understandable. We can go along with the view that man is egocentric, heavily coloring human effort with self-interest; we certainly subscribe to faith in God. With an equal degree of realism we understand that this current mood is neither permanent nor inevitable. The divinely ordained self-interest of man makes him appear hopeless only because it has been misinterpreted and misdirected. The entirely normal desire to make the most out of life, properly understood and exercised, can lead to rich self-fulfillment and realization of the highest moral and spiritual values.

The great havoc of our age has been wrought by *lack* of faith in man rather than by too much of it. The forces that threaten destruction put their faith in states, dialectics, political parties, programs of destruction for those who differ, in anything, except man. Much of the suffering in life, the disorientation and neurotic unreasonableness, stem from man's frantic effort to recover his lost ego. Man's vision of his true self-interest has been perverted by false standards of success and by unsound values. Faith in the highest values and in God, needs to be emphasized—but not by depreciating man. The downgrading of human nature will not lead to the enthronement of the Divine nature. The humiliation of man will not increase confidence and joyful striving to achieve higher values. Judaism pins its faith on the potential goodness of man.

3. *Religious naturalism*

Establishment of the Kingdom of God by a supernatural God is, according to the religious naturalists, contrary to the criteria of modern thought and, furthermore, acts as a deterrent to its realization by man. Naturalism is a conception of God's sovereignty that functions as an aid to the regeneration of society through direct human agency, independent of a reliance on miraculous intervention. Trust in the sovereignty of God implies faith that in mankind is manifest a power (God) which operates for the regeneration of human society. God's Kingdom on earth will be established, but only by the efforts of man upon whom rests ultimate responsibility for its realization. Men cannot improve their lives by accepting existing conditions as final or by trying to change the essential nature of things; men must study nature and, in conformity with natural law, adapt the selected means to the desired ends. God manifests Himself through man's initiative and active striving to transform the conditions under which he lives. Ultimately, God will become sovereign in human society. As treated by the religious naturalists, the establishment of the Kingdom of God demands no revolutionary change in human nature and no miraculous saving act of a supernatural God. (See Mordecai M. Kaplan's *Meaning of God* and Jack J. Cohen's *The Case for Religious Naturalism.*)

The naturalist position is a fine statement of social principle and humanitarianism with religious shadings. It clarifies the meaning of Godhood in man and of the immanent aspects of God in social life. These positive principles deserve to be stressed. But, in the process of strengthening man, they depersonalize and de-emphasize God. By magnifying the role of man and reducing God's, which is the reverse of the existentialist tendency to magnify God and reduce the role of man, the religious naturalists fall into the same kind of error.

Traditional Judaism, in a sense, is a combination of the religious naturalists' view that man and Immanent God can achieve redemption within the context of history, and the existentialists' view that man may fail to convert society and requires the miraculous intervention of the Transcendent God. History is a gradual fulfillment of the purpose for which God created the world. Man works in partnership with God for this fulfillment. Partial fulfillment has meaning in the light of the ultimate goal; partial redemption suggests the possibility for complete redemption.

CHAPTER XIII

The Soul

Why Have Men Believed in the Existence of the Soul?

The need to explain the mystery of life, the difference between life and death, may have prompted, as it does still prompt, first thoughts regarding the soul. Ancient man postulated anima or spirits. These anima gave life to matter; their departure left matter inert or dead. Anima distinguished the living from the dead. Whether we term it anima, energy, elan vital, spirit, soul or breath of life, the basic idea is the same: a life-giving force enters and departs from matter. This force transcends, survives, and exists independently of matter.

Consciousness is another phenomenon that has prompted man to recognize the existence of soul. Although man consists of matter undergoing physical and chemical changes, he possesses an additional indefinable component that cannot be duplicated or even remotely approximated in a laboratory: awareness. Awareness in all its aspects is soul. Matter reacts with matter to form new products; physical and chemical adjustments are continually resulting in modifications of one kind or another. But matter itself, physical or chemical, has no consciousness of self or of the new and modified aspects of itself. Man alone is aware of process and change, of a dynamic self, of the existence of others and of his need to relate himself to these others and finally, in spontaneous response, to a Cosmic Being, God. This awareness prompts man to think in terms of soul.

Conscience is still another affirmation of the validity of the soul concept. It is inconceivable that any configuration of atoms should result in human conscience—the ability to distinguish between right and wrong, and to feel duty-bound to do the right. The *functioning* of the conscience may be explained in psychiatric terms but the *origin* of man's moral nature cannot be explained except in terms of soul.

There are qualities and urges in man—creativity, special talents, aesthetic responses, persistent quests for further understanding and truth, religious and philosophical leanings—that can be accounted for only by the belief that man is endowed with a soul. It is difficult enough to explain the soul but it is even more difficult to account for the complex personality of man without postulating a soul.

What Does Judaism Teach About the Soul?

Where the Jewish tradition discusses the unknowable, it deliberately allows the widest possible latitude for differences of opinion. Therefore, on the *exact* nature of the soul, tradition maintains a prudent silence. Many opinions are recorded: none is declared authoritative and final. The tradition teaches but, at the same time, seems to say there is much we do not know and still have to learn.

What Are Some of the Opinions on the Nature of the Soul Expressed in the Bible?

The soul is referred to by five different words in the Bible. Each expresses something about the character of the soul:

1. *Nefesh*—sometimes translated as vitality, sometimes as personality. In Deut. 12:23, it refers to the blood, that which carries life through the body. *The soul is the bearer of life in the person, that which makes him alive biologically.*

2. *Ruach*—generally translated as spirit or wind. It refers to that element which enables man to be aware of and to commune with God. This term, more than any other, suggests the content and meaning of the phrase "in the image of God." The *Ruach* in man brings him into kinship with the

Ruach Hakodesh (the Holy Spirit): it lifts him above the physical plane and leads him to contemplate the eternal verities—truth, goodness, and beauty. *The soul is the bearer of the divine in man, that which makes him alive spiritually.*

3. *Nishamah*—generally translated as breath or psyche. This term usually refers to the spiritual quality of man, after the spirit, *Ruach*, of God has been breathed into him. Thus, the *Ruach* makes man a *Nishamah*, a psychical being. *The soul is that which makes man alive psychologically.*

4. *Yechida*—translated as one or unique. The limbs of the body are in pairs and even those organs that are single have many qualities in common with all the rest. Only the soul is one and unique in the body. *The soul is that which makes man unique among all created things.*

5. *Chaya*—translated as living or surviving. Everything decays but the soul lives on; the body dies but the soul survives. *The soul is that which gives man immortality.*

Apart from the terminology referring to the soul, the Bible expresses a number of ideas regarding the soul and its nature. The soul is the divine breath that animates the body, the motive force of all vital activities; its exit from the body results in death. Aside from its life-giving force, it is the seat of the emotions, the agent of thought, the source of moral sentiment, the residence of memory, the center of personality. The soul comes from God but it is *not* an emanation or a part of Him; it is a special and unique creation. Whether the soul pre-exists the body and what its condition and place before birth may be, the Bible does not tell. The Bible seems to imply that man is born, body and spirit, at the same time. Similarly, the Bible says very little about what happens to the soul after the death of the body.

The Bible's interest centers on man as a unity, a combination of body and soul, which manifests itself in an individual, self-conscious, and personal life. It concerns itself with the acts of man as a joint functioning of body and soul for which the total man is held responsible. Responsibility is not divided between the physical and spiritual components of human nature; the one is not condemned nor is the other exalted in comparison. The total man is held responsible and accountable in the Bible.

What Did the Rabbis Teach About the Soul?

The Rabbinic views on the soul are based on the Bible but derive also from the Rabbis' own observations and from ideas stimulated by contact with Greek and other thought, which were then brought into agreement with Biblical teachings.

1. The Biblical conception of man, a combination of earthly body and divine soul, was further developed by the Rabbis. They said that God created the body from the earth and into it he put a soul from heaven. Therefore, Man is related to the heavenly and to the earthly beings, both of which preceded him in the order of Creation. According to the sages, God created *heaven and earth* on the first day, then proceeded to create alternately one thing above and one below: on the second day, the firmament above; on the third, the seas below; on the fourth, the heavenly lights above; on the fifth, the aquatic creatures below. Only one day remained for the completion of Creation. God said, "If I produce anything above, earth will be displeased; if I produce anything below, heaven will be dissatisfied." What did He do? He created man's body from the earth and his soul from heaven.

This distinction between "heavenly" and "earthly" has nothing in common either with the Greek concept of spirit and matter or with the associated Christian idea that the soul as spirit is holy and good whereas the body as matter is corrupt and evil. Such thinking was altogether foreign to Biblical and Rabbinic reflection.

2. The soul requires the body and depends on it in order

to perform its functions in this life. Yet, it *is* considered the more significant part of the combination, for it survives the body. Whereas the body has a beginning and an end (mortal), the soul has a beginning but no end (immortal, but not eternal like God). The soul is the element which makes man aware of kinship with God; it is the animating principle and source of man's ability to reason, to know, to will and to love. Rabbi Simeon, a Palestinian teacher of the third century, summarizes some of the views of the Rabbis in reference to the relationship between the soul and the body as follows:

"The soul fills the body as God bears the world. The soul outlasts the body as God outlasts the world. The soul sees and is not seen as God sees and is not seen. The soul is pure in the body as God is pure in the world."

The phrase "pure in soul and body" was used very often by the Rabbis to protest against vilification of the flesh. They objected vigorously to the idea of the incompatibility of body and soul and to the notion that the soul, when incorporated in the body, had "fallen" and must be "saved." According to the Rabbis, the soul's destiny is *not* to live apart from the body and to find happiness for itself in fellowship with God, but to unite with a body in order to achieve a purposeful union of the two—the righteous man. For that object was the world created by God.

3. According to some of the Sages, the soul returns to God in the same condition as it came from God. Its proper functioning may become impaired, as when man becomes ill or is injured physically or mentally, but the soul itself remains whole. This view is reflected in the morning prayer: "My God, the soul with which Thou hast endowed me is pure. Thou hast created it. Thou hast formed it. Thou hast breathed it into me. Thou dost preserve it within me, and Thou wilt hereafter take it from me and wilt restore it to me in the life to come. So long as there is soul within me, I give thanks before Thee, Lord my God and God of my

fathers, that Thou art the Sovereign of all creation, the Lord of all souls. Lord Who dost restore the soul to the dead, blessed art Thou."

Some of the Rabbis felt that man can pollute, corrupt, and even impair the soul. This is the implication of the rabbinic comment on Ecclesiastes 12:7, "And the spirit returneth unto God Who gave it." "As He gave it to you in purity so return it in purity." (Shabbas 152 b)

When Does the Soul Come Into Existence?

Judaism has an assortment of answers to this question:

1. *From the Talmud*
   A. "In the Seventh Heaven are stored the spirits and souls yet un-united with a body." (Chagigah 12b) Other scattered references teach the pre-existence of the soul. According to a frequently expounded view, all souls were created at the same time as the world.

   B. God unites a soul with a body but opinions about the time of this union differs. Some say it occurs at the time of procreation, others after the embryo is full grown. Some Jewish law seems based on the assumption that the child is not in possession of a soul until thirty days after birth, or later.

2. *From Rabbis of the Medieval Period*
The soul does not enter the body from without; it is created with and in the body. The medieval Sages were concerned lest the dualistic thinking characteristic of the philosophy of their times infect Jewish theology. This preoccupation will be treated at greater length in a section below.

How Are Body and Soul Related?

When God created man, He made him flesh and spirit, dust and soul, a touch of earth and a spark of heaven, in the image of animal and in His own image. His body together with his senses, emotions, powers of thought, drives and goals, make up a single whole. If God combined body and soul, then the proper state for both is in perfect union. Even where Judaism is logically compelled to accept the dualism implied in the death of the body and continued survival of the soul, it logically concludes that a reunion of body and soul will occur "at the end of days" (Resurrection of the Dead).

Judaism tries to avoid comparative evaluation of the body and soul. It emphasizes the union and proper functioning of the body and soul in natural compatibility. It views with disfavor any philosophical tendency that divides man into flesh and spirit and sees the two as being in conflict with each other. Assertion of supremacy of flesh over spirit, or of spirit over flesh, is a denial either of the spiritual or material aspects of life. Judaism opposes all views that deny either of the two aspects, that see the two as being in conflict, that recommend a truce between them, or that advocate the annihilation of the flesh or derogation of the soul. The Hasidim put it this way: The soul should not boast that it is holier than the body for both were created by God, and only in and through the body can it perform its function. The body also should not brag even though it supports the soul, for when the soul leaves, the flesh falls into decay.

Do Jews Today Believe that Man Has a Soul?

Unlike the Jews of the Rabbinic and Medieval periods of our religious development, Jews today like Jews of Biblical times are not deeply preoccupied with the soul. There is a tendency to simply assume that man has a soul but little effort, if any, is expended by the average Jew or by our theologians to define its nature. This is true in varying degrees in the three branches of Judaism:

ORTHODOXY

The belief in a traditional concept of the soul is a definite part of the theological outlook of the Orthodox. However, because there is diversity of opinion in the tradition itself, there is no positive, authoritative concept of soul even among the most traditional-minded Jews today.

REFORM

Reform Jews are inclined to reject the traditional conception in favor of a poetic interpretation of soul as a symbol of man's spiritual stature. They have difficulty thinking of the soul as a distinct entity and in accepting the traditional "mythology" which describes the soul as the spirit of God literally breathed into man. Nevertheless, they do speak of the immortality of the soul. Reform Judaism looks to modern psychological study of man where it hopes, eventually, to find a conception of soul in harmony with the scientific study of man as well as with the poetry of religion.

CONSERVATISM

Conservative Judaism, like Reform, is watching and studying advances in the field of psychology, particularly psychiatry, in the hope that new insights, reconcilable with traditional Jewish thinking about soul, may be discovered. The speculative Rabbinic and Medieval view of the soul as a distinct entity enjoying an independent existence in the after-life is still retained because Conservatives are markedly reluctant to discard traditional concepts. However, there is a pronounced shift back to the Biblical idea of man in Conservative orientation.

RECONSTRUCTIONISM

The Reconstructionists, a group that started as the left wing of the Conservative movement and has been joined by a growing number of Reform rabbis and thinkers, redefines the soul in terms of its functions rather than its abstract nature. This group strives to harmonize Jewish religious thinking with modern thought and, despite its nontraditional concept of the soul, may add significantly to its development and revitalize its use in modern Jewish religious thinking. "If we want to improve the health and growth of the human body, we have to learn all about the body and about the conditions under which it thrives. . . . What health and growth are to the human body, God is to the human spirit (soul). For God to function as a reality in the life of man and to influence his character and his conduct, we have to concentrate on the nature of the human spirit, or that phase of man's nature which has to do with his becoming fully human." This brief quotation, out of context, does not do justice to the author's conception of the human spirit or soul but it indicates how seriously the Reconstructionists discuss the soul. To them it is not an abstraction for sterile metaphysical speculation, but the crux of the religious life.

Do Jews Believe That Man's Soul Needs to be Saved?

Judaism does not believe that the soul is threatened in a way requiring outside rescue. It is not chained in a prison from which it cannot liberate itself or gripped by a fate from which it cannot shake itself loose. The soul needs no saving because it is not lost; it needs no raising up because it is not fallen; it needs no liberation because it is not the victim of enslavement. Religions believing in the doctrine of Original Sin believe that the soul needs to be saved. Judaism does not believe in this doctrine.

What Is the Doctrine of Original Sin?

It is the belief that, in the beginning, life was perfect. Then, some early man committed an act of abhorrent sacrilege thereby bringing down a curse upon himself and all his descendants. ("In Adam's fall, we sinned all.") Guilt and anxiety, suffering and death, are now the punishment of all men for all times due to the sin of this one man. Every soul born into the world is tainted with this original sin.

What Sparked the Belief in Original Sin?

The best way to understand any religious belief is to appreciate the reasons for its popularity, the need it fills and the fact of life it tries to explain.

1. *The need to believe in God's justice*
A just God surely created man in a state of purity and perfection since He expected man to live in harmony with Him and to do His Will. Man in his original state must have been innocent, immortal, and destined to enjoy perfect bliss.

2. *The need to explain man's sinfulness*
Since man has obviously fallen from his original state, he must have sinned by disobeying and rebelling against God. The first transgressor brought down the curse of guilt, suffering and death upon all who came after him.

3. *The need to explain how perfect man came to his downfall*
In order to solve one theological problem, namely, how man created in innocence could become sinful and perverse, mystical religions created another, namely, the enigma of a Satan who contended with God for man's soul, and won. Satan tempted, enticed, and led man astray from obedience to God. Man's soul became blemished as a result.

4. *The need for a second chance*
The blemished soul can be restored to its original purity. Decontaminated, the soul can be reunited with God. Man has a second chance, if not in this life then after death in the next life.

How Does Traditional Christianity Explain Original Sin?

In the beginning, God breathed into Adam a perfect soul. Adam, tempted, disobeyed God's command not to eat of the Tree of Knowledge and lost both paradise and his soul. Preoccupation with the lost soul brought forth the following tenets:

1. The soul is confused, contaminated, and weighted down by the immorality of Adam's sin. Sinful man cannot save his own soul. It can be saved only by the Grace of God. Therefore, God the Father sent His only begotten son, Jesus, to be a sacrificial atonement for the original sin of Adam which mars the souls of all men. Those who believe in Jesus share in the atonement of his death—just as previously they shared in the guilt of Adam—thus erasing the stain of their sin with the blood of God's sacrifice.

2. The body with which Adam sinned is a filthy garment of flesh which entombs the soul like a carnal dungeon. Body and soul are locked in conflict and the body has supremacy over the soul. Man cannot save his own soul, free it from the chain of bodily sin that holds it in bondage. To free the soul of man God has offered man His saving sacraments. These sacraments, Baptism, etc., have the power to purify man's soul. In a state of purity, the saved soul can return triumphantly to God after the death of the body. Therefore, death is better than life for it is the saved soul's opportunity for liberation and reunion with God.

How Does Modern Christianity View Original Sin?

Modern liberal Protestantism almost liberated itself from the morbid preoccupation of traditional Christianity with the doctrine of Original Sin. It had developed a vigorous and optimistic social outlook. However, the disillusionment of the cold war era has converted most of the champions of Christian liberalism to an existentialist neo-orthodoxy. They have resumed the pessimistic refrain of Original Sin, albeit in a highly sophisticated and profound form. Man is helpless to save himself. Even his best efforts to do good end in evil: his scientific, social, political, philosophical, moral and spiritual efforts are doomed by the paradoxes that are inherent in existence. All his actions of mind, will, emotion are tainted by his sinfulness. Confidence in achieving self-fulfillment and determination to find solutions to the problems of existence are evidence of sinful pride. Striving for righteousness, he becomes self-righteous; achieving knowledge, he becomes arrogant; faith in man becomes egocentricity; virtue, self-flattery; charity, vanity and condescension; mercy, superiority; reason, rationalization and self-justification. Something deep within man's soul taints everything he attempts; his very successes are failures. His only hope is to admit that he cannot save himself.

Even such a brilliant and enlightened spirit as Reinhold Niebuhr, the leader and ideologist of liberal Christianity, has endorsed the doctrine of Original Sin: "The universal inclination of the self to be more concerned with itself than to be embarrassed by its undue claims may be defined as 'original sin.' The universality of the inclination is something of a mystery."

Why Don't Jews Believe in Original Sin?

Overtones of belief in original sin may be discerned in early Judaism as well as in Christianity. The idea, in one form or another, is to be found in nearly all ancient religions. The Biblical story of Adam's disobedience and banishment from the Garden of Eden can be interpreted as the basis of the idea for the "fall" of man and "original sin." This is precisely how Christianity does interpret it. This interpretation may well have had some currency among Jews in the pre-Christian era. Some suggestions for the belief in an original fall that made all men "fallen" may be found in the Jewish tradition. Even in Talmudic times some sages held to this view. One group of sages pictured Adam as saying, "You die on your own account, not on mine." (Tanhuma Hukkat 16); another group said, "You die because of the sin of the first man" (Deut. R. 9:8). The majority adhered to the former interpretation. "Why was only one man created at first? That virtue and vice may not be attributed to heredity." (Tosefta Sanhedrin 8:4)

The idea of original sin was rejected by the vast majority

of the sages and the Jewish people as a whole. Jewish commentators on the Bible point out that the story of Adam attempts to explain how death, not sin, came into the world. This explanation for the death of the body is completely unrelated to and not to be confused with the Christian doctrine which condemns the whole human race to a "spiritual death" from which man can be saved only by faith in the risen Christ.

All interpretation is subjective selection. Christianity selects from the story of Adam's sin the interpretation of original sin; Judaism uses the same story to teach us, in the words of the renowned first Chief Rabbi of Israel, Abraham Kook, "that man though he *is capable of* attaining a high stage of perfection and thus prove himself worthy of glory and bliss, *can forfeit* all if he corrupts his ways, bringing thereby suffering upon himself and upon many generations that come after him." Judaism draws from the Adam story the lesson that sin drives man from God's presence. Without God, the world becomes a wilderness instead of the Garden of Eden that it can and should be.

The Sages, who rejected the belief in original sin, were not blind to the persistence of sin in man. They knew well enough that "there is no man who sinneth not." For them, the partial truth in Original Sin was overshadowed and negated by the more important positive truth: that interpreting life as a fall implies pessimism and fatalism. Their faith in God compelled them to reject the concept of original sin in favor of a trust in the promise and meaning of life.

We reject the doctrine of original sin because:

1. It introduces a morbid note which is alien to the Jewish mentality and stamps most of man's efforts as futile. Judaism has always had an optimistic outlook; the tradition has encouraged men to believe in their God-given power to rise morally and to achieve spiritual progress.

2. It clashes with our belief in free will. The Jewish

tradition has withstood every philosophy which condemns man to a pre-determined fate over which he has no control or for a deed he did not commit. Despite abundant evil, many unpleasant memories of past failures, and realistic awareness of our limitations, we have never faltered in our belief that men are free to change that which is evil into that which is good.

CHAPTER XIV

The After-Life

Why Do People Believe In Life After Death?

At least four reasons may be discerned for the persistent and universal belief in some form of survival after death:

1. *It helps overcome the haunting fear that life is unimportant.*

To shake off this fear, man engages in a creative drive to leave his mark on the world. In a leap of faith to transcend time and space he attempts to make this life purposeful and meaningful in terms of the hereafter. The fear that death reduces man to nothingness, making his strivings transient and pointless, is partly overcome by the triumphant perspective that life has ultimate meaning in the hereafter.

2. *It invests life with enduring significance.*

Belief in the hereafter gives man reassurance that the "here" must have meaning, and quickens his resolution to invest this life with enduring significance.

3. *It satisfies the desire for total self-fulfillment.*

All of us die before achieving maximum moral and spiritual development. Death cuts us down before we have had a chance to complete our life's work and to attain cherished goals. The self needs the hope for survival in order to sustain enthusiasm and efforts for self-fulfillment through enterprises that may not be completed in one's lifetime. The self desires the promise of fulfillment beyond the grave.

4. *It upholds a morality predicated on justice.*

The belief in an after-life is a logical requirement for

the ultimate vindication of justice. Experience in this life often contradicts the principle of justice and yet the human conscience asks men to build the whole structure of moral life on the premise that justice is indispensible and ultimately irresistible. In social ethics, we defer the vindication of the basic principle of morality to the future when the good society will be realized. For the individual, moral conduct must often look for its rewards in an after-life.

What Has the Jewish Tradition Said About the After-Life?

1. *The early Biblical view*
The Bible emphasizes life in *this* world. No doctrine of the hereafter is expressed in the Torah. There is, however, an occasional vague reference to the concept of an after-life. The Bible speaks of *Sheol,* land of shadows; *Dumah,* land of silence; *Belijaal,* land of no return; *Neshiyah,* land of oblivion. From these terms, it may be inferred that the Bible ascribed to man survival beyond the grave in some kind of shadowy existence. Other biblical references pointing to belief in a life after death are: a prohibition to communicate with the dead; regulations governing burial of the dead; Jacob's lament that he would go down to his son in *Sheol;* Abel's unavenged blood crying out in protest from the grave. Expressions for death like "being gathered to their people" and "sleeping with their fathers" all seem to point to an ancient Hebrew belief in a continuation of life beyond the grave. Jews of the early Biblical period gave the after-life no emphasis beyond envisioning a shadowy future existence. The accent was on concern for man's history and destiny in this life.

2. *Expressions from the later Biblical books*
The center of interest in the later Biblical books does not change but there is greater concern with the after-life, more detailed descriptions, and some expansion of the idea:

Reunion in the after-life—Death separates loved ones

and the after-life reunites them. The concept of community existence, having its origin in the family grave, is gradually extended.

Equality in the after-life—The Prophet Ezekiel (Ch. 32) speaks of a large number of nations gathered in *Sheol*: great and small, master and servant, lie huddled together in dreamlike consciousness. Isaiah, Ch. 14, gives a striking portrait of the great Babylonian King descending into *Sheol*: The shades of former earthly royal beings greet the fallen monarch, who had threatened to destroy Israel, with some satisfaction, "So, thou too art weak as we."

Relationship between the living and the dead—Contact between the living and the dead and the memory of earthly life are indicated in some parts of the Bible. The Prophet Samuel is called up from the grave by Saul. He appears, dressed in his earthly garb, fully acquainted with what has been going on in the camp since his death, and with a foreknowledge of what is to come in the future, including Saul's fate. The Prophet Jeremiah speaks of Rachel weeping in her grave for her exiled children. On the other hand, Job, in Chapter 14, affirms that both the dignities and the indignities of this life are forgotten in the grave and Ecclesiastes suggests that even consciousness is destroyed—dust returns to dust and nothing remains.

Return to life—In some of the later Biblical writings is expressed the opinion that there is no return from the grave, but side by side with this appears the view that God slays and makes alive, brings down to the grave and raises up the dead to life again. Here are to be found the beginnings of a debate about the resurrection of the dead which raged at a later period. Job asks, "If a man dies, shall he live again?" However, he does not answer the question he poses. Ecclesiastes replies with an unequivocal negative and denies all hope for a future life. But resurrection of the dead is expressed as an eager expectation in some of the prophets;

it is the reward of those who lived a meritorious life on earth; the wicked perish forever.

In other words, there is no uniform view on the after-life or any of its aspects.

3. *The Rabbinic or Talmudic views*

In harmony with the views expressed in the later Biblical writings, the Rabbis developed further the belief in the after-life. They called it the *Olam Ha-Ba*, the World to Come. The belief contained the following basic elements:

Immortality—Life does not end with death. This life is preparation for the next life, in another world. There was no official view on the nature of the next life and the other world. Differing constructions were current but on one thing the Sages were agreed: the soul lives on in a spiritual world.

Reward—Man does not receive exactly what he merits in this life. Since there must be perfect justice in the moral order, man will be compensated in the after-life: good will be rewarded, evil punished. On the nature of the reward and punishment, the Sages expressed many views but made no authoritative pronouncements and formulated no dogmas. There was agreement on the continuity of life beyond the grave, a life of great moral significance and spiritual fulfillment.

Resurrection of the dead—This is the belief that for the Final Judgment, after the advent of the Messianic Age, God will resurrect the bodies of the dead so that body and soul may be judged together. "They sinned together and merited together, therefore let them be judged together." Body and soul suffered and sacrificed together during their earthly sojourn in order to hasten the coming of the Kingdom of Heaven on earth. They were separated by death but will be reunited in the life of eternal bliss, a life without pain, evil or death in an *Olam Hadash*, A New World.

This belief was challenged by many. Even those who wanted to believe it found themselves wondering, as did Job,

"If a man dies, shall he live again?" How can the decayed body be reconstituted? To these questions the Sages replied, "If God created a living being out of that which was not alive, He can surely recreate a body that was once alive." "The mystery of re-creation is no greater than the mystery of creation." "If what never existed before exists, that which once existed can exist again."

The New World—Each individual life is followed by an after-life of compensation and fulfillment; similarly, society in this world will be followed by an *Olam Hadash,* a new and perfect world where society as a whole attains the divine purpose for which it was created. In this way, according to the Rabbis, history's fulfillment—the divine principle governing the whole order of creation—will be accomplished.

Belief in the after-life of the individual, combined with belief in an after-life for society, formed a doctrine of ultimate destiny known as *Olam Ha-Ba,* the World-to-Come.

The Olam Ha-Ba—Everything has a purpose. Under God's providence, purpose leads to fulfillment. The *Olam Ha-Ba* is the fulfillment of the *Olam Ha-Zeh* (this world). The Rabbis reminded the people that the World to Come was beyond human knowledge and warned against fruitless speculation concerning details of the *Olam Ha-Ba.* They believed implicitly in an after-life and The World to Come but stressed the moral and spiritual tasks of this life as the center of Jewish religious concern.

To summarize, the early Biblical view was *this-worldly*; the prophetic and Talmudic, *new-worldly*; part of the Talmudic and the Medieval orientation was *other-worldly.* In the Modern period, there is a swing back to a this-worldly and new-worldly outlook. Today, in the so-called post-modern period, we are witnessing a growing infatuation with other-worldliness.

What Is the Modern View of the After-Life?

Modernists tend to deny existence beyond the grave because it is not subject to proof or deductive reasoning. However, many modernists cautiously concede the possibility of a life beyond this world despite their feeling that the idea is compounded of myth and wishful thinking. Myth can, and often does, house a truth. Wishful thinking is not necessarily unrealistic; reason does not destroy the possibility of an after-life. However, reluctant to accept a supernatural order of immortality, the modernist finds evidence for a kind of reasonable imperishability even in the natural order:

Biological transmission—We enjoy a measure of immortality through our descendants, who inherit our physical and psychical characteristics.

Social immortality—Our ideas and tangible works remain a lasting influence on our family, friends and society.

Jewish immortality—Some part of each individual Jew is kept alive in the Jewish people and its faith. So long as Jewish ideas and prayers and convictions endure, so long as institutions and causes with which Judaism is identified flourish, we ourselves survive.

With some reluctance, most modernists go beyond naturalistic immortality and accept the traditional view that something of the human personality survives the grave. They, like the traditionalists, call this imperishable something, the soul. They avoid trying to define the soul and the nature of its immortality but are in agreement with the Psalmist that the body returns to dust but the spirit returns to God. Thus, the modernist neither vigorously denies, nor does he affirm, the possibility of Heaven and Hell, Resurrection, Final Judgment and the Rabbinic description of *Olam Ha-ba*. He simply believes in man's immortal soul.

How Can We Explain the Tradition's Casual Treatment of the Doctrine of Immortality?

Judaism's morality was focused on the tasks and duties of this life. The Torah defined the major concern of the Jew in terms of daily and immediate choices between good and evil. This concern crowded out excessive preoccupation with rewards in an after-life. The Jew satisfied his quest for self-realization by meeting head-on the immediate challenges that confronted him each day, and through fulfillment of *Mitzvos.* He was confident that his children and descendants would carry on the tradition and that they would, eventually, share the Jewish people's coming to glory. He carried eternity in his heart even though he had no immortality in his creed, for he trusted God implicitly.

Judaism had no desire to move in its thinking beyond this life's experience: its present was unspeakably precious since it was hallowed by an intense piety and delight in its God-faith. The Jew loved this life, a life of worship, service, devotion and obedience to God. And he did not fear death. A man content with the presence of God in this life is not inclined to speculate idly about his future beyond the grave.

Too, Judaism's monistic view of man refused to separate him into a body and a soul. The body was considered God's handiwork and indispensable to life; yet the body perished and decayed at death. How was the future life to be conceived? There was a little doubt that God somehow "causes to die and to live again" but excessive speculation concerning the precise nature of this phenomenon was sharply discouraged as a diversion that could be misleading and dangerous.

Furthermore, Judaism had lived through many civilizations whose religions were closely associated with all kinds of beliefs about the dead. Its strong opposition to the pagan cult of the dead and to ancestor-worship, and its determination to shun any kind of association with such practices, made Judaism deliberately avoid too much speculation concerning the life after death.

According to Judaism, What Is the Relative Importance of This Life as Compared with the After-Life?

Four positions are possible:

1. Affirm the reality both of this life and of the hereafter.

2. Deny the meaning both of this life and of the hereafter.

3. Affirm the reality of this life, and deny the hereafter.

4. Deny the importance of this life, and affirm the hereafter as the true reality.

Judaism has held only to the first position, with important qualifications.

How Does Judaism Qualify Its Belief in an After-Life?

1. The focus of man's purpose and interest is in this life, to work out on earth a life of the fullest possible moral and spiritual development.

2. Concern with the hereafter must never be used as an excuse to evade the conflicts, problems, and responsibilities of this life.

3. Faith in reward and punishment being worked out in the after-life must not be exploited to justify and perpetuate suffering.

4. An after-life of eternal joy without responsibilities and useful exertions is a concept which is morally intolerable. It prompted the Rabbis to say, "The righteous find rest neither in this world nor in the world to come."

5. It is not in man's power to define the hereafter or to describe its nature; speculation regarding these matters should be discouraged.

Should a Jew Today Adhere to a Belief in the Hereafter?

Yes, for at least four good reasons:

1. Anything that adds meaning to life is good. Belief that life extends beyond the grave makes the life of this world even more significant.

2. The death of a loved one is often an agony to those who remain behind. Death can appear as a cruel, senseless end to many untold hopes and dreams. Belief in a life after

death removes much of the sting of death and makes continued living endurable and reasonable for the survivors.

3. Belief in an afterlife, where Divine righteousness is totally realized and where the individual can realize fully the powers with which he has been endowed by God in this life, adds impetus to our strivings after goodness and self-fulfillment.

4. If belief in a hereafter is conceived as fulfillment of promises; if it vindicates God, redemption, and continuity; and if it encourages expectation, initiative, moral achievement, a deeper faith and a more profound reverence for the holiness of life, it is worthwhile. If it brings about apathy, resignation to suffering, and disinterest in the moral issues of life; if it comes to be regarded as a bribe or a warning threat, it is unworthy.

What Should a Jew Believe About the Hereafter?

Judaism has no authoritative doctrine on the hereafter. A Jew has only to cling to the basic elements and main characteristics of the traditional view (even though he may not be able to accept it in all its details) in formulating his belief:

1. Something in the nature of man was always considered imperishable.

2. Opinions on the nature of the after-life were always diverse and undogmatic.

3. Both extreme views were rejected: an *other-worldliness* which detracts from the significance of this life and a *this-worldliness* which denied the possibility of an after-life.

4. Enthusiastic acceptance of this life and the conviction that man's conduct in this world has significance beyond this world were not considered mutually exclusive principles.

Did Jews Ever Believe in Heaven and Hell?

There is no mention of Heaven and Hell in the Bible. There is reference only to *Sheol*, one single abode for all the dead, both righteous and wicked. It was known as the land of no return: all men go there after death but none returns to the land of the living. It was believed to be a place of darkness and decay, deep down in the earth. It was not a place for punishment or reward, it was not a place reserved for the worship of God. In most of the books of the Bible, *Sheol* is a concept of after-life destiny entirely without hope; death is the final and unalterable fact of life. But in two of the books of the Bible, Isaiah and Daniel, *Sheol* is no longer a place into which there is only an entrance and from which there is no exit: there are suggestions of a resurrection of all the dead and a judgment to follow. The good will be remembered: God will "wipe away tears from every face and bring back to life the spirits of the departed"; "But the dead will live, their bodies will rise. Those who dwell in the dust will awake and will sing for joy." (Isaiah 26:19) With one blow Isaiah's faith shatters the gates of *Sheol* for the release of the righteous; Daniel, delivered from the den of lions and the fiery furnace, declares that "many of those who sleep in the land of dust shall awake, some to everlasting life and others to everlasting reproach and contempt." (Daniel 12:2)

The terms "Heaven" (for reward) and "Hell" (for punishment) entered the vocabulary of Jewish belief only after the solution to the problem of reward and punishment was relegated to the hereafter. This belief became widespread during the days of the Second Temple. However, there was some reservation and doubt, even outright objection in some quarters. And, on the nature of heaven and hell, the form and duration of reward and punishment, there was certainly no unanimous opinion.

In order to link the idea with the Bible, the Rabbis selected for the places of reward and punishment names from the Bible. *Gan Eden* (Garden of Eden), where Adam and Eve lived in innocence before sinning, a place of pleasure and plenty, was the term given to Paradise or Heaven;

Gehinom, a Biblical reference to a valley near Jerusalem associated in pre-Israelite days with the constant burning of great fires on altars dedicated to Moloch by idolatrous worshippers offering up human sacrifices, was the term given to Hell. A vast literature described vividly the pleasures of *Gan Eden* and the torments of *Gehinom* in physical terms. However, the teachers of the tradition were not in agreement about the teachings contained in this literature. Many statements in the Talmud, for instance, interpret rewards and punishments in a spiritual sense. In one of the discussions cited, the Rabbis debate whether or not there is a *Gehinom* at all. Some held that there was no *Gehinom*; others interpreted the *Gehinom* idea in divers ways. Some maintained that God caused the sun to shine upon the righteous and the wicked; the righteous are healed, the wicked destroyed by that same sun. Rabbi Judah b. Ilai contended that there is neither *Gehinom* nor a consuming-healing sun but the wicked are burned up by a fire which issues from themselves. What Rabbi Judah suggested here, and others elsewhere, is that wickedness causes its own punishment and destruction: Hell is within the wicked and of their own making. A later scholar expresses it similarly, "It is not the wicked that are in Hell, but Hell is in the wicked."

There were those who believed in eternal physical punishment, primarily by fire. According to Mishnah Eduyot, Ch. 1, the judgment of the wicked in Hell is limited to one year. But some sages of the School of Shammai, known for its severity and pessimism, held that there were two classes of grave sinners: one, after its punishment in Hell, suffered complete annihilation of the soul; the other suffered eternal punishment. Many of the sages could not get themselves to accept the idea of a merciful God inflicting eternal damnation on anyone. One of the popular beliefs was that even the souls of sinners, after punishment and purification, entered Paradise. The majority believed that even God's punishment of the wicked is for the purpose of rehabilitation and redemption. The wide range of opinion from denial to the varying forms of acceptance, and the refusal of the Rabbis to arrive at any one authoritative conclusion, would indicate that belief in Heaven and Hell was not considered essential to Jewish theology. The Rabbis elected to be ambiguous deliberately. It was in accordance with their view that preoccupation with, and dogmatism about, what preceded and what follows this life is spiritually unhealthy. Also, they wished to emphasize that the Jew must be motivated in good conduct by obedience, in reverence and love, to the Commandments of God, not by the fear of Hell or the hope of Heaven.

Do Jews Today Believe in a Physical Heaven and Hell?

Whether a Jew believes in Heaven and Hell is a personal matter. The belief was never a dogma of our faith; it was not a unanimously respected doctrine and even those who accepted it had their reservations. Today, Hell has dropped completely out of the vocabulary of Jewish teaching and preaching. Certainly no modern rabbi preaches Hell and Damnation, and these words do not figure in our religious instruction.

However, belief in Heaven enjoys some credence among Jews. The association of a Heaven with the justice of a merciful and loving God is hard to resist. The Orthodox retain the belief; the Conservative Movement retains the prayers in which the belief is expressed but more often than not regards Heaven and Hell figuratively or poetically, rather than literally. Reform Jews believe in the concept of immortality but avoid description of the after-life in specific and concrete terms and reject the belief in a physical Heaven and Hell. Kaufmann Kohler, in his *Jewish Theology,* expresses the Reform interpretation of the tradition: "When the rabbis speak of Paradise and Hell . . . these are only metaphors for the agony of sin and the happiness of virtue."

All three branches of Judaism believe in a Righteous Judge and in Divine Judgment. Therefore, all accept the idea of reward and punishment: the *Orthodox* spell it out boldly; the *Conservative,* vaguely; the *Reform* are reluctant to say anything except that the Providence that watches over us and judges us lovingly in this life, will continue to do so in the future life.

Heaven and Hell never stimulated the Jewish imagination to dwell on possible forms of reward and punishment. The major concern has always been, and is still very much, the religious effort to remove hell from this world and to build a heaven on earth.

Have Jews Ever Believed in Angels?

Malach, the Hebrew word for angel, means a messenger. The word appears in the Bible but is used to describe a human messenger sent by a king or leader to perform a human mission. In such instances, there is no implication of divinity. Occasionally, the phrase *Malach Adonoy,* messenger of God, is also a reference to a human messenger. However, this same phrase is used to denote a celestial being, an angel. In the Bible, there is reference to a Heavenly Court with God as King and angels as His servants.

The following observations in regard to belief in angels in Biblical times may be made:

1. The belief in angels was not important. The angels were never central factors in any of the great events of the Bible.

2. Most of the books of the Bible make no reference, or only rare reference, to angels.

3. Most of the prophets omit angels completely; only a few make frequent and elaborate reference to them.

4. Mostly, the angels appear as decorations or figures of speech to glorify God. No single angel even has a name until the comparatively late Book of Daniel.

Angelology did originate in the Bible but its real development was in Rabbinic literature:

1. Their number was increased greatly until there were millions of them.

2. The angels were divided into different classes.

3. More of the angels were given distinct individuality and specific names.

4. The Rabbis held that the angels were created on the second day or fifth day of the Creation, not on the first day, in order to avoid the suggestion that they helped create the world.

5. Angels were more active and their functions clearly defined.

6. The nature of angels came under lengthy discussion.

The following conclusions may be drawn from the many references to angels in Talmudic literature:

The belief in angels was undoubtedly taken seriously by some of the sages. Yet, in the thinking of many of them, it played no significant role. Some of the Rabbis did not concern themselves at all with the belief in angels. They neither contested nor affirmed the belief. It simply did not figure in their thinking.

Actually, the belief in angels was never a matter of doctrine. It was a way of expressing the idea that God has many messengers to execute His Will. The motive underlying Rabbinic angelology was not to invent intermediaries between God and the world. In fact, they objected to the idea of intermediaries because of a strong conviction that God is immanent, near to man. Their purpose was the glorification of God.

A popular practice of addressing prayers to angels developed among the people but was condemned by the Rabbis. A trace of it is present in the popular Sabbath Hymn *Sholom Aleichem* ("Peace be unto you, ministering angels of peace"). The practice of invoking the help of angels was also opposed by the Rabbis but survives in some Orthodox prayer books in the prayer recited before retiring: "In the name of the Lord, the God of Israel, may Michael be at my right hand, Gabriel at my left, before me Uriel, behind

me Raphael, and above my head the divine presence of God."
A number of prayers contain references to the angels, as
messengers of God and as members of His heavenly retinue,
singing His praises.

In the Middle Ages, the rationalistic Jewish philosophers
downgraded the belief in angels but the Kabbalistic or mystical literature of the same period developed the belief in
angels to its peak of elaboration. Apparently, in the Middle
Ages as in the Talmudic and Biblical periods, some believed
in angels and others were little, if at all, concerned. Belief
in angels was never considered basic or indispensable to
Judaism.

Do Jews Today Believe in Angels?

Today, Jews have definitely turned away from belief in
angels and reverted to the rationalistic view of the late
prophets and some of the Medieval Jewish philosophers.
Angels still figure in our religious poetry and appear in
some of our prayers but they are not a matter of intellectual
or spiritual concern. Most of the Orthodox still retain the
old liturgy in its entirety but attach little, if any, significance
to the angelic adornments of the mystical passages. Some
Orthodox do believe in the existence of supernatural beings,
i.e., angels. Conservative prayer books eliminate most of the
Kabbalistic references to angels but retain the older prayers
like the *Kedusha*, in which angels are pictured as singing
God's praises in Heaven. Reform prayer books have virtually
eliminated all references to angels.

The popular belief among non-Jews that the souls of the
righteous become angels was never part of the mainstream
of Jewish thought. Apparently, the Jew could not picture
himself becoming an angel. The contemporary Jew has at
least retained this bit of humility. He *can* accept the interpretation, expressed by Maimonides in his *Guide for the
Perplexed*, "Anyone entrusted with a mission and engaged in
the work of the Lord may be called an angel, a messenger of
God."

CHAPTER XV

Contemporary Moral Problems

How Has Judaism Reacted to Emerging Moral Problems?

Jews found themselves in a variety of cultures and changing societies throughout the ages. Consequently, new moral problems arose. Earnest efforts to help the Jew deal with them, brought forth a whole body of philosophical and moral writings: the Talmud, Midrash, Codes of Jewish Law, and Responsa literature, Books of Responsa—collections of current questions examined in the light of traditional beliefs—have been produced by Jewish scholars and sages in the past and continue to be produced in our own day.

The tradition evolved slowly and continually to meet the spiritual requirements of morally sensitive people. When a community, or even one Jew, raised a question, it became the subject of discussion in Jewish communities all over the world. It was analyzed: different ways of understanding the question itself were considered; underlying values and principles were examined; and implications of the possible alternatives were set down. In the letter and spirit of the Torah, based on the teachings of the sages as recorded in the *Halacha,* conclusions were drawn. Answers did not always come through clear, unambiguous, and final. More than one acceptable answer might develop, or only a tentative statement. This allowed for flexibility and greater understanding.

In this chapter, we examine some moral problems of our

own times. What do scholars have to say about them in the light of traditional Jewish belief?

What Is Abortion?

Abortion is the deliberate termination of a pregnancy by physical, chemical, or surgical procedures. If the termination is spontaneous or accidental, it is a miscarriage.

Is Abortion Right or Wrong?

One extreme position in contemporary debate regards abortion as a personal problem to be resolved by a pregnant woman and her doctor. The decision may be based on convenience, physical, psychological, or economic need. The abortion must be performed safely by a competent practitioner. Neither politics nor morality need to be considered.

The other extreme regards abortion as murder. When abortion is willfully induced, woman and doctor are guilty of homicide. It is a criminal act punishable by law. The embryo or fetus is a human being with a "right to life."

The key issue of these extremes hinges on whether embryo or fetus is a human being. It is a factor, also, in the Jewish position which holds with neither extreme. Let us consider it briefly.

Is the Embryo or Fetus a Human Being?

"At what stage is soul joined to the fertilized ovum." This question goes back to antiquity. The Greek philosophers differed in their answers. According to Plato, the rational soul accompanies conception. According to Aristotle, the soul is infused on the 40th day after conception for the male, and on the 80th day for the female. The Stoics believed that the soul entered at birth.

Where Does Judaism Stand on This Issue?

In rabbinic literature, the fertilized ovum is regarded as "mere fluid" until 40 days after conception. After 40 days, it is part of the mother's body and not a separate entity. In Jewish law, the unborn fetus is not a person.

On What Authority Is the Jewish View Based?

In the Bible, Exodus 21:22-23, two men are fighting. A pregnant woman is pushed by one of them, and miscarries. The man responsible for the mishap is required to pay compensation for injuring the woman. Had the woman died, the penalty would have been "a life for a life." From this the rabbis inferred that the Torah does not regard the fetus as a living person.

A talmudic statement (Mishnah Oholoth 7:6) gives further support. "If a woman is having difficulty giving birth, and her life is in danger, we may remove the fetus surgically, even limb by limb, because her life takes precedence; but if the greater part has already emerged, we may not touch it because we may not take one person's life for that of another."

Jewish scholars in the post-Talmudic period leave no doubt that abortion is permitted when the mother's life is directly endangered by the fetus. The various Codes of Jewish Law written in the Middle Ages reflect this. Commenting on this Mishnah on abortion, Maimonides reasoned that abortion is permissible because the embryo is like one who is pursuing the mother to kill her. Other rabbis, following Maimonides, agreed that a direct threat to the life of the mother justified abortion. Another medieval scholar, Rashi, commented on the very same case. He stated that so long as the fetus does not enter "the air of the world" it is not a living person. Most Rabbis who followed the authority of Rashi even sanctioned abortion for indirect threats to her well-being. Under certain circumstances, a pregnancy might be terminated for the sake of the woman's physical or mental health, or for the sake of other children in the family.

What Is the Rabbinic Position on Abortion in Our Own Time?

If a woman's health, physical or mental, might be seriously impaired by carrying the fetus to term, many rabbis would not oppose abortion. Where the possibility of severe malformation exists due to the woman's having contracted rubella or having taken a drug like thalidomide, or if the pregnancy is a product of rape, adultery, or incest, many rabbis would not discourage abortion. When the Nazis decreed that Jewish women who were pregnant forfeit their lives, rabbis in the death camps encouraged abortion to save lives.

Why Do Rabbis Reject the Idea of Abortion-on-Demand?

As a general rule, abortion is considered an extreme measure and the decision must take into account the moral implications. Unless there are compelling reasons to justify abortion in a particular case, the Rabbis are opposed to it for several reasons:

1. The fetus possesses a potential for life. It may not be destroyed on whim or for convenience.

2. The fetus is a partial person. Its destruction without cause goes counter to some biblical and talmudic teachings.

3. Indiscriminate, uncontrolled destruction of the unborn diminishes our humanity and the sanctity of life-in-the-potential.

4. Should the abortion require a surgical procedure, it

would wound. A wound may be inflicted only for therapeutic purposes (Baba Kama 91b).

5. Abortion presents some danger. Jewish law forbids placing one's life in jeopardy unnecessarily.

BIRTH CONTROL

What Is Birth Control?

It is a way to regulate child bearing through contraception. The dictionary defines contraception as "artificial prevention of the fertilization of the human ovum."

What Is the Traditional Jewish Position on Birth Control?

In general, the tradition is opposed to it. Contraception was viewed as a form of self-destruction or depravity. Judaism requires the Jewish people to *perpetuate* itself. Jewish children are the Jewish future; the Jewish family is basic to the transmission of the Jewish religio-cultural heritage from generation to generation.

Contraception violates the first positive commandment in the Torah: "be fruitful and multiply." Onan "spilled his seed on the ground" to prevent conception and died for this sin (Genesis 38:9-10). Rabbis of the Talmud and later scholars did not deviate from this stand; they did interpret the basic commandment to permit contraception where it was clearly necessary and desirable.

When Is Contraception Permitted?

No Jewish law forbids a woman to use a contraceptive device. In practice, women resorted to contraception only for compelling reasons. The Talmud (Yev. 12b) permits or even requires the use of a tampon by minor, pregnant, or lactating women. Reference is also found to some kind of oral contraceptive that produced temporary, or even permanent, sterility (Yev. 8:4). If a pregnancy might endanger the life, or even health, of the mother, she was justified in taking contraceptive precautions. The rabbis were quite liberal about the latter, especially if the commandment of procreation—having a son and a daughter—had been fulfilled.

A woman's use of contraceptives was encouraged during times of famine, persecution, and extreme danger. During the Holocaust, rabbis counseled birth control when consulted by women in the death camps.

May a Man Practice Birth Control?

According to the Rabbis, the command to "increase and multiply" was given to man, not to woman. Jewish tradition disapproves of celibacy. Life is diminished for the man who avoids all sexual relations; he has rejected God's blessings and his Jewish responsibility.

Marriage, and sex in marriage, are tender, loving experiences that enlarge and enrich the human heart and mind. Jewish law forbids the use of all forms of contraceptive by the male. His life is not endangered by pregnancy, and it is incumbent on him to produce children, to raise a Jewish family.

Is Sterilization By Surgical Means Approved?

For the male, it was disallowed except for therapeutic reasons. Mutilation is forbidden. Moreover, the biblical command to him is "to increase and multiply." Even if he has fathered a son and a daughter, and wishes no more children, he must not make it impossible, through surgery, to ever have additional children.

If the woman's life depends on surgery that makes her

sterile, the surgery is a therapeutic measure. Mutilation and sterilization are incidental to it and unavoidable.

What Is the Jewish Position on Population Control?

Adam and Eve were commanded to "increase and multiply and fill the earth." Jewish tradition dictates that man's duty and privilege is to enter into marriage, to procreate, and to assure continuance from generation to generation. Population expansion within the Jewish group was natural and necessary to assure survival of the Jewish people, and to promote its God-given and humane values.

Jewish tradition also recognized circumstances which warranted population control:

1. If famine threatens, it is permissible, and almost obligatory, to control conception.

2. In crowded ghettos into which Jews were locked, and from which they could not flee in times of persecution, the obligation "to increase and multiply" was declared fulfilled if a son and daughter had already been produced.

3. If the family's physical and spiritual well-being is at stake, Jewish law does not disallow limitation of its size.

4. If child-bearing is harmful to the woman, she may use contraceptives. Her life must be made secure, even if it requires abortion. To preserve it, all the laws of the Torah —except idolatry, adultery, and murder—may be suspended. Not more life, but better quality of life, is at the heart of Jewish tradition. By extension, the number of births should be limited where the life and well-being of mankind is threatened by over-population.

What Is the Position of Rabbis Today on Population Control?

Like all sensitive, intelligent people their opinions differ. Some Reform and Conservative rabbis are involved in planned parenthood and population control movements; others feel strongly that the Jewish population should not be unduly curbed voluntarily, not after the Nazis reduced our numbers so radically.

Orthodox rabbis and many Conservative rabbis favor large Jewish families precisely because of rampant population explosion all over the world. How else insure the survival of Judaism?

What Is the Jewish View on Organ Transplants?

The idea of organ transplants is new. As mechanical devices are perfected, the problem itself may become academic. The decision to try to save a life through organ transplant is debatable. Below, we shall mention very briefly some factors to be considered.

1. *Transplant from a living donor.*
The life of the donor is as sacred as that of the recipient. Mutilation of a healthy body must be avoided. Judaism would say that no life may be endangered, shortened, subjected to disfigurement, or sacrificed through removal of a healthy organ for the sake of another person.

2. *Transplant from a dead body.*
Where prompt removal of the organ after death is crucial, certainty of death is required. Jewish law forbids the hastening of death, also the needless mutilation of a dead body.

3. *A moral speculation.*
Who shall receive an available part or organ if several candidates are equally suitable recipients? The Jewish approach might be to choose the individual most likely to survive and to benefit from it. If this cannot be known in advance, scholarship and meritorious deeds would be the determinants, not wealth and influence, because wisdom

and virtue serve society's finest needs.

What Is Euthanasia?

The word itself simply means "happy death." It is used in reference to an act or method of causing death painlessly in order to end the suffering of the incurably afflicted. In cases of severe deterioration of physical and mental powers, of hopeless brain damage, of terminal cancer, and so on, may the life of the sufferer be shortened? Civil law at the present time demands that life be prolonged by all means; no patient may be "put out of his misery."

What Is the Jewish View on Euthanasia?

In Jewish belief, only God may decide who shall die and when. Man may not shorten his life, a sin for which there is no atonement, let alone that of another. It is sacrilege. A "mercy killing," the popular expression for euthanasia, is murder according to most Jewish scholars.

Life may not be cut off. Neither does our religious belief compel us to prolong and increase agony forcibly through technological procedures which postpone death but cannot conceivably save life.

The dying day of Rabbi Judah the Prince, author of the Mishnah, is discussed in the Talmud (Ketubot 104a). Rabbis had gathered in ceaseless prayer to keep him alive. His devoted servant, knowing how he suffered and aware that the case was hopeless, prayed that the privilege of death should be granted to him. When the rabbis persisted in praying that he live a little longer, the servant woman hurled a huge earthen jar from the roof to distract them from their prayers. Her action is noted with approval in the Talmud.

Some Jewish scholars say that in exceptional cases the patient may be permitted to expire without artificial life support systems which only prolong agony without hope; and that this would be the will of a compassionate God: to alleviate suffering.

CAPITAL PUNISHMENT

The Torah stipulates the death penalty for murder, for certain sins against God, and for certain crimes against society. In biblical times, the law of "a life for a life," the so-called *Lex Talionis* (latin for "law of retaliation"), was comparatively moderate. Let us compare it with practices that prevailed in the ancient world.

Throughout history, sovereigns imposed death capriciously and at will. It might be for stealing bread, for inadvertently crossing the path of a royal entourage, for even lesser offenses or for no known offense. In civilized Athens, Socrates was put to death for "offending the gods." In the Roman empire, a father could legally put his own child to death; it required no justification. In these and in other lands, unwanted babies were abandoned to die of exposure. Kinsmen of a slain individual—even where the death was known to be accidental—could, and were expected to take the life of the slayer.

How Did the Torah Delimit and Discourage Capital Punishment?

The Torah made it difficult to impose a death sentence. Sins and crimes that warranted death were spelled out clearly and in detail, and a recognized court of law had to make the judgment. The judgment had to take into account motives for the crime, and the circumstances. Those who were guilty of *involuntary* manslaughter could flee to a city of refuge. Moses assigned six cities to which "shall flee thither and live he who killeth his neighbor unawares and hated him not in time past." (Num. 35:13, Deut. 19:9) In these cities, he was immune from persecution and could lead a normal life and make a living. The judgment also required that at least two witnesses come forward to testify.

Jewish history does not record any instances of capital punishment for many offenses listed and described in the Torah as punishable by death. Apart from the legal aspects, social pressures operated against it. For example, if conviction meant death by stoning, the accuser or witness had to cast the first stone. Parents who had brought the accusation of incorrigible sinner against a son, had to be the first ones to carry out the death penalty of the court.

How Did Rabbis of the Talmud Restrict Capital Punishment?

A Torah law was never nullified by the Rabbis. However, requirements for conviction were so severe that the death penalty was hardly possible. For instance, when eyewitnesses testified, they had to declare that they were at the scene of the crime, had forewarned the accused of the consequences, and had tried to restrain him.

Why Did Rabbis of the Talmud Tend to Restrict Capital Punishment?

We can only guess. In the abstract, they all subscribed to it. They recognized that it was legal, in the Torah, and necessary to declare certain transgressions punishable by death. It could hardly have been a big issue in a small community where social pressures kept people in line.

During the Roman occupation, when the Sanhedrin was already stripped of its authority to try capital cases, the Rabbis commented on capital punishment. In the Talmud (Mishnah Makot 11:10), the following is recorded:

A Sanhedrin which executed one person in seven years was called a destructive court. Rabbi Elazar says, "Once in 70 years." Rabbis Tarfon and Akiva say, "Were we members of the court, no man would ever be executed."

Rabbi Simeon ben Gamliel reprimanded his colleagues because "such leniency would have made you responsible for the proliferation of murderers in Israel."

They believed that God does not desire the death of the sinner, only that he turn away from his evil ways and do good. They tended, therefore, to interpret the death penalty as a deterrent.

What Is the Position of Rabbis Today?

There is probably no more unanimity today than there ever was. But, increasingly, rabbis of all three branches of Judaism favor the abolition of the death penalty. Keeping the death penalty on the statute books, but imposing it only in rare instances is more in harmony with the spirit of traditional Judaism.

AUTOPSY

What Is Autopsy?

Autopsy is the examination and dissection of the body after death. It is usually done to ascertain the cause of death, to trace damage done by the disease, or to learn more about the disease.

Why the Reluctance to Permit Autopsy?

To those who cherished the deceased in life, the thought of having the body disfigured after death, cut into,

and dismembered can be abhorrent. This natural aversion
to autopsy was reinforced by Jewish traditional beliefs.

Which Beliefs Reinforce Jewish Aversion to Autopsy?

1. *The body belongs to God.*
The body is sacred: God's creation, forged in God's im-
age, residence of a Divine soul. It is "the property of God"
(Maimonides, Hilchot Retzach 1:4), His handiwork.
Therefore, it is to be treated with reverence in death as in
life.

2. *The body must be respected.*
Even in death the body must be clothed in dignity. It
should not be exposed, carved up like a carcass, or handled
like an impersonal object. It should be consigned to un-
disturbed rest in the grave.

3. *The body must not be exploited.*
For the living to derive any kind of satisfaction or profit
from a corpse was anathema. Among Jews, robbing graves,
using human skin for lampshades, and so on, would be unthinkable.

4. *Resurrection.*
The dead turn to dust, and from dust God will ultimately resurrect the dead. Nonetheless, this belief made
disfigurement or dismemberment of the dead unacceptable.

Is There Authority or Precedent for Autopsy in the Tradition?

In the Talmud (Chulin 11b), discussion in one case
centers on whether autopsy should be performed. Was he
murdered or did the man die of natural causes? The decision of the sages was to permit autopsy in order to establish

the cause of death, rather than risk the life of a man suspected of murdering him.

The question of whether autopsy should be permitted for medical research did not come up for discussion until the 18th century. Ezekiel Landau and Moses Sofer, prominent authorities, concluded that it is permitted if the findings might save the life of a person *on hand,* known to be a victim of a like malady. They ruled out autopsy to teach anatomy, for student practice, or for the general advancement of medical science.

What Is the Position of Orthodox, Conservative, and Reform Judaism on Autopsy Today?

General Orthodox rabbinic opinion permits autopsy only where it may save the lives of patients *on hand.* Yet, increasingly, Orthodox rabbis are taking into account the changed circumstances of society, our accelerated communications, and our advances in medical science which make possible immediate use of findings for a sufferer in any part of the world.

General Conservative rabbinic judgment is similar to that of the liberal Orthodox. The area of approval is further broadened to include observation of the effects of new drugs, and where reasonable doubt points to an incorrect diagnosis.

Reform rabbis, and many Conservative also, generally assume that an autopsy may lead, directly or indirectly, to knowledge that will ameliorate suffering or save lives. If the attending physician can justify the procedure, they permit it. Indiscriminate surrender of bodies to postmortem examination is not approved. Routine autopsy would diminish respect for the dead. Reduced regard for the dead would lessen regard for the living and for the whole body of traditional values that make us and keep us humane. For the Reform, the deceased may even be cremated but they may not be desecrated.

May a Jew Donate Part or All of His Body to Science?

During his lifetime, while in full possession of his faculties, an individual may decide to donate parts of his body after death, e.g., cornea of the eye, for transplant or for scientific study. How would rabbis react to this desire?

Some strict Orthodox might object. They would permit post-mortem surgery and removal of a part of the body to save a life but not to save sight. Liberal Orthodox, Conservative, and Reform rabbis would probably respect the wishes of the dead. They would reason that the part removed lives on, and to save a person's sight is, in a sense, to save his life.

Donating the whole body is another matter. Very few rabbis would permit—if they could—the body to be cut up for study; to be fragmented and treated like a carcass. Repugnant in itself, it would violate Jewish law and the spirit of Jewish belief on which the law was based. Some Reform rabbis might sanction extensive post-mortem on condition that the remains be treated with reverence and buried, or cremated, like other bodies.

WAR

What Was the Early Jewish Attitude Toward War?

From earliest biblical times it is clear that war was not to be waged for material gain or for asserting or extending power. It was a last-resort solution. Some examples:

1. Abraham said to Lot: "Let there be no strife between us for we are brothers." He urged Lot to stake out whatever grazing area he chose, then removed himself to a place that did not intrude on it (Gen. 13:8-9).

2. When Abraham defeated the kings in an engage-

ment undertaken to release Lot from captivity, he refused to benefit from the victory beyond freeing Lot. "I will not take a thread nor a shoe-latchet, nor aught that is thine." (Gen. 19:23)

3. On their way to the Promised Land, the Children of Israel requested peaceful passage through various lands. When it was not granted, they skirted the area, advancing toward their destination by a longer, roundabout route. When their rear was attacked by those who had denied them a direct route, they engaged in punitive warfare.

No glory was attached to military victories. Examples:

1. In a rabbinic legend, God rebukes the angels for rejoicing over the drowning of Egyptians in the Red Sea as they pursued the Children of Israel. "My children are drowning," He cried, "and you rejoice!" The life of the "enemy" is just as precious in the sight of God as the life of any of His creatures.

2. King David was denied the privilege of building the Holy Temple in Jerusalem because his hands were blood-stained from the battles in which he was involved.

Was War Ever Considered Desirable in Jewish History?

War was never considered desirable. War to extend the borders of the land, to enhance its greatness, or to increase its prestige was forbidden. It required the permission of the Sanhedrin and permission was never granted.

Two kinds of war were considered necessary.

1. *Divinely Ordained War.*

It was commanded in the Torah to:

A. Exterminate the seven idolatrous nations of the land of Canaan which had been promised to the Jewish people for a homeland; and,

B. Blot out the memory of Amalek, the archetype of inhumane action against the Jewish people in biblical times.

These commands were never carried out by Moses or his successors. The Rabbis of the Talmud were troubled by this Divine command to commit genocide. Finally, they interpreted it as a stern warning against idolatry and immorality and declared it "lapsed" for this reason: The specific peoples against whom they were directed were no longer distinguishable. The Assyrians had deported and mingled the peoples when they conquered Palestine in 722 B.C.E.

2. *The Obligatory or Just War.*

A clear-cut, direct, and immediate threat to the survival of the Jewish people demands action. When attacked, we must save ourselves from annihilation. The wars against the Romans and the Greek-Syrians in their midst and on their borders are examples of obligatory wars. In our own day, Israel's wars against the Arab forces are obligatory if the Arabs rule out peaceful relations and seek to destroy the Jewish nation.

How Was the Destructiveness of War Circumscribed?

In the Torah are regulations for humanizing war and placing limits on its destructiveness. Based on these references, Rabbis of the Talmud formulated principles that became part of the Jewish tradition. Five examples follow.

1. Peaceful settlement of disputes must be attempted. "One may not wage war against any people whatsoever until one has first offered them peace, whether it be a permissive war or a war of obligation" (Maimonides *Mishne Torah* Kings VI,1). Only after possibilities for avoiding armed conflict have been exhausted may war be resorted to.

2. "When thou goest forth against thine enemies, thou shalt keep thee from every evil thing" (Deut. 23:10). This

verse, together with other biblical references of this nature, was interpreted by the rabbis to preclude brutality, looting, sexual license, debauchery, and even foul language. Conquered peoples could not be exploited for forced labor; prisoners of war could not be hurt or mutilated; the bodies of those slain in battle were not to be desecrated by stripping or disfiguring them. All such acts were forbidden.

3. The enemy should be spared needless loss of life. A beleaguered city should be surrounded on only three sides to allow inhabitants to save themselves by flight. (Num. 31:7; Maimonides, *Mishneh Torah* Kings VI,7; and Nachmanides who counted it as one of the 613 commandments of the Torah "to deal mercifully even with our enemies in time of war . . . and this is a *mitzvah* for all generations.")

4. "When thou drawest nigh unto a city to fight against it, then proclaim peace unto it. . . . And if it will make no peace with thee, but will make war against thee, then thou shalt besiege it" (Deut. 20:10-12). Based on this, undeclared wars were prohibited. "A declaration of war must precede by two or three days the opening of hostilities" (Sifre on Deut. 20:10-12).

5. "When thou shalt besiege a city a long time . . . thou shalt not destroy the trees thereof by wielding an axe against them. . . . For is the tree of the field man, that it should be besieged of thee?" (Deut. 20:19) A fruitful place must not be turned into a wasteland. Trees and earth are God's creations and are to be preserved.

In the Tradition, Who was Exempt from the Draft?

When the Jewish nation was under attack, and survival was at stake, "all that were able," including women, could be conscripted. It was a moral duty to serve.

In a war where men went out to do battle, provision was

made for deferments and exemptions on moral and humane grounds:

1. Deferments were allowed for

a. The male, until the age of 20.

b. The newlywed, one year in which "to cheer his wife."

c. Whoever had built a new house, until he could dedicate it suitably.

d. Whoever had planted a vineyard whose fruits had not been gathered, until he could enjoy the fruits of his labor.

e. Whoever had already betrothed a wife but not taken her, until he fulfilled the mitzvah.

f. The self-confessed "fearful or fainthearted," until he overcame his fears, and in his own time.

2. Exemptions from conscription for

a. Women, and everyone under 20 years of age.

b. All who were permanently disabled.

In his book, *Government Law in Israel,* published in 1952 in Jerusalem, Rabbi Simon Federbush maintains that "fearful and fainthearted," according to the Talmud, applies to those who are afraid to die, to those who fear that they may commit transgressions while fighting, to those who feel doomed on account of serious guilt-feelings, to those who would rather be slain than slay another. They were excused from fighting. Those who were relieved from active service, for whatever reason, but were physically able, repaired roads and performed other noncombatant services away from the battlefield.

ATOMIC BOMBS, NUCLEAR WEAPONS, POISONS

Does Anything in Jewish Tradition Reconcile Us to the Use of Atomic Bombs, Nuclear Weapons, Biological, and Chemical Poisons?

In the Torah we read about whole cities and peoples,

even the whole world, destroyed in a single disaster from which no one could save himself. What did these disasters have in common? In each, God Himself made the decision and inflicted the punishment. God judged, and God carried out His own terrible judgment.

From the story of Noah we learn that God gave the inhabitants of the earth time to reconsider their ways. He forewarned them. After the flood, God pledged never to visit such total devastation upon the world again.

Fire and brimstone were rained down on the cities of Sodom and Gomorrah in total destruction. According to the biblical account, God would have spared these wicked cities if even ten righteous men could have been found in them.

The story of Jonah teaches that even the most wicked are not beyond redemption. God does not want to make "return" impossible; God does not want to destroy. Jonah of Tarshish was instructed to go to Nineveh, a great distance over land and sea, to warn the inhabitants to repent of their ways. Jonah tried to evade an assignment that seemed so hopeless. When he finally brought the warning, the inhabitants heeded it, were remorseful, made atonement, and were spared. Thus, God may send man from afar in the effort to save lives, not to decimate them.

God's wrath is aroused by barbaric conduct: torture, slow and painful killing, mutilation, lack of respect for the human personality. Peoples were blotted out for persisting in their inhumanity. God made the judgment.

On the basis of traditional Jewish belief, the use of weapons and other instruments that annihilate men and all growing things without discrimination would be forbidden. Such agents dehumanize those who wield them; they are immoral; they do not put limits on the destructiveness of war.

LAW AND ORDER

What Is the Traditional Jewish Stand on Law and Order?

The tradition is unequivocally for law and order. The Rabbis of the Talmud taught that "the law of the land is the law." They exhorted Jews to pray for the welfare of the governments under which they lived. To obey the law is the duty of the good citizen. They held that even bad government is better than no government because in a state of chaos men might "swallow each other alive." If there is to be order, laws have to be enacted and enforced.

At the same time, these rabbis taught that "the law of the state is the law when it promotes the welfare of the state" (Baba Kama 113b). When laws and their enforcement work against the people's welfare, the state itself is guilty of undermining respect for law and order.

What Was Indicated for the Jewish Living Under Tyrannical Government?

A corollary of belief in God is belief in Divine justice. The Jews was advised "not to despair of retribution" (Ethics of the Fathers 1, 7), to believe that justice would ultimately prevail. He might take peaceful measures to change the situation or make it more tolerable (mind and soul are unfettered and under the individual's sole dominion). Violence was recognized as inviting counter-violence, non-productive at best and excessively retaliatory at worst.

Was Civil Disobedience Ever Approved?

Jews lived by the law of the countries where they lived. Two classes of law, however, could be circumvented, ignored, or quietly resisted:

1. Edicts that did not apply to all inhabitants alike; and,

2. Laws which required violation of important religious principle or practice.

Under the kings of Spain, France, and Germany specific laws discriminated against Jews and did violence to their religious conscience. From the Talmud and medieval responsa literature we know that rabbis advised resistance to and evasion of "illegal laws." The monarch's power to make and enforce the law did not depend on Jewish approval. All one could do was exercise practical ingenuity and bide one's time in patience and in faith. Forcible resistance was not even considered, let alone approved.

In line with Jewish tradition, he can debate issues, criticize intelligently, reprove vigorously, act to change wrong or immoral policy through the established order. He can engage in "controversy for the sake of Heaven" as did our ancestors.

He may not destroy or undermine the government itself lest chaos ensue. Evil, selfish and greedy seekers of power use forces of legitimate discontent to promote chaos. This can result in a tyranny far more oppressive and repressive than what went before it.

HOMOSEXUALITY

What Did Judaism Say About Homosexuality in the Past?

"Thou shalt not lie with mankind, as with womankind; it is abomination. . . . Defile not ye yourselves in any of these things; for in all these things the nations are defiled, which I cast out before you." (Lev. 18:20)

Two incidents involving homosexuality are reported in the Bible. In Gen. 19:5, the Canaanites of Sodom demanded that Lot, Abraham's nephew, surrender his male visitors so that they might have carnal knowledge of them. In Judges 19:22, "certain base fellows . . . spoke to the master of the house, the old man, saying: 'Bring forth the man that came into thy house, that we may know him.' " The base fellows' were men of Gibeah which belonged to the Tribe of Benjamin. In both incidents, virgin daughters were offered to save the male guests from molestation. Homosexuality was rated more sinful than heterosexual rape. In both incidents, the cities themselves, Sodom and Gibeah, were destroyed for their wickedness.

In Sifra 9:8, Rabbis of the Talmud noted that homosexuality was widespread among Egyptians and Canaanites but regarded as abhorrence by Jews. During a discussion on safeguards and restrictions to prevent homosexual relations, the rabbis ruled that they were not necessary because Jews did not engage in them (Kiddushin 82a).

In the Middle Ages, Maimonides, a codifier of Jewish law and also a physician, held that "Jews were not suspected of practicing homosexuality."

Why Did Judaism Condemn Homosexuality?

Several reasons for the Torah ban are rooted in the tradition:

1. It is contrary to nature, a perversion. The God of nature equipped man and woman with bodies designed uniquely for relations with each other.

2. It violates the biblical law against "spilling the seed in vain."

3. It is a denial of the prime purpose of sex: to enable husband and wife to build a family.

4. It damages family life in cases where one marriage partner deserts in order to cohabit with someone of the same sex.

5. It had associations with the gross immoralities practiced by peoples in the ancient world.

INDEX

244